Dilemmas of Development

Dilemmas of Development: the social and economic impact of the Porgera gold mine, 1989–1994

Colin Filer (editor)

Australian
National
University

E PRESS

ANU
E PRESS

Published by ANU E Press
The Australian National University
Canberra ACT 0200, Australia
Email: anuepress@anu.edu.au
This title is also available online at http://epress.anu.edu.au

National Library of Australia Cataloguing-in-Publication entry

Title: Dilemmas of development : the social and economic impact of
            the Porgera gold mine, 1989-1994 / Colin Filer, editor.

ISBN: 9781922144416 (pbk.) 9781922144423 (ebook)

Notes: Includes bibliographical references and index.

Subjects: Gold mines and mining--Social aspects--Papua New Guinea--Porgera.
          Gold mines and mining--Economic aspects--Papua New Guinea--Porgera.
          Porgera (Papua New Guinea)--Social conditions.
          Porgera (Papua New Guinea)--Economic conditions.

Other Authors/Contributors:
          Filer, Colin.
          National Research Institute (Papua New Guinea)
          Australian National University. Resource Management in Asia-Pacific.
          Australian National University. Asia Pacific School of
          Economics and Management.

Dewey Number: 338.274109953

First published by Asia Pacific Press, 1999
This edition © 2012 ANU E Press

Contents

Tables, figures and maps

Tables

Figures

Maps

Currency conversion table

US dollars per PNG kina, 1988–98 (year end)

Year	US$
1988	1.2100
1992	1.0127
1994	0.8485
1996	0.7553
1998	0.4700

The following symbols are used
.. not available
- zero
. insignificant
n.a. not applicable

Contributors

Glenn Banks initially became involved in the Porgera Social Monitoring Programme while studying for his doctorate at the Australian National University. He now teaches in the School of Geography and Oceanography at the Australian Defence Force Academy, University of New South Wales.

Aletta Biersack has been engaged in detailed ethnographic studies of the Ipili-speaking people since 1974. Her most recent fieldwork in the Porgera area has been primarily concerned with the social impact of the mine. She holds a teaching position in the Anthropology Department at the University of Oregon.

Susanne Bonnell was employed by the Porgera Joint Venture from 1989 to 1991, initially in the position of Technical Training Officer (Relocation) and later as Assistant Superintendent (Social Development). Since leaving the company she has worked as an independent consultant on various mining projects in Papua New Guinea, including her two periods of collaboration with Glenn Banks on the Porgera Social Monitoring Programme.

John Burton initially became involved in consultancy work for the mining industry while teaching at the University of Papua New Guinea. His more recent work has been carried out under the auspices of his own consulting company, Pacific Social Mapping Pty Ltd.

Colin Filer also taught at the University of Papua New Guinea, where he helped to establish the university's business arm (Unisearch PNG), before joining the National Research Institute as the Head of what is now its Social and Environmental Studies Division in 1995.

Abbreviations

AIDS	Acquired Immune Deficiency Syndrome
BCL	Bougainville Copper Ltd
CIC	Community Issues Committee
CODE	College of Distance Education
CSIRO	Commonwealth Scientific and Industrial Research Organisation
DEC	Department of Environment and Conservation
DTIGSC	Department of Trade and Industry Goods and Services Committee
EMMP	Environmental Management and Monitoring Programme
FIFO	fly-in/fly-out
HIV	Human Immunodeficiency Virus
IMF	International Monetary Fund
IPI	Ipili Porgera Investments Pty Ltd
LDC	less developed country
LMP	Lease for Mining Purposes
LNC	Landowners' Negotiating Committee
MCH	Maternal and Child Health
MIM	Mount Isa Mines
MOA	Memorandum of Agreement
NYMP	National Youth Movement Programme
PDA	Porgera Development Authority
PLA	Porgera Landowners' Association
PJV	Porgera Joint Venture
PMV	public motor vehicle
PNG	Papua New Guinea
PNGBC	Papua New Guinea Banking Corporation.
PPYA	Porgera Paiela Youth Association
PWA	Porgera Women's Association
RDU	Rapid Deployment Unit
SEIS	Social and Economic Impact Study
SML	Special Mining Lease
STD	sexually transmitted disease
WEPS	Wambao Enga Pii Sikulu
WIPS	Wambao Ipili Pii Sikulu

Acknowledgments

Glenn Banks wishes to thank Benedict Imbun, formerly Teaching Fellow (now Lecturer) at the University of Papua New Guinea, and the student fieldworkers who assisted in one or more of the questionnaire surveys undertaken in the Porgera area—Londe Powell Imbun, Nick Kakapae, Mogola Kamiali, Jiro Kandoiya, Micheal Leamon, Norit Luio, Garry Sali, John Samboek, and Martin Sabrini. The Environment, Business Development and Community Relations staff of the Porgera Joint Venture provided valuable back-up and assistance on site: particular thanks should go to Nick Currey, Des Fanning, Don Flaganan, Rob Goldsmith, Laurie Martin, Jim McNamara, Greg McNee, Bill Muntz, Opis Papo, Jonathan Paraia, Fritz Robinson, Charlie Ross, and the inimitable Noel Walters. Bill Muntz and Don Flanagan both commented extensively on an early draft of the business development study (see Chapter 7). Many other people at Porgera (government employees, trade store owners, and other private individuals) helped to provide the information presented in this volume. In Port Moresby, Colin Filer helped with design of the survey forms and with the management of the Social Monitoring Programme in 1993 and 1994, while accommodation was provided by Michael Wilson and his family. The report presented as Chapter 3 of this volume received the benefit of proof-reading by Jean Kennedy, comments from Susanne Bonnell, and production editing by John Burton. John Burton of Pacific Social Mapping and Robin Hide of the Department of Human Geography at the Australian National University both commented extensively on an early draft of the report presented as Chapter 5 of this volume, while Bryant Allen, Chris Ballard, and Michael Bourke lent their considerable experience to the interpretation of my observations during informal conversations. Tracey Hansen assisted with data entry, proof-reading and moral support throughout the period of this study. The maps contained in this volume were all produced by Keith Mitchell of the Cartography Section in the Department of Human Geography at the Australian National University.

Susanne Bonnell is especially grateful to Charlie Ross, Noel Walters, Laurie Martin, Fritz Robinson and Nick Currey for organisational and administrative assistance. They, together with Des Fanning, Don Flanagan, Bill Muntz, Greg McNee, Jonathan Paraia and Annie Robinson, provided valuable input, lively discussion and good companionship during the period of her fieldwork. For the relocation survey (Chapter 4), she is indebted to Mogom Tili and More Aliana who assisted with the interviews; to members of the Porgera Women's Association who provided the network for organising visits to the relocation houses; and especially to the owners and occupants of the ninety-six relocation houses for their generous cooperation. Graham Taylor, then Porgera District Manager, also gave freely of his time to support this project, provided access to government reports, and facilitated interviews with public servants in Porgera. She also thanks Glenn Banks for his comments on her original report, Kathleen McGregor for editing and production work, and Judy Duggan of Lismore for her insight and moral support.

Aletta Biersack is particularly thankful to Stephen Hepworth, Kurubu Ipara, Jeffrey Puge, Graham and Gelmer Taylor, Morep Tero, and Father Andrew and Father Ed for their hospitality, logistical support, and information and ideas, during her fieldwork in 1996. At the National Research Institute, with which she was affiliated during this period, her thanks go to Anou Bourrey, Colin Filer, Wari Iamo and Michael Laki. Glenn Banks has participated in several fruitful conversations, sharing insights and research findings. The Porgerans at Tipinini and Porgera Station were most generous with their time and knowledge, and she is grateful to these and to her many Paiela friends for their intelligence, tolerance, and excellent company.

The editor wishes to acknowledge the financial support of the Mineral Resources Development Company of Papua New Guinea and its former Managing Director, Charles Lepani, for the National Research Institute to undertake a review of socioeconomic impact studies in the mining sector. This publication constitutes part of that undertaking.

Papua New Guinea, with Porgera highlighted

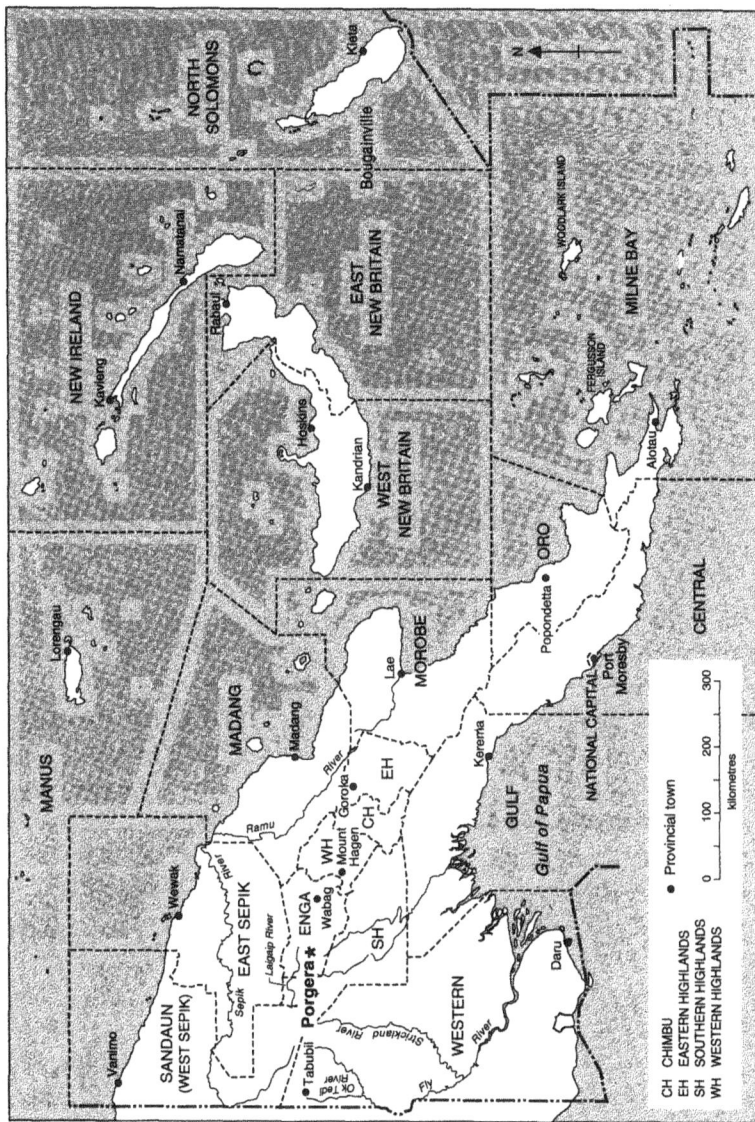

1

Introduction

Colin Filer

The main purpose of this volume is to publish, and thus to publicise, the factual material contained in a series of consultancy reports commissioned by the Porgera Joint Venture (PJV) between 1992 and 1994 (Banks 1993, 1994a, 1994b, 1994c; Bonnell 1994). These reports dealt with the social and economic impact of the Porgera gold mine on the population of the Porgera Valley during the period which had elapsed since the Government of Papua New Guinea (PNG) signed a Mining Development Contract with the PJV in April 1989. They were commissioned as part of what became known as the Porgera Social Monitoring Programme, which was itself intended to satisfy some of the conditions which the PNG Department of Environment and Conservation (DEC) had attached to its approval of the company's Environmental Plan (NSR 1988) and Environmental Management and Monitoring Programme(PJV 1991). The substance of these reports has been revised and edited to form Chapters 2–7 of the present volume. The last two chapters have been specially commissioned from two other social scientists who have studied the social impact of the mining project, and who were asked to provide their own comments on the design, management and output of the Porgera Social Monitoring Programme.

The Porgera Social Monitoring Programme, 1992–94

Condition 21 of the Porgera Environment Plan approval requires the PJV to undertake 'periodic studies of the socio-economic impacts of the mine development on the people directly affected by the mine'. Condition 22 states that 'the Company shall report to Department of Environment and Conservation on the studies in 21 above as part of the approved Environmental Management and Monitoring Programme'. By the time that this second approval was granted, the construction phase of the mining operation was almost complete, and the PJV had already commissioned one of the contributors to this volume to undertake a census of the local population (Burton 1991), which had been rapidly swollen by immigrants from other parts of Enga Province.

In May 1992, the PJV's Environment Manager, Charlie Ross, asked the University of Papua New Guinea's business arm, Unisearch PNG, to propose a more comprehensive programme of work to monitor the social and economic impact of the mine. In my capacity as the Unisearch Projects Manager, I promptly sought the assistance of my former university colleague, John Burton, whose previous consultancy for the PJV had also been undertaken through the university's business arm. Burton's original proposal, submitted in June 1992, had two main components.

- The first was for him to resume and complete the social mapping and census exercise which he had started under the previous contract, and which the PJV's management had apparently placed on the proverbial back burner (see Chapter 9).
- The second was for the PJV to commission Glenn Banks, then a PhD student at the Australian National University, to study the local economic impact of the mine, with assistance from Engan staff and students at the University of Papua New Guinea.

In discussion of this proposal, it transpired that the PJV had already made a separate arrangement with Susanne Bonnell, who had previously been employed in the company's Community Affairs Division, to collect 'social statistics' in the mine impact area, and her work was then absorbed into the design of the overall programme. Glenn Banks and his team began their first period of fieldwork in November 1992, but it was only in March 1993 that DEC staff were finally persuaded to convene a Steering Committee which retrospectively approved the terms of reference for both of these consultancies. The meeting in question was attended by representatives of the PJV, the PNG Department of Mining and Petroleum, the PNG Department of Finance and Planning, the Department of Enga Province, and the Porgera Landowners' Association. Susanne Bonnell, John Burton and I were also present at that meeting, and after further consultation with Glenn Banks, we finalised the design of the Porgera Social Monitoring Programme, and presented our proposals to the PJV in June 1993 (Burton and Filer 1993).

However, for reasons discussed at greater length in Chapter 9 of this volume, the only elements of this programme which had borne fruit by the end of 1994 were those which had already been initiated in 1992. After completing the first report of the 'Economic Modelling Project' in May 1993 (Banks 1993), Glenn Banks went on to produce three more reports in February, July and December 1994 (Banks 1994a, 1994b, 1994c). Revised versions of these reports appear as Chapters 3, 5, 6 and 7 of the present volume, in that order. Susanne Bonnell presented her own findings on 'Social Change' in a single report (Bonnell 1994) which was submitted to the PJV in August 1994. The findings of her study are presented as Chapters 2 and 4 of the present volume.

The documented impact of the mine

According to Banks (1996:223), the Porgera gold mine, from a technical and financial point of view, is 'one of the most spectacular successes of the mining industry in recent times'. Annual output of gold reached a peak of almost 1.5 million ounces in 1992 (the first full year of production), but fell to about 850,000 ounces per annum in 1995 and 1996 (PJV 1997). The value of this output was almost K500 million in 1992, but was still more than K440 million in 1996, due to the slide in the value of the kina which began in 1994.

According to the national census, the Porgera Valley had a resident population of approximately 10,000 in 1990 (excluding mining company personnel), most of whom appeared to belong to ten 'traditional' rural communities outside the limits of Porgera government station. This was almost twice the number recorded in 1980, which shows that there had been substantial immigration into the area during the exploration and construction phases of the project (Burton 1991). No-one knew how many people were living in the Porgera Census Division by 1993, but Banks (Chapter 5) makes a

Map 1.1   Porgera mine impact area

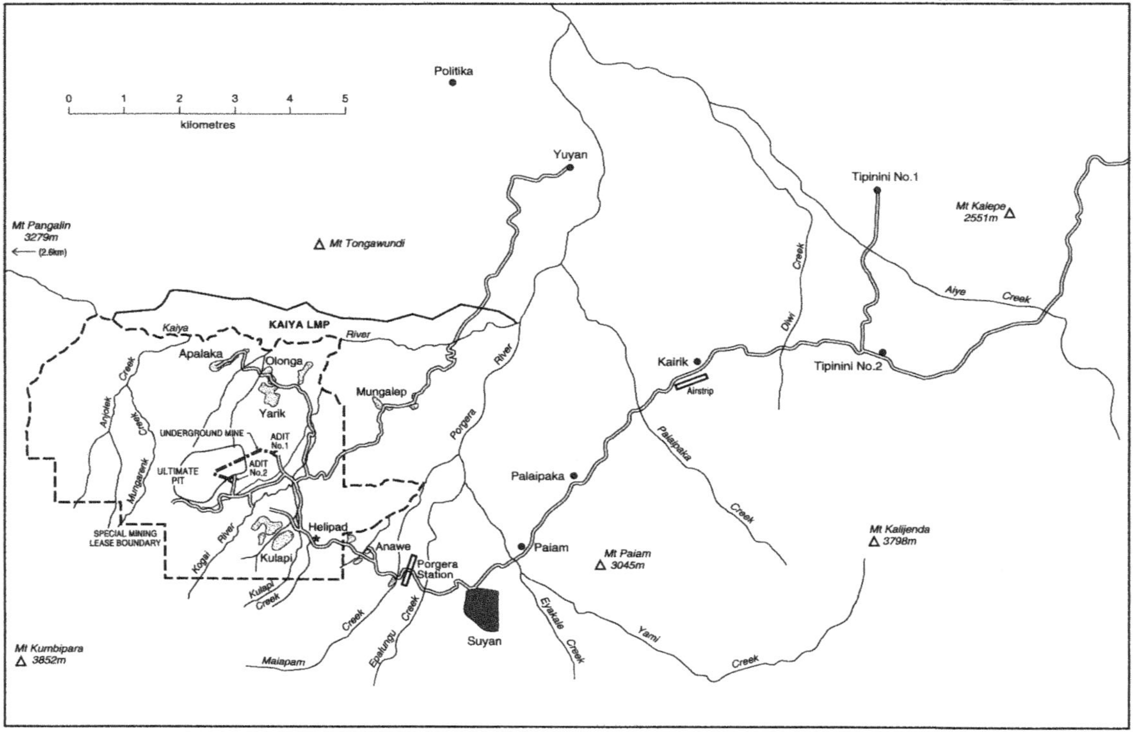

Source: Banks, G., 1994b. *Kaiya River LMP Socio-Economic Baseline Study*, Porgera Social Monitoring Programme Report 4, Unisearch PNG Pty Ltd for Porgera Joint Venture, Port Moresby.

(probably conservative) estimate of 12,000. By the end of 1994, over 4,000 of these people had been 'relocated' by the PJV in order to make room for the development of the mine (Banks 1996). By that stage, almost 3,000 hectares of land had been leased from local landowners for this purpose (see Map 1.1).

By the end of 1996, the PJV had paid about K40 million to local landowners in the form of general compensation for relocation and environmental damage (Banks and Bonnell 1997a),[1] and had spent another K13 million on various forms of community infrastructure in the Porgera Valley, aside from the K11 million which was spent in various parts of Enga Province under the national government's Tax Credit Scheme. By that point in time, about K35 million had been paid out in royalites, of which K24 million had accrued to the Enga Provincial Government, while the remaining K11 million had been shared between local landowners and the Porgera Development Authority. The number of Engans (including Porgerans) directly employed by the PJV had risen from 638 in 1990 (out of a total workforce of 1,191) to 1,141 in 1996 (out of a total workforce of 2,087). The gross value of 1,942 business contracts awarded by the PJV to Porgeran companies in the period from 1992 to 1996 was approx-imately K70 million. By the end of 1996, the PJV had also spent another K20 million on various forms of education and training, much of which was directed towards the population of the Porgera Valley (PJV 1997).

These figures provide some indication of the sheer scale and intensity of the social and economic impact of the Porgera mine on the Porgera Valley. The studies conducted under the Porgera Social Monitoring Programme provide a more detailed picture of the outcomes of this process, as they were observed in 1993 and 1994.

In Chapter 2, Bonnell illustrates the dramatic transformation of the physical environment, including the construction of the mine and its associated infrastructure, the creation of the new 'towns' of Suyan and Paiam, and the construction of schools, health facilities, roads and bridges, and Kairik airstrip (see Map 1.1). She then proceeds to discuss some of the major social changes which accompanied this transformation. Local health services, for example, were greatly improved, when measured in terms of the growth of facilities and staff to deal with curative medicine, but the demands of Porgerans for this kind of medicine, combined with weakness in the government system, led to a corresponding neglect of the field of preventive medicine. By

1993, there was an obvious need for community health extension programmes to deal with sexually transmitted diseases, basic hygiene issues, family planning, substance abuse and environmental sanitation.

Porgera's educational bases did not really take off until the construction of new schools and classrooms in 1992. While the growth of facilities, especially community schools, was impressive, there was a major quality of education problem due to unacceptably high pupil-teacher ratios in Grade 1 and the lack of curriculum materials. But by 1993, Porgera did have the necessary mix of educational institutions to cater for most of the pre-tertiary education needs of the population: vernacular pre-schools, community schools, an international primary school, technical high school, vocational centre and College of Distance Education.

Bonnell found that the impact of large amounts of cash, especially in the form of compensation payments, had a negative impact on women and on marriage. Adultery, abandoned wives and children, and domestic violence became major concerns. At the same time, loss of land for food gardening purposes led to specific forms of economic hardship for many women living in the Special Mining Lease (SML).

The deteriorating law and order situation was found to be the main problem affecting the quality of life in Porgera. However, at a time of rapid social change and breakdown in traditional clan discipline, the government system had little to offer. While the national government had got more directly involved in the business of mining, the PJV had been simultaneously forced to become more involved in providing government services. By 1993, it was evident that a number of other problems would need further attention during the life of the mining project: the distribution of benefits to children of the SML landowners, a non-mine-related economic base for 'life after the mine' in Porgera, and the ongoing debate about commuter mining.

In Chapter 3, Banks focuses his attention on the mine-related economic base which had developed by the end of 1992. The main sources of direct income to local people in that year were wages, royalites, compensation (despite a decline from the peak year in 1991), and other fees, and together amounted to just under K7.5 million. Business contracts to the value of K35 million had been awarded to locally-based companies since the start of construction. Local employment with the PJV was over 450, while five large local firms dependent (directly or indirectly) on the PJV employed another 300 local employees.

Yet only some of the value of these inputs into the local economy was retained within Porgera and re-spent or redistributed there. Much of it was either spent on trade store goods sourced outside the area, whose prices had the added impost of transport from distant distribution centres, or given to 'wantoks' from outside Porgera, or transferred to other towns to purchase large items, such as vehicles, which could not be obtained in Porgera. As a result, the rate of local capital accumulation was hardly any greater than it was in other parts of Papua New Guinea which were peripheral to the main centres.

Banks also found that there were significant economic inequalities within Porgera—between communities, between men and women (female income being less than a third of male income), and between individuals, with the most affluent 10 per cent of his survey sample earning 60 per cent of the income, and the bottom 50 per cent earning just 2 per cent of the income. Another notable feature was short-term temporal variations, with regular fortnightly 'pulsing' of the economy, and longer-term fluctuations in the value of PJV inputs.

In Chapter 4, Bonnell concentrates on the social impact of the PJV's relocation programme. She recounts the way in which the Relocation Agreement was negotiated directly between the landowners and the PJV as part of a larger compensation package, and goes on to tell how 420 families were moved into relocation houses between 1989 and 1993. Relocation provided a large number of people with a dramatic improvement in their standard of housing, and the benefits were certainly appreciated by the majority of home owners. Relocation houses have locked people who were previously more mobile into their new places of residence. The growing population density of the newly created relocation villages, which was due to high birth rates and the immigration of relatives, had brought about a shortage of food gardening land and other forms of environmental degradation. At the same time, the relocated families exhibited high rates of marital breakdown, which were associated with a substantial increase in the practice of polygyny amongst the men who had reaped the economic rewards of their status as SML landowners.

In Chapter 5, Banks provides a more detailed account of the problem of population pressure which Bonnell mentions in both of her chapters. He found that subsistence agriculture continued to be the base of the Porgeran economic system for the bulk of the population , which meant that mine-derived money was still only a 'second garden' for many Porgerans. In the SML, he found the potential for a looming crisis in the agricultural system, as population increase and loss of land combined to place pressure on the existing subsistence base. Particular problems were already being experienced in two of the relocation villages which he cites as case studies. The immigrant population , which accounted for roughly 40 per cent of the population of the valley, and was certainly an integral part of the Porgeran economy, was clearly contributing to the rapid increase in pressure on subsistence resources.

In Chapter 6, Banks provides another case study of the Kewai people resident in the Kaiya 'Lease for Mining Purposes', which was about to be added to the total area leased by the PJV because of the predicted physical impact of a new waste dump. The relatively marginal position of the Kewai in relation to the development of the mine was reflected in the fact that incomes and assets were generally lower than in other parts of the Porgera Valley, with alluvial mining providing the major source of income. Access to the area was difficult, and residents had to travel some distance to reach health and education services. There was little evidence of population pressure on the agricultural land resource. However, the Kewai were about to lose a significant proportion of their lower altitude land and gardens to the spoil from the proposed dump. A new compensation and relocation agreement was intended to ensure that, in return, they would receive significant benefits in the form of cash payments, some relocation homes, a road, and various other items of infrastructure.

In Chapter 7, Banks enlarges on some of the points made in his first report (Chapter 3), by detailing the growth and development of the business sector at Porgera since the start of construction in 1989. Despite large amounts of cash compensation and business contracts with the mine, an increasingly skilled and sophisticated population , and the assistance of the PJV Business Development section, the business sector at Porgera had not developed as it might have done. A number of constraints were impinging on businesses at Porgera— economic, financial, educational, cultural and land-related. Some of these could be expected to diminish over time. Contracts were a particular focus for the local community, but they had not provided the anticipated benefits to the community, largely because of a poor understanding of what a contract is.

The influence of 'custom' on the impact of the mine

Neither Banks nor Bonnell is an anthropologist, and both authors were therefore reluctant to engage in an extended discussion of the traditional culture and social organisation of the Ipili-speaking people who inhabit the Porgera Valley. Yet we still need to recognise that the local landowners and their sundry 'guests' have by no means been purely passive recipients of the 'impacts' visited upon them. Indeed, as I have previously argued

> the word 'impact' needs to be treated with some caution, mainly because it suggests that relationships between the project and its social environment are not only dramatic but strictly unidirectional—as if the project were a stone thrown into a pond, and all the ripples in the pond should then be seen as the results of this particular event. In order to recognise the possibility of interaction between the project and its social environment, we should also think of the project as a big fish swimming in the pond, rather than a stone thrown into it, and thus allow that other, smaller fish can also make some ripples of their own (Filer 1996:59).

The relationship between the PJV and the local population has been characterised by a level of noise, and even occasional violence, which may owe as much to the traditional 'political culture' of this part of the central highlands as it does to the social and economic impact of the mine itself (Filer 1997a).

Then again, it might owe something to the previous history of contact between the indigenous population and various external forces. As Bonnell points out in Chapter 2, the Ipili of Porgera had already been adapting to changes resulting from trade, warfare, disease and famine before the European invasion began in the 1930s. The documented history of events which have since influenced Ipili society includes the 'first contact' patrols which marked the beginning of the modern area, local involvement in a millenarian 'cult' imported from another part of Enga Province, early gold prospecting activities in the Porgera Valley, the establishment of a government patrol post, the arrival of Christian missionaries, the construction of the road linking Porgera to Lae, the escalation of large-scale mining exploration, and the Mount Kare gold rush of 1988.

If it is still possible to disentangle the effects of recent history and ancient tradition, we should have to ascribe a substantial part of the

Porgeran reaction to 'development' to a form of traditional social organisation which seems to reflect the peripheral position which Ipili-speakers formerly occupied within the wider 'culture area' which is dominated by the far more numerous Enga-speaking population to the east and Huli-speaking population to the south. The flexibility of the rules or principles by which Ipili 'clans' recruit their members received a good deal of attention in Burton's (1991) social mapping study

- first because of the problems which had already arisen from the tendency of company and government personnel to treat these 'clans' as if they were corporate descent groups with clearly demarcated social and territorial boundaries; and
- second because the absence of such demarcations had enabled thousands of *epo atene* ('come stay') people to justify their presence in the impact area by reference to distant ties of kinship with the people who were officially recognised as the 'true landowners'.

In Chapter 8, Aletta Biersack explores the ramifications of this flexible form of social organisation in greater detail, showing how it functions as a form of resistance to the complex process of territorial demarcation, group incorporation and economic stratification which has been set in train by the development of the mine, and how it serves to explain some of the aggressive postures adopted by community leaders in their dealings with the mining company. In this way, she is able to cast new light on some of the evidence of 'social disorder' discussed in the earlier chapters by Banks and Bonnell.

From this account, we are led back to the problem which John Burton articulates in the final chapter of this volume, which is the PJV's failure to invest in a deeper understanding of 'traditional' Porgeran society during the exploration and planning phase of the project. More to the point, perhaps, Burton and Biersack might both agree that there is even more of a puzzle in the fact that this apparent lack of interest has continued to the present day.

Social monitoring programmes as a matter of policy

In the period preceding construction of the Porgera mine, the PNG government and the industry itself had shown little or no interest in monitoring the social impact of mine construction and operation anywhere in PNG. Neither of the industry's two main operators, Bougainville Copper Limited (BCL) and Ok Tedi Mining Limited, were required to take any responsibility for this activity under the terms of their separate agreements with the state. The government had made a commitment to monitor the social impact of the Ok Tedi mine when construction work began in 1980, but this was soon forgotten. A belated study of the social and environmental impacts of BCL's Panguna mine (AGA 1989), which was undertaken during the period in which the PJV was negotiating its various agreements with the national government and the local landowners, came far too late to prevent the outbreak of the Bougainville rebellion and the end of BCL's mining operations (Filer 1990). On the other hand, the rebellion itself prompted a new wave of interest in the question of whether social monitoring programmes could help to prevent the relationships between mining companies and local communities from deteriorating beyond the point of no return.

As the stormclouds gathered over Bougainville, PNG's National Executive Council coincidentally decided that the production of 'socio-economic impact studies' of all kinds should no longer be the sole responsibility of government, or the joint responsibility of government and developer, as had previously been the case, but should henceforth be part of the developer's responsibility to comply with the *Environmental Planning Act* of 1978.

However, the DEC has never yet been able to produce any detailed set of guidelines regarding the manner in which questions of social impact are to be addressed in an Environmental Management and Monitoring Programme. Developers have been left to formulate their own answers to these questions, with the result that quite different mechanisms for monitoring and mitigating social impacts have been adopted in respect of successive mining projects, without any consistent or concerted input from government. Although the DEC has normally required the establishment of a Social Impact Monitoring Committee in respect of each project, with a brief to identify and address social issues through the resources of its members, there has been no policy framework or procedural mechanism for relating one issue to another, for recognising causal connections between social impacts and mitigation measures, or for resolving differences of opinion on the way that social problems should be handled.

In 1992, the European Union agreed to fund a Mine Monitoring Project within the DEC which was intended, amongst other things, to strengthen the department's own capacity to monitor the social impact of mining projects by appointing specialist field staff to a newly established Social Policy Unit. This experiment has not been a great success. The new unit has not had the human or financial resources to conduct any kind of effective research programme, but the tantalising prospect of eventually doing so has diverted its staff from the task of policing and evaluating the research programmes funded by the mining companies themselves, and from seeking the active collaboration of other government or non-government organisations in putting their recommendations into practice. Mining companies have been left with the impression that social monitoring programmes are things which they fund and organise for their own internal use, and if funds are in short supply, they do not need to organise them at all.

In the absence of any clear guidelines from government, there is still little evidence that mining companies are developing a consistent and sustained approach to the design and implementation of social monitoring programmes. Instead, we find a mixture of idiosyncratic organisational responses to specific social settings and community demands. This is not so surprising when one considers that

- mining projects differ from each other in several basic dimensions, especially their scale and their duration, which affect the nature and extent of their social impact; and
- their local social environments also vary in several basic dimensions, from the experience of colonial administration to local forms of leadership or current patterns of development.

On the other hand, the companies also share some organisational features which make it difficult for all of them to adapt to the problem of social impact mitigation or risk management in the somewhat peculiar local environments which they encounter in Papua New Guinea.

In Chapter 9, John Burton presents a detailed analysis of the causes and consequences of this 'performance evaluation gap', with specific reference to the development of the Porgera project. As he points out, the mining companies have commonly failed to develop the 'new competencies' which are necessary to bridge this gap because of the typical separation of an 'environmental monitoring' section or division, which is normally run and sometimes exclusively staffed by natural scientists, and a 'community affairs' section, which is normally staffed by individuals with 'local knowledge'. It is then left to the general manager to make the cerebral connections between these two limbs of the corporate body, but the most senior levels of project management in this sector are normally reserved for engineers or accountants, and these individuals have even greater difficulty in understanding the concepts and methods of applied social science than do the natural scientists and public relations personnel who work at lower levels in the hierarchy. This corporate blind spot therefore duplicates and reinforces the lack of appropriate expertise in relevant government departments.

Comparison of the Misima and Porgera projects, both of which have been developed under the conditions laid down in the *Environmental Planning Act*, shows how the same operator (in this case Placer Dome), presumably guided by the same general conception of its aims and objectives, is liable to adopt quite different approaches to the problem of social impact monitoring in different local contexts (Filer 1998). In the Misima case, the company initially left its own community affairs staff to do all the social impact monitoring work (if such it can be called), without any assistance from external consultants. Their reports to the DEC consisted primarily of a record of the benefits which the company had provided to the local community, and the minutes of meetings between the authors and various community representatives. In the Porgera case, as this volume testifies, there has been greater recognition of the need for external assistance in the design and implementation of a social monitoring programme, because the community affairs staff have been totally absorbed by the day-to-day business of fighting the metaphorical fires created by a far more menacing collection of local stakeholders. On the other hand, as Burton explains in Chapter 9, the vagaries of this struggle seem to have produced a situation in which the programme is continually interrupted or fragmented by the limited attention span of senior management. It is tempting to attribute the whole of this contrast between Porgera and Misima to the difference in political style, and even political strength, between the two local populations surrounding the respective mines, but part of it is also due to the difference between the size, the likely duration, and the actual profitability of the two projects.

Even where mining companies recognise that 'social monitoring' is something which they cannot do by themselves, as part of the routine practice of managing 'community affairs', there is a tendency for company managers and government officials to treat the monitoring and mitigation of social impacts in the same 'mechanical' way as the monitoring and mitigation of bio-physical impacts, by assuming that the work consists essentially of measuring those 'things' for which quantitative data are already available or can readily be acquired. The resulting pile of numbers may obscure some of the most important factors in the social dynamics of a project impact area, providing little or no guidance to the formulation of mitigation or risk management strategies. The changing attitudes and values of the local community are an unpredictable but essential element in determining the very nature of the impacts which they experience, and the choice of strategies for dealing with them. One cannot simply establish social impact 'thresholds' which are comparable to something like an acceptable particulate level, and then require the 'triggering' of specific mitigation strategies as these thresholds are approached, since the nature of the problem and its solution will nearly always be a matter for negotiation between the interested parties.

Burton makes the same point in Chapter 9, when he argues that the mining companies which fund and organise social monitoring programmes need to transcend the attitude which merely looks for the least cost of compliance with government standards. To which we may add the need for all interested members of the local community to have access to all the outputs of such work except insofar as this would constitute a breach of corporate confidentiality. Consultant social scientists experience a conflict of interest in the conduct of such work, which is typically revealed by the refusal of community representatives to accept the 'objectivity' of their findings, and the failure of government representatives to act on their recommendations. Both of these revelations have been characteristic of the Porgera Social Monitoring Programme from the time of its inception. The organisation of such work must therefore make allowance for various forms of 'feedback' to take place between the measurement of change in the project impact area and the evaluation of relationships between all stakeholders in the development process—including its managers and regulators. This means 'speaking truth to power', and that truth may not always be welcome.

In our long experience of organising or undertaking this kind of work for mining companies in Papua New Guinea, Burton and I have done our best to ensure some mutual recognition of the need to place the results in the public domain, and to use these results in a broader discussion of corporate policy. While the companies have had some trouble in formally ensuring this freedom, because of their own obligations to shareholders, they have normally been prepared to acknowledge that 'secret' social monitoring studies are self-defeating. The PJV's endorsement of the present publication is a pleasing example of such transparency.

The Porgera Social Monitoring Programme, 1996–97

At the end of 1994, the Porgera Social Monitoring Programme entered a two-year period of hibernation, during which I secured the PJV's approval to begin the long task of preparing the reports for publication. For reasons unconnected with events at Porgera, completion of this task has been delayed to the point at which it has been necessary for me to convert the present tense, as used in the original consultancy reports, into the past tense, which now makes their findings seem like a contribution to the early history of the Porgera mine. However, the issues raised by the social and economic impact of the project over the last five years have been no different to those which were raised in the first five years of its existence. The more important question is the one which Burton raises in Chapter 9, which concerns the continued absence of a consistent institutional approach to the documentation and mitigation of these impacts.

While Burton attributes this lack of consistency to the organisational culture of the mining company, some part of the blame, in this particular case, would appear to be due to the failure of the DEC to sustain its own role as the notional coordinator of the Porgera Social Monitoring Committee. In August 1996, the PJV once again took the initiative, by asking Glenn Banks to submit a proposal for a second phase of the Porgera Social Monitoring Programme. His proposal observed that the first phase of the programme had comprised a series of 'one-off' reports, without the elements of coordination and feedback which had been a central feature of its original design (Burton and Filer 1993), and went on to argue that these elements should be more firmly embedded in the design of a second phase. In particular, he emphasised the potential significance of the programme as a 'community development planning tool', as well as a means of compliance with the government's environmental regulations, and revived the argument for regular (annual) reports which would not only monitor the activities of all the major stakeholders in the impact area, but would also supply recommendations for action to be taken by all of these stakeholders. At the same time, he suggested that the definition of the impact area be expanded to include the Lagaip-Strickland river system, downstream of the mine, and the powerline linking the mine to the Hides gas plant, because groups of downstream and 'upstream' landowners had both been embroiled in conflict with the PJV over the distribution of compensation and benefits from the project.

In November 1996, three members of the original design team—Banks, Bonnell and myself—assembled once again in the offices of the Community Affairs Division to hammer out the details of this proposal. At this stage, the new mine manager raised the possibility of subsuming the Social Monitoring Programme within the remit of the 'Stakeholder Monitoring Committee' which had recently been formed, on the company's initiative

- to address the conflicts which had arisen over the downstream impact of the waste material being discharged into the Porgera River
- to implement the recommendations contained in the CSIRO's report on the bio-physical dimensions of this impact (CSIRO 1996; see also Chapter 9); and
- to establish a new forum for dialogue between the PJV and those non-government organisations which had been taking the company to task on this issue.[2]

Although we were prepared to include the Lagaip–Strickland river system in our own definition of the impact area, we found this suggestion to be inappropriate, because the geographical distribution of social and economic impacts could not be equated with its bio-physical impact on the river system, and the institutional mechanisms required to mitigate these impacts would therefore need to involve a different set of stakeholders. In particular, we argued that the social and economic impacts of the mine were still concentrated within the Porgera Valley or (more broadly) within the Porgera District, and many of them had little or nothing to do with the discharge of waste material into the Porgera River.

This argument was accepted by PJV management—not least because one of the most contentious issues at that time was the company's desire to maintain the 'fly-in/fly-out' system of commuter mining (see Chapter 2) against local demands for the further development of Payam township to accommodate a larger proportion of the project workforce. The company was hoping to resolve this issue by exchanging a reduction in the number of commuters for a local undertaking to reduce the incidence of 'law and order' problems which would otherwise dissuade its employees from taking up residence in the township. The Social Monitoring Programme was seen as one of the devices which might assist in setting the terms of this reciprocal arrangement, and then making sure that both sides kept to their respective parts of the bargain. At the same time, the company recognised the need to address a variety of other issues which had been documented in the first phase of the programme, and our own design of the second phase was built around the need to determine what had or had not been done to implement the long list of recommendations appended to those earlier reports. For this reason, we proposed that each Annual Report would henceforth be accompanied by a Draft Action Plan which would continually update this list of recommendations, and which would then cease to be a mere draft once it had gained the acceptance of all the stakeholders represented on the Social Monitoring Committee. As in the design of the first phase (Burton and Filer 1993), it was envisaged that more detailed studies of specific problems, such as demographic change or 'law and order', would be commissioned by the PJV as part of the agreed Action Plans, and that their findings would then be absorbed into subsequent Annual Reports.

Once again, the design document was accepted by PJV management. Banks and Bonnell then set about collecting the data required for the 1996 Annual Report, which was duly submitted to the company, along with a Draft Action Plan, in July 1997 (Banks and Bonnell 1997a, 1997b). Some weeks later, both documents were presented to a meeting of the Social Monitoring Committee, whose membership had now been extended to include the Porgera District Administration, Porgera Development Authority, Porgera and Paiela Local Government Councils, Porgera Landowners Association and Porgera Women's Association, as well as the PJV, the DEC, the Department of Mining and Petroleum, and the Department of Enga Province. Agreement was reached on most of the measures proposed in the Draft Action Plan, which was then redrafted as the Action Plan in September 1997 (Banks and Bonnell 1997c). But we do not know how many of the planned actions have since been taken, because the consultants have not yet been asked to produce an Annual Report for 1997, let alone for 1998, nor have we yet seen any sign of the detailed studies which they recommended.

Rather than speculate on the reasons for this second period of hibernation, I shall simply note that our own reason for not including a revised version of the 1996 Annual Report as a separate chapter in the present volume is that we thought this ought to constitute the first substantive chapter in a second volume devoted to the findings of the second phase of the Porgera Social Monitoring Programme. Besides which, we have yet to secure the PJV's approval for publication of this material, and there is reason to believe that the volume of noise and heat which has been generated by some of its recommendations would cause the company to hesitate. On the other hand, there is also reason to expect that further studies of the social and economic impact of the mine will be undertaken during the course of the next decade, whether or not these are commissioned by the PJV, and we trust that the publication of this volume will serve to encourage and guide the formulation of these studies.

Notes

1   This is much higher than the 'official' figure of about K18 million contained in the company's own information booklet (PJV 1997), but there are good reasons to suppose that Banks and Bonnell have got closer to the mark.
2   This committee has since been renamed the Porgera Environmental Advisory Komiti, and presently includes three company representatives, three government representatives, four non-government organisation representatives, with an independent chairperson acceptable to all parties (see Atkinson 1998; Van den Brand and Parkop 1998).

2

Social change in the Porgera Valley

Susanne Bonnell

This chapter is based on the observations which I made during my
period of employment with the Porgera Joint Venture (PJV), from
February 1989 to October 1991, and an additional 11-week period of
fieldwork in the Porgera area between October 1992 and May 1993,
conducted as part of the Porgera Social Monitoring Programme.
According to the terms of reference established for my own
contribution to this programme, I was to

- describe and provide information on the changes which took
  place in the social environment of the Porgera mine impact
  area from the end of 1988 to the present (i.e. to mid 1993)
- identify undesirable impacts and trends and where possible
  recommend strategies to eliminate or minimise these
  impacts and trends; and
- identify existing and potential resources in the community,
  government and PJV which could be utilised for long term
  social development strategies for the mine impact area.

Fourteen separate components of the Porgera social environment were
simultaneously identified as the objects of my study, from 'relocation
and settlement patterns' through to 'socially disruptive influences'.

My study is thus concerned with the processes of social change
from the beginning of 1989 to mid 1993. Although the Special Mining
Lease (SML) was not granted until May 1989, the building and

occupation of the relocation houses which were provided to many of the local landowners really marks the beginning of the construction phase of the Porgera mine. My study of the history and impact of the relocation programme itself turned out to be a major component of the report which I presented to the company, and the findings of this study are presented as a separate chapter of this monograph (see Chapter 4). It should also be noted that my own study was primarily concerned with the social rather than the economic impact of the mine, because my fellow consultant, Glenn Banks, had been commissioned to produce a separate study of the economic impact (see Chapters 3, 5 and 7). The main areas of overlap between our studies are those which concern the impact of development on subsistence agriculture and the impact of outsiders on the Ipili people of the Porgera Valley. At the same time, Banks is more concerned with the way that social and economic impacts were seen from the male point of view, while my own study tends to emphasise the female viewpoint. This difference is understandable and arguably appropriate. Although both sexes were concerned with the full range of socioeconomic considerations, women were more concerned with matters affecting the family and the community, while men were more concerned with economic gains and losses.

The main sources of information for my study were government and PJV records, interviews with individuals and groups, a relocation survey and a separate survey on the marriages of those who had been relocated. The two-volume 1987 Pacific Agribusiness report—*Social and Economic Impact Study:Porgera gold mine* (hereafter referred to as the SEIS)—was to be used as the baseline study. Besides the SEIS, I reviewed a number of other reports which discussed the local social environment prior to construction of the mine, notably those of Talyaga (1984), Jackson (1987), and Robinson (1988, 1991).

Both company officials and public servants in Porgera were very cooperative (and patient) in providing access to documents which might contain information relevant to this study. The main problem was trying to collect data on health, education and crime. There were virtually no government records in Porgera prior to 1991 containing any meaningful information. The situation improved with the 1991 Annual Report for Porgera District and the 1992 Annual Report was even more comprehensive. The Porgera Development Authority (PDA) records appeared to be complete and accurate. Due to protocol problems, however, I was forbidden access to provincial government statistics on health and education in Wabag and told not to interview provincial public servants located there. By the time this problem was sorted out, the buildings which would have contained this information had been destroyed by the fire which followed the suspension of the Enga Provincial Government. Police in Wabag kept no crime statistics. I was never able to find out if the data I was looking for existed or not. Fortunately the very informative Enga Six Year Education Plan (1992–97), written in 1991, had been widely distributed. Otherwise, the search for the elusive data which should have existed as part of the standard national data collection system (I was not looking for state secrets) was time consuming and frustrating.

Apart from the survey interviews conducted in the relocation houses (see Chapter 4), I interviewed a wide variety of other individuals, including public servants, PJV employees, church leaders, school teachers and heads of various organisations. I attempted to seek out as wide a range of opinion as possible. Those with anti-mine sentiments appeared to speak quite frankly. My visits coincided with those of Father Phil Gibbs (a well-known Catholic priest who had done genealogical work in the area) and Chris Ballard (a researcher from the Australian National University in Canberra) who gave me some very interesting insights into the evolutionary context of certain changes occurring in Porgera.

A study of this kind necessarily has serious limitations. The broad terms of reference combined with a one-person research approach means that a lot of areas were not investigated or were incompletely investigated. It is hoped that the breadth of my study does something to compensate for its lack of depth. I have tried to show the various ways in which the development of the mine had either directly or indirectly introduced social benefits and social costs. The presence of the mine may also have accelerated social trends which were already present. However, it must also be stressed that many of the social problems identified in this study were not unique to Porgera—they were national problems. These included: a high birth rate which showed no sign of decreasing; the large percentage of population under the age of 15, which put further stress on the already stressed health and education systems; an increasing law and order problem; the breakdown of clan discipline; trade stores; alcohol abuse; and domestic violence. My original report to the PJV contained a long list of recommendations which were intended to spark discussion and debate between Porgerans themselves and the staff of relevant national and provincial government agencies, as well as those of the mining company, which might lead to an improvement in the socioeconomic situation of Porgera District and Enga Province. These recommendations have not been included in the published version of the report, in case they serve to embarrass some of the relevant stakeholders, but the reader will not find it difficult to infer their general character from the findings presented here.

The Ipili of Porgera

This brief sketch is intended to highlight aspects of Ipili culture and the impact of events since foreign intrusion in 1938. While the development of the mine has led, either directly or indirectly, to considerable change in Ipili society, change and adaptation have always been a feature of any existing culture. Prior to European intrusion, Ipili society would have been adapting to changes resulting from trade, warfare, disease and famine. Although Pacific Agribusiness (1987), Gibbs (1977), Meggitt (1957) and Biersack (1980, 1982, 1987, 1991) have written at greater length and depth about aspects of Ipili culture, there is still a need for a more comprehensive anthropological study of the Ipili of Porgera.

Environment and culture

The Ipili are a cultural and linguistic group located in two census divisions of the Porgera District of Enga Province. The Eastern Ipili of Porgera occupy land of a generally higher elevation than the Western Ipili of Paiela. The disadvantage of malaria prevalent in the Paiela area is offset by the less productive land of the Porgera area.

The Porgera Valley is characterised by steep mountains at altitudes ranging from about 1,800 to 3,500m. Soil fertility is variable, but generally of poor quality compared with the rest of Enga Province. Both the altitude and soil fertility limit the types of crops which can be grown. Porgera has an average annual rainfall of about 3,500mm, with no marked dry season. This high rainfall is linked to extensive cloud cover, particularly at higher altitudes (see Chapter 5). The high rainfall often leads to soil saturation and landslides. The average daily temperature of 11–22° celsius varies little throughout the year. The Porgera Valley is also characterised by low wind speeds, and there have been no reported frosts in the area.

The origins and length of occupation of the Ipili are not known. It has been suggested that the Ipili originated from migrations westward from Enga and northwards from the Tari basin. While there are many similarities with their neighbours, there are also striking differences in terms of kinship, land tenure, beliefs and ceremonies.

The Ipili practise a form of cognatic kinship in which individuals trace their descent through both male and female links to a founding ancestor (Burton 1991:10). An Ipili is therefore a member of many descent groups. This form of kinship offers a great deal of flexibility for land usage rights. As the Ipili were subsistence horticulturalists, this would be particularly advantageous where soil fertility is poor. On the other hand, cognatic kinship divides an individual's loyalties between various descent lines. This reduces the possibilities for a strong clan leadership system, and tends to fragment society into smaller groups. Leadership, as in other parts of the highlands, is achieved as opposed to inherited. The Ipili had male leaders who were big men, *akali andane*, and wise men, *nembo yene*. These leaders had accrued wealth, spoke well, interpreted events, and advised on the best course of action. But the outside influences of cash and education has led to a conflict between traditional values and new forces (Pacific Agribusiness 1987[1]:19). Today, the road to becoming a big man is through success in business or politics or, as is usual in PNG, the combination of both.

Recent history

European intrusion into Porgera has mainly been from three sectors: mining, government and Christian missions. It was generally accepted that Porgera's first contact with the outside world was the Taylor/Black patrol of 1938. Banks (Chapter 3) suggests that the first European intruders were the Fox brothers on an 'unauthorised expedition' in 1934. Gibbs (1977:11) reports that the arrival of James Taylor and John Black had a profound impact on the Ipili of Porgera

> Older men told me of their fearful reactions when they first witnessed the arrival of the 'redmen'. The 'redmen' were immediately thought to be yama or spirits and women and children were sent to hide in the forests while some of the men killed pigs as propitiatory offerings. Aircraft were used for reconnaissance in conjunction with the patrol and people told me how fearful they were of these noisy flying objects. Men also told me that several people were shot and killed by the patrol.

Although the Taylor/Black Hagen–Sepik patrol was a government exploration patrol, gold prospecting also featured as part of the patrol's activities. It was during this patrol that gold colours were found in the Porgera River. John Black wrote in his diary on 31 March 1939, 'After finding gold today I am not elated but rather awed with the dangers of wealth if it should turn out to be wealth' (Handley 1993:3). Although Black was of course referring to himself, it was somewhat prophetic in view of the future impact of gold wealth on the lives of the Ipili.

The next recorded impact on the Ipili was the cult from Lyeimi about 1942 (Meggitt 1957; Gibbs 1977). A Taro Enga prophet appeared preaching change, and carried the message that the earth was going to end and the people who practised the new way of life would go to live in the sky. This millenarian cult paved the way for the acceptance of Christian missionaries who carried a similar message.

After World War II, and while the Ipili were still under the influence of the Lyeimi cult, the first gold prospectors entered the Porgera Valley. Jim Taylor, who was then a District Officer in the Central Highlands, issued permits to enter Porgera to Joe Searson, Mick and Jim Leahy, Elphinstone and John Black. This expedition ran out of supplies and failed to find gold. Joe Searson remained behind in 1946 and settled among the Ipili people. There was a minor gold rush in 1948, which resulted in a number of European miners seeking their fortune (Pacific Agribusiness 1987[1]:6). The Ipili were introduced to a cash economy by these early prospectors, and they purchased goods at a local trade store which was opened by Jim Taylor, who also had mining leases in the area. The Ipili learned the skills to become alluvial miners themselves.

During the 1950s, Catholic and Lutheran missionaries made regular patrols to Porgera. Shortly after Porgera was de-restricted in 1962, the first permanent Christian mission stations were established. Catholic missionaries acquired land for their stations at Mungalep and Tipinini (see Map 1.1). Lutheran missionaries acquired land at Yuyan, then located near the government's patrol post and airstrip, which had both been established in 1961. Apostolic missionaries took out leases at Anawe and Ingau, and the Seventh Day Adventists at Yendakali and Kairik. Missionaries played an important role in the early social and economic development of Porgera. They introduced new vegetables and cash crops, built roads, promoted cash cropping and sawmilling, and established schools and health facilities (Pacific Agribusiness 1987[1]:7).

In the 1960s, mining leases were granted to companies for exploration. Companies involved in early exploration included Bulolo Gold Dredging, which was amalgamated with Placer in 1966, Mount

Isa Mines, Anaconda Australia, and Ada Explorations. In 1972, the four-wheel-drive vehicular track reached Porgera from Laiagam. This led to further intrusions and influences from the outside world, and no doubt assisted in the intensification of local mining activities in the 1970s. Initial involvement of the Ipili in alluvial mining began when they were hired as labourers for the colonial gold works. Later, Ipili alluvial gold miners worked on existing leases on a tribute basis, sharing profits with expatriate leaseholders. This tribute system lapsed in 1983, after a major gold strike at Waruwari triggered a gold rush. By this time, Yuyan had become a major informal gold buying centre, and Ipili miners panned gold which they sold directly to official or unofficial buyers. Gold became known as the 'second garden' for the Ipili.

In 1988 there was a major, and totally Melanesian, gold rush at Mount Kare, only a day's walk from Porgera. Here many Ipili from both Porgera and Paiela made and lost fortunes. The events of Mount Kare will no doubt become legends to occupy night time story-telling in Ipili households for years to come.

The Ipili and the Porgera Mine

By 1993, the development of the Porgera mine could already be broken down into five stages, each of which could be characterised by different attitudes and responses to change, particularly from the SML landowners as well as the wider community.[1]

The exploration stage lasted until about 1987. The change from individual prospectors to company mining leases and the escalation of exploration activity were relatively gradual and benign. Porgerans benefited from increased employment and trade. Knowledge was increased, producing a greater desire for the perceived benefits of the outside world. This change was easily absorbed and the gains exceeded the costs. Mining activity injected some cash into the economy primarily in the form of wages and some compensation. Profits from alluvial mining were an important source of cash.

In the pre-construction stage, from 1987 to mid 1989, the possibility of a mine became a reality. Tension increased in the community. Different vested interest groups, both within and without the SML and Porgera District, jockeyed for support and negotiated for benefits, often exacerbating the unrealistic expectations of benefits to be acquired. Landowners shifted, built, and planted to increase their chances for compensation. Disputes over land boundaries escalated, as did conflicts between the young and the old for leadership. In 1988, tension was defused to a certain degree by the Mount Kare gold rush, which divided the energies of many SML landowners and offered alternative possibilities for non-SML landowners. In Porgera itself, preparations for mining injected more cash into the economy in the form of wages and increasing compensation payments. The large compensation payments began just as cash from Mount Kare was decreasing at the end of 1988.

In the construction stage, from mid 1989 to 1991, tension between the landowners and the PJV was increased by the insensitivities and carelessness of the 'fast tracking' construction contractors who were rearranging the Porgera geography. No amount of education or familiarisation trips to other mines can really prepare people for the impact of the loss of use (or permanent loss of land), for the impact of a large work force, and the indecent haste of construction. This was a period of maximum social disruption. Anger was directed towards the mine by people who either received no benefits or benefits below the level of expectation. Mining activity injected a great deal of cash into the local economy in the form of wages, business contracts, and compensation payments, while income from Mount Kare largely ceased. Categories of 'haves' and 'have-nots' were created, leading to jealousy and greed.

The first phase of operations, which began in 1991, was a period of adjustment, adaptation and re-evaluation. Cash income from wages and compensation was still significant but already declining. Royalty payments began, but there were fewer business contracts after construction had been completed.

The second phase of operations, which showed signs of emerging in 1992, was characterised by the anger of the children of the first generation of landowners who felt cheated by the greed or ignorance of their parents. Cash availability was greatly reduced: wages and royalties were the major source of cash income, but business contracts continued to diminish in value. The SML landowners were placed under additional stress by the problem of having so little time to adjust to the anger and frustration of their children.

Urban development and physical infrastructure

The Ipili of Porgera felt left out of the many changes taking place in Papua New Guinea. The mine represented the chance to catch up and enter the modern world. This led Porgerans to focus their energies on demands for physical infrastructure and economic gains. Anger and frustration continued to boil to the surface as limitations of finance and institutional capacity failed to cope with the seemingly endless list of demands for buildings on and near the government station and permanently closed Porgera airstrip.

Towns and urban services

The Porgera government station was established in 1961 by a land purchase from the Maipangi clan. The amount of land purchased, while adequate for the time, was not adequate for all the services and facilities needed for a town to service a large mine. From late 1989 to April 1991, Porgera Station experienced a building boom: several new residences, a guest house (Mountain Lodge), a police station with cells, a community centre, a women's resource centre, an office complex for the PDA, plus improvements to the health centre. There were also several improvements to the community school on land adjacent to the station but under a lease to the Lutheran church. In April 1991, there was a major landslide which lasted a couple of weeks. The slide destroyed the airstrip, the new police station and the women's centre, and threatened many other buildings before the ground stopped moving.

While growth had been substantial, there were still several amenities that Porgera Station did not have, even in 1993.

- Public toilets. Given the number of people who were congregating in the town on pay fortnights in an area with endemic typhoid, this was a major concern.
- Public telephones. The national government gave an undertaking in the Development forum that the Post and Telecommunications Corporation would be directed to install public phones within six months of the signing of the forum agreements in May 1989. Phones anywhere in the Porgera area were problematic in 1989. Public telephones were installed in Suyan for the use of PJV residents in 1991. But the delay in installing public phones at Porgera Station angered landowners and public servants alike.
- Post Office. This was also promised under the Porgera forum agreements. A post office agency was acquired by Ipili

Porgera Investments' (IPI's) Sullivan's Store (later known as Supa Store) but since it operated out of Wabag it did not work. The PJV took out a box, and even altered its new address on stationary and business cards, but since the postal agency was inefficient the company ceased using it. In May 1993, public servants in Porgera still had to drive to Wabag to pick up mail—another source of frustration for themselves and local landowners.

With the subsequent development of Paiam township, it was assumed that a post office with public telephones would be constructed there, but there would still be a need for public toilets at Porgera Station.

In 1989, Westpac operated limited banking services from a container located in the yard of Sullivan's store. Bank agents did not always arrive for their scheduled fortnightly visits, which were meant to coincide with both PJV and government paydays. At that time, the government cash office also served as a Papua New Guinea Banking Corporation (PNGBC) agency which offered limited savings account transactions (for example with a maximum K200 withdrawal), but it was frequently unmanned. At a time when Porgerans had large amounts of cash from selling gold excavated at Mount Kare and from the large PJV compensation payments of 1989, the limited banking services did not support efforts to encourage savings. The armed hold-ups at the Westpac container certainly were a problem, but no more so than the armed hold-ups in other parts of the country. In 1990, the PNGBC opened a full branch in Porgera. Initially there was much chaos, as everyone who had Westpac accounts changed over to PNGBC, but this bank provided a much needed service. The bank manager was a popular guest speaker at women's leadership courses, and did a lot to encourage women to save their share of the compensation payments made for the Paiam land purchase.

As there was insufficient land at Porgera Station for urban growth relating to mine development, the national government purchased land at Paiam to cater for this need. The proposed services and facilities represented a new beginning, and even Porgera's entry into the 'modern world'. The development of Paiam Town was the responsibility of the PDA and the Enga Provincial Town Planning Board. Funding for public buildings came from various tied grants. The standard of commercial buildings was likely to be problematic. History has shown that most Engans and Porgerans do not invest in real estate in Enga Province because of the risk factor, so it was not clear in 1993 how successful the town would actually be. It promised to provide even more amenities (including a hospital, high school, and recreational facilities) to draw even more outsiders into the Porgera area. Some Porgeran leaders had an unrealistic picture of a peaceful, integrated town with no fences and a strict building code to ensure attractiveness. Yet one had only to look at the neighbouring towns of Laiagam, Tari, Kandep and Wabag to see the difficulties ahead: steel buildings with unsightly security fences; buildings burned and destroyed in payback or random violence; betel nut stains, graffiti and overflowing rubbish bins and litter.

Suyan, the other 'township' in the area, was really not a town at all—it was an accommodation compound for PJV employees. The land had not been purchased but had been leased by the PJV from the Aipakane clan. By mid 1993, Suyan consisted of six eight-room 'motels', 44 eight-room 'bunk houses', 30 three-bedroom married houses (of which 16 were actually occupied by families), a mess and an indoor sports complex. Many Porgerans were resentful that Suyan was a fenced enclave rather than an open, integrated town, but it was ironic that the very Porgeran leaders who wanted the fence removed from Suyan (and wanted no fences in Paiam town either) had fences around their own homesteads.

In 1993, the Porgera Local Government Council was operating a truck for rubbish collection in Porgera and Suyan, and was due to extend this service to the new Paiam township. Collecting rubbish is one thing—disposing of it is another. The problem of rubbish disposal was a mixture of the NIMBY ('not in my back yard') factor and the general instability of land in the Porgera Valley. Initially, the council was adding to the unsightly nature of Porgera Station by dumping rubbish into the Maiapam creek at the edge of the station. Furthermore, the council was not providing a rural village service, and this meant that rubbish disposal was a growing problem in the relocation areas (see Chapter 4).

Road construction

The equation 'roads equal development' has a long tradition in PNG. Indeed roads do bring access to services and provide the means for marketing cash crops. Porgerans, like people of any other neglected area of Papua New Guinea, are keen for road development. There are two perspectives on road development in Porgera—one is the PJV's need for a lifeline to the coast, and the other is Porgerans' own desire for access.

The responsibility for the upgrading and maintenance of the Highlands Highway as far as Wabag has been the responsibility of the PJV. The road to Lae is the mine's very vulnerable lifeline. Indeed, if there had been no mine in Porgera, it is quite reasonable to assume that the Maip road would have collapsed, leaving the Porgerans without road access to Wabag, Mount Hagen and Lae. As popular as the upgrading of the Porgera–Wabag–Hagen road has been, the Porgerans have long wished for alternate access to Mount Hagen through Tari in order to ensure free access to Mount Hagen when clan tensions in the Laiagam District make road travel hazardous. While the road to Tari would provide an alternate route to Mount Hagen and Lae, the downside is that it would probably bring in more outsiders from the Southern Highlands and alcohol for the black markets which flourish in Porgera.

Road links to Paiela (under construction in 1993) are also a mixed bag of benefits and disadvantages. While many Paielans wanted easy access to Porgera and the benefits thought to derive from this access, some Paielans did not want the road. While it would possibly provide the means for some Paielans to live only part-time, as opposed to full-time, in Porgera, and would open up potential for agricultural development (betelnut comes to mind), some Paielans rightly felt that they would pay too high a price in social disruption. On the other hand, the bridge and road access to Yuyan and Politika was undoubtedly popular, since the people of Yuyan felt slighted once their position as the commercial centre for gold-buying shifted to Mungalep and Alipis.

People, both landowners and outsiders, gravitate to roads. Nowhere was this more apparent than along the Tipinini–Kairik–Paiam–Suyan corridor. The same trend had also become a problem on the Waile Creek road. Yet the main problem with road development was the demand for instant construction. This was simply not feasible, and the outcome was that, in order to meet these demands, inadequate money was budgeted for road maintenance. The Yuyan road was barely trafficable in a four-wheel drive vehicle in May 1993. Another problem with the indecent haste of road construction is that machines tend to be used in situations where hand labour contracts could be issued. Hand labour may be slower, but it does spread the wealth.

The most unusual feature of roads in and around Porgera was that some were literally paved with gold. Stockpiles of ore of too low a grade to be economically processed in Porgera were crushed and used to surface roads. Whenever this happened, people risked the danger of the dump trucks to try their luck mining the road.

Despite all the road-building activity, most local people still walked long distances, and often pedestrians were often overlooked in the demands for roads. Pity the pedestrian in Porgera. Heavy traffic made the roadside dangerous, as well unbelievably dusty when dry (two hours without rain would do), and muddy when wet. This dust and danger was a source of constant complaint from landowners and the Porgera Women's Association. The sealing of the road at Paiam town, and from Suyan to the mine site, made life easier for the pedestrian, and proposals had been made to construct pedestrian foot paths from Kairik to the minesite.

Both the PDA and PJV supported efforts to construct footbridges over rivers. Footbridges are a tremendous advantage for dangerous creeks and rivers, although they were not always utilised. One day, at the footbridge at the end of the Suyan relocation road, I watched in apprehension as a woman with *bilum* and baby on her back led her other children across the river. She was only about 100 metres from the footbridge. People do not change habits easily.

Commuter mining

Porgerans wanted a residential mining town to be built as one of the conditions for their approval of the mine. This requirement is contained in the Porgera forum agreements, as well as the Mining Development Contract between the State of Papua New Guinea and the PJV. Under the Mining Development Contract, the PJV is required to actively promote the residence of mine operations personnel in the Porgera area.

In 1993, most PJV employees were still working a shift of 20 days on and ten days off, commuting to and from their place of recruitment by plane or road. This arrangement is normally called commuter mining, but tends to be known in PNG as 'fly-in/fly-out' (FIFO) because of the fact that most employees commute by plane or helicopter. The FIFO issue has been a longstanding grievance of the Porgeran landowners.

The PJV constructed Kairik airstrip as required under the mining agreements. Opening of the airstrip was delayed due to arguments over the standard of the airstrip—both basic construction standards and the question of how the design limited the category of aircraft which could use the strip. Another source of grievance concerned terminal facilities. It was left to the PDA, the managers of the airstrip, to develop facilities for regular passenger services. The PJV constructed a terminal for its own employees who departed daily on charter flights. At this facility, everyone had to suffer the indignity of being searched for alcohol on the way in and gold on the way out.

Table 2.1 shows that the PJV had 720 non-Porgeran staff in 1993, and another 376 non-Porgeran award employees. It is not known how many of these employees were married. By May 1993, the PJV had constructed 30 married houses at Suyan, of which 15 were occupied by the 2 per cent of staff employees who were residing permanently in Porgera with their families. The remaining non-Porgeran work force was commuting by plane or road.[2]

The primary reason that Porgeran landowners wanted employees to reside in a town in Porgera was so that they could profit from business spin-offs. A second reason, though not often heard, was that, if most PJV employees and their families lived in Porgera, this would demonstrate a commitment by the PJV to remain for a 'long time'. The PJV's preference has obviously been for commuter mining. I say 'obviously' because the company could have made more efforts to comply with its commitments to urban development. While much of the PJV's cautious approach could be attributed to economics, the company had some other very valid reasons.

- The primary reason was the law and order situation. The PJV could not guarantee the safety of its employees. To add families would have made the situation even more difficult.
- Many non-citizen and coastal employees would not be willing to move their families to Porgera because of the law and order problem and lack of amenities.
- Another factor was the availability of land at Suyan and Paiam. Full compliance would have required further land acquisition, which might not have been in the best long-term interests of landowners.

There also appeared to be a lack of commitment by the national government to ensure that the PJV (in which it had a 25 per cent stake) actively promoted the residence of mine staff in the area. In one of his 1992 reports on the implementation of the Porgera forum agreements, the Porgera District Manager, Graham Taylor, wrote that the national government

Table 2.1   PJV employees by category and place of origin, March 1993

Category	Origin	Number
Staff	Porgeran	20
	Other Engan	78
	Other Papua New Guinean	224
	Non-citizen	418
Award	Porgeran	364
	Other Engan	189
	Other Papua New Guinean	187
Trainees	Porgeran	125
	Other Engan	41
	Other Papua New Guinean	20
Total		1,666

Source: PJV records.

has not written to the Board of Management of the PJV outlining its requirements in this matter. Whilst we recognise that the PJV is taking steps to locate its staff in Porgera despite the constraints that exist, the onus in this matter is one for the National Government to spell out to the PJV what basic facilities the Government will bring to Porgera, what it will do to bring serenity to the place (and this must include reducing the migration in of squatters) and what timetable, what standard of houses it expects the PJV to put up. The National Government can not ensure the promotion of residence of mine personnel without giving a direction to the PJV and allowing the PJV to respond to the policy and the landowners to respond. This matter is unclear.

Members of the Porgera Landowners Association expressed concern in quarterly review meetings that the delays might lead to non-implementation; and they were right.

Health

The difficulty in obtaining health data was extremely frustrating. I was initially denied access to information in Wabag. By the time this difficulty was overcome, the information had been destroyed when the provincial government office complex was burned to the ground in early 1993. Despite the fact that health staff in Porgera were very cooperative, reports on file were patchy. I was unable to locate any annual reports for Porgera District for the years 1987, 1988 and 1990, and for some reason, at the last minute, was denied access to maternal and child health data. Maternal and child health information was not included in the Porgera District Annual Reports for 1989, 1991 and 1992. By 1993, record keeping at the Porgera Health Centre had greatly improved due to the efforts of the new medical officer, Dr Padraig Kramer. A computerised system had also been introduced by Dr Michael Hohnen at the Anawe Medical Centre.

Besides the absence of health data, another problem in examining the health situation in Porgera was the lack of recent and reliable census information. With the unknown number of outsiders moving into Porgera, population projections previously used were meaningless. No one knew how many people were living in Porgera Census Division, nor the sex and age breakdowns which would be necessary to analyse infant welfare clinic coverage, supervised births, family planning acceptors, disease frequency and so on. In hindsight, time would have been more profitably spent investigating the aid posts in Porgera instead of pursuing the fruitless paper chase.

Anecdotal evidence supports the impression that health services in Porgera deteriorated from 1987 to 1989. As a result of the Mount Kare gold rush, many of the staff of both the Porgera and Paiela health centres and the aid posts left to try their luck on the gold fields. Health services in Paiela were reportedly the hardest hit. In addition, in early 1989, tribal fighting and tensions between clans in the Laiagam and Porgera districts led to frequent closures of the Porgera Health Centre because most of the health staff were non-Porgeran Engans. A further problem was shortage of drugs, which was (and still is) a nation-wide problem. From mid 1989, as a direct result of mining development, the health services in Porgera began to improve. The first improvement was long overdue maintenance on the health centre undertaken by the PJV's construction contractors. In mid 1989, the PJV's medical officer, Dr Michael Hohnen, arrived. In order to strengthen rather than compete with the government health services, he conducted clinics at the health centre and provided much needed medicine. His presence undoubtedly prevented many deaths during the 1989–90 typhoid outbreak as well as the continuing problem of infant pneumonia. This arrangement remained in place until the government medical officer, Dr Padraig Kramer, assumed duties in Porgera in 1991, thus fulfilling another of the long-awaited provisions of the 1989 forum agreements between the government and the landowning community.

Health facilities and staffing

According to the 1992 Annual Report, the Porgera Health Centre had 40 beds and a staff of 23 headed by a medical officer. There was no classification of staff by qualifications—for example Health Extension Officer, Nursing Officer and Community Health Worker. The 23 staff included six casual workers who I assumed to be the cook, cleaners and driver.

PJV's Anawe Medical Centre provided medical and occupational health services to PJV employees, contractors and subcontractors— approximately 1,800 people altogether, including local Porgeran employees. The centre staff would also treat referrals from the Porgera Health Centre and would treat emergencies presenting at the mine site gate. The staff of the centre included two medical officers, three health extension officers, one anaesthetic technician/nurse/first aid trainer, one ambulance driver/first aid trainer, and three aid post orderlies/ nurse aids. The centre was better equipped than the Porgera Health Centre and provided services to a much smaller population. Because the centre was not a government facility, it had the organisational capacity to hire and fire staff and to obtain the drugs and equipment needed to provide an effective service.

Construction on the new multi-million kina Paiam Hospital commenced in early 1994. This facility was negotiated by Porgera landowners as part of the Porgera forum agreements. The desire for such a major facility was a reflection of Porgerans' desire for curative medicine when what was really required was more preventive medicine. While there was no question that Porgera health facilities needed improvement, there were good reasons to think that the plan for this hospital was inappropriate for local needs. The anticipated benefits of the new hospital were

- an improvement in diagnostic facilities which should prevent people from shopping around for 'cures' in Mount Hagen and Lae
- an improvement in operating facilities
- an improvement in labour wards and maternity facilities
- a possible improvement in staff morale (if improved housing were also provided); and
- the availability of dental treatment.

On the other hand, criticisms of the proposed hospital included the following points

- it was a high-tech flashy solution which did not address the basic problems of health care
- it might attract even more outsiders to Porgera
- it would be difficult to keep clean
- it was not clear who would be running the hospital, and if the government were running it, that would be another problem
- given the general reputation of Enga Province and the prevailing attitude of some Porgerans towards the existing health staff, it would be difficult to recruit new outside staff for the hospital
- it would be costly to operate.[3]

The Porgera hospital thus showed every indication of becoming an administrative and financial nightmare. Another concern would then be the community response when the unrealistic expectations of the benefits of this hospital were not realised.

In 1987, aid posts servicing the Porgera Census Division were located at Politika, Yuyan, Mungalep, Tipinini, Pakoandaka, Kairik, Yapatep and Waruwari (mine) (Pacific Agribusiness 1987). In 1993, the aid posts were located at Politika (unmanned), Nekeyanga, Mungalep, Tipinini, Pakoandaka, Kairik, Yapatep, Kulapi and Yarik. The Waruwari aid post was moved to Yokolama #2 in 1989, until the Anawe Medical Centre was completed on the plant site in 1990. As mentioned above, aid post services in the district were severely affected by the Mount Kare gold rush. There was a great deal of subsequent improvement and upgrading of aid posts and houses for aid post orderlies in all of Porgera District by the PDA under the PJV's Community Facilities Grant. In addition, as part of the relocation agreement, the PJV constructed aid posts and relocation houses for the government supplied staff at Yarik and Kulapi. The old aid post at Kairik, which was vandalised and virtually destroyed, was located on the site of the new airstrip.

Disease patterns

The leading causes of admissions to the Anawe Medical Centre were pneumonia, malaria, typhoid and trauma. The leading in-patient diagnoses at the Porgera Health Centre from May 1992 to February 1993 were pneumonia, diarrhoea/gastroenteritis, measles, typhoid fever, obstetric problems and anaemia (see Table 2.2). Typhoid was no longer as prevalent as it had been in the recent past. Dr Michael Hohnen (pers. comm.) reported that in 1989/90, 40 per cent of

Table 2.2   In-patient diagnoses at Porgera Health Centre, May 1992 to February 1993

Diagnosis	ICD Code	Frequency	Percentage
Pneumonia	321	287	21.78
Diarrhoea/gastroenteritis	016.1	149	11.31
Measles	042	109	8.27
Typhoid fever	011	80	6.07
Obstetric problems	39 to 41	71	5.39
Anaemia	200	62	4.70
Oral candidiasis (thrush)	?	45	3.41
Influenza/URTI	312	35	2.66
Heart problems	25, 283	31	2.35
Assault injury	E 551	30	2.28
Open wounds	50	29	2.20
Dysentery	016.2	26	1.97
Eye problems	23	20	1.52
Chronic obstr. airways disease	323	20	1.52
Skin problems	42	17	1.29
Perinatal problems	45	17	1.29
Pelvic inflammatory disease	372	16	1.21
Ear problems	24	15	1.14
Musculoskeletal problems	43	15	1.14
Internal injuries	49	15	1.14
Fractures	47	14	1.06
Scabies	079.1	11	0.83
Psychiatric problems	21	8	0.61
Meningitis	220	8	0.61
Malaria	052	6	0.46
Accidental injury	E 52	6	0.46
Miscellaneous bacterial diseases	03	6	0.46
Motor vehicle accident	E 474	3	0.23
Abortion	380	2	0.15
Cancer	08 to 14	2	0.15
Miscellaneous viral diseases	110	1	0.08
Leprosy	032	1	0.08
Tuberculosis	02	0	0.00
Other		161	12.22
Total		1,318	100.00

Source: Dr P. Kramer.

patients spending the night at health centres were being treated for typhoid.

The main diagnoses among out-patients at Anawe Medical Centre were respiratory diseases, diarrhoea and influenza. As was the case with Porgera Health Centre, domestic violence-related injuries were common, but were not separately recorded. The Porgera Health Centre's 1992 Annual Report recorded 29,617 treatments at the out-patient clinic. Dr Kramer indicated that out-patient data, including diagnoses, was unreliable for a variety of reasons, but that the main out-patient diagnoses would have been respiratory diseases, cuts and sores, diarrhoea and other gastrointestinal diseases, and that injuries from domestic violence were common. It may also be noted that there were eight cases diagnosed as psychiatric problems during this period. While not viewed as a major problem, this diagnosis was probably on the increase due to the demands of the church, alcohol, marijuana, and stress in a rapidly changing society.

From May 1992 to February 1993, there were 23 in-patient deaths at Porgera Health Centre, the causes of which are shown in Table 2.3.[4] It can be seen that pneumonia was the main cause of childhood admission and death. Children who died in hospital usually had a poor nutritional status and poor immunisation record, and tended to present late. Of a total of 354 under-five admissions, 19 (5.4 per cent) died after an average admission duration of 2.7 days. Of these deaths, eight (42.1 per cent) died within 48 hours of admission, before any effect from antibiotics could be expected.

The general trends in the pattern of disease may be summarised as follows

- scabies had declined due to improved water supply in relocation houses
- childhood pneumonia was still a serious problem
- typhoid, although endemic, had stabilised
- asthma was increasing along with the abuse of ventilators
- dental problems, especially in children, were on the increase due to the junk food syndrome
- new clustered living patterns and increased personal mobility were causing the spread of communicable disease such as measles
- domestic violence injuries were frequent, fracture of the ulna being the most common.

Table 2.3 **Causes of death at Porgera Health Centre, May 1992 to February 1993**

Age group	Cause of death	Number
Perinatal	Asphyxia	2
Neonatal	Neonatal sepsis	1
Infant	Pneumonia	10
	Measles	2
Toddler	Septicaemia	1
	Pneumonia	1
	Gastroenteritis	1
School-age	n.a.	0
Adult	Typhoid fever	2
	Cerebral malaria	1
	Chronic obstr. Airways	1
	Lung cancer	1
Total		23

Source: Dr P. Kramer.

Maternal and child health services

In 1987, infant welfare clinics were conducted at Yapatep, Alipis, Suyan, Porgera Station, Waratore/Apalaka, Inginene/Politika, Palipaka/Paiam, Pakoandaka, Tipinini, Yuyane, Kairik, Anawe, Kakandaka, Mungalep (Pacific Agribusiness 1987). In 1993, clinics were conducted at Yapatep, Suyan, Porgera Station, Apalaka, Palipaka, Paiam, Pakoandaka, Tipinini, Yuyan, Kairik, Anawe, Kakandaka, Mungalep, Panandaka, Yarik, Kulapi. The 1993 clinic locations reflected changed settlement patterns. For example, Alipis village no longer existed, but there was a higher density of people in the Panandaka area. Kulapi and Yarik were newly created relocation villages.

The main activities undertaken in the monthly village clinics were the immunisation and weighing of babies. Clinic schedules were followed more regularly after the provision of transport by the PDA. The clinic nurses reported no major problems except that mothers working at the mine were not bringing their babies to the clinic. No problems were reported with regard to the immunisation programme, which covered Triple Antigen, Sabin, Pigbel, BCG and Measles. The government was out of Hepatitis B vaccine, which is needed to prevent liver cancer, and which is normally given to infants to reduce the disease pool. Protein energy malnutrition amongst children has not been a major problem in Porgera, but there was probably some under-reporting in the clinics due to inaccurate weighing methods— for example weighing an infant in a *bilum* and not subtracting the weight of the *bilum*. Anecdotal evidence suggested there might be an increasing problem of malnutrition due to parents feeding infants and toddlers chocolate milk and lolly water. Junk food was certainly contributing to an increase in dental problems in young children.

As there was no qualified midwife, antenatal clinics were only conducted at the Porgera Health Centre. A cultural constraint to an antenatal programme in Porgera was women's shame to admit they were pregnant during the first trimester. Although there were 193 supervised births recorded at the health centre in 1992, it is not known how many unsupervised births there were in this period. Complaints about the conditions for giving birth at the health centre were often brought up at meetings of the Porgera Women's Association. Women did not want men to attend them during childbirth, and some (not all) of the staff treated the women in labour with contempt. These were justifiable concerns that could have been solved by the recruitment of a competent and caring midwife.

No data were available on the number of family planning acceptors. Staff at the family planning clinic appeared to be competent in their job and had the standard range of family planning methods available. Most women in the community appeared knowledgeable with regard to the benefits and methods of family planning, with Depo Provera being a popular option. Family planning services were not offered to single women or to married women without the consent of their husbands. This was not an outdated moral response, but a very pragmatic decision based on fear of payback from husbands or fathers. A common complaint from women was that they were tired of always being pregnant. Women lost control over their reproduction with the breakdown of the post-partum sex taboo. In Porgera there are no known traditional methods of contraception or abortion other than magic spells.

Sexually transmitted diseases

According to the SEIS, there were 18 recorded cases of sexually transmitted diseases (STDs) at the Porgera Health Centre in 1986, and 26 for the first quarter of 1987. It was felt that the low incidence was due to people travelling to Wabag or Mount Hagen for treatment. It was also predicted in the SEIS that there would be a considerable increase 'with the influx of a transient population of predominantly single males'. However, it is arguable that the subsequent increase in STDs was attributable to the Mount Kare gold rush. There was a rich storehouse of anecdotal evidence concerning the prostitution at Mount Kare, as well as the excesses of the successful Porgeran miners on their trips to Mount Hagen, Port Moresby, Australia and the Philippines.

Porgera Health Centre records indicate that 531 STD cases were treated in 1989, 201 in 1990, 520 in 1991, and 523 in 1992. The unusually low figure in 1990 was attributed to the loss of relevant records. The records contained no breakdown by sex or by disease (gonorrhoea, syphilis and donovanosis). The STD figures from the Anawe Medical Centre show a marked increase in 1992, from a reported 4–6 per month in 1991 to a total of 523 for 1992 (which is coincidentally the same number recorded by the Porgera Health Centre in the same year). The 1992 total was divided between 422 cases of gonorrhoea, 88 of syphilis, and 13 others. The increase was attributed to non-Porgeran national employees on field break not being treated in their home areas because government health centres had run out of the standard treatment. There was a decrease again in 1993, with a reported 173 cases up to 20 June (gonorrhoea 147, syphilis 25, and others 1). This decrease was attributed to greater awareness as a result of the medical staff giving health lectures on STD/HIV, and to the increased purchase of condoms from the medical centre (Dr M. Hohnen, pers. comm.). Most of the diagnosis for STDs at both health centres was clinical, but deemed to be fairly accurate. The Anawe Medical Centre figures are probably more reliable than the Porgera Health Centre figures due to the latter's problems with recording—as well as some suspected 'back door' treatment.

By 1993, there were no known cases of HIV in Porgera, but testing was not being done at either health centre. All overseas staff working in PNG were required to undergo HIV testing in order to obtain work permits. Diagnosis of AIDS in a 'payback' society would be a problem, and this was an argument against routine testing for HIV. With the high STD rate and the two confirmed deaths from AIDS in Laiagam (*Post Courier* 22 January 1993), it is probable that the HIV virus was already present in the Porgera population.[5] There was a lot of gossip in Porgera about confirmed AIDS cases and the need to build a special house for 'these AIDS people' in order to isolate them from the community. In 1993, the government's own STD/AIDS education effort was limited to those attending the STD clinic.

Health extension programmes

Staff at the Anawe Medical Centre began a health education programme in 1992. The programme included monthly lectures to the PJV staff (including over 500 Porgerans) in 16 locations throughout the mine site, and the 'Health Corner' feature in the PJV's *Ipili Wai Pii* monthly magazine. Topics covered by mid 1993 included personal hygiene, typhoid, nutrition, smoking, heart disease, STDs and first aid. PJV's Social Development staff had also done some health extension work (primarily with women) during the relocation programme and through the Porgera Women's Association. This focused on scabies, infant and child feeding, STDs and family planning, and on hygiene to prevent typhoid. At the Porgera Health Centre, some health advice was being given during treatment at the STD clinic, and also to women who attended the maternal and child health services and family planning clinics, but there had otherwise been no community level health extension programme conducted between 1989 and mid 1993.

The 1991 Porgera District Annual Report mentioned the formation of a 'Health Committee', and the 1992 Report mentioned that it had been disbanded, but neither mentioned its function. It was suggested that this committee might be reformed under the Porgera Local Government Council as part of a larger exercise to revitalise that body. Local government councils do have the power to make and enforce health rules, which then gives a health committee some teeth. It was not difficult to think of a list of topics which might have been included in a community level health extension programme for the Porgera area, to be implemented by a Health Extension Officer with the assistance of other medical personnel and even the PJV's media unit. Existing networks for implementation of the programme included the local government councils, aid posts, infant welfare clinics, literacy schools, youth and women's associations and their member groups, churches and schools.

Health care delivery problems

The health care delivery problems existing in 1993 could be summarised as follows

- Government provision of drugs and equipment ranged from inadequate to non-existent (for example the lack of Hepatitis B vaccine in the country). Porgera Health Centre obtained assistance from the Anawe Medical Centre with X-rays and oxygen. Due to efforts and finance from the PJV and PDA, drug shortage was no longer a problem. However, there were still problems with drug theft, the unnecessary use of antibiotics, and petty pilfering of equipment by staff and patients.

- Although there had been significant improvements with regard to maintenance of staff housing since 1989, staff housing was still inadequate.
- In-service training still needed to be improved.
- Medical staff of the Porgera Health Centre had been verbally and physically abused by members of the community. Working under constant threats and intimidation was one cause of low staff morale.
- Nearly 85 per cent of the staff at the Porgera Health Centre were non-Porgeran Engans who were traditional enemies of the Porgerans. Some of the staff were blatantly contemptuous of the Porgerans, whom they regarded as inferior. Although one could recognise a need to transfer these staff and seek a better staff mix, this was likely to be difficult because coastal people are reluctant to work in the highlands.

Education

As with health services, the development of the Porgera mine was the catalyst for a significant improvement in education services in Porgera District. Porgera's poor educational situation received further setbacks in 1988 as a result of the Mount Kare gold rush, when teachers and students left to try their luck on the gold fields. However, after 1991, there were dramatic improvements in education for the whole district

- an increase from four community schools in 1986 (Porgera, Yuyan, Paiela and Tokopa) to ten in 1993 (Porgera, Yuyan, Tipinini, Mungalep, Apalaka and Paiam in Porgera Census Division, and Tokopa, Paiela, Alumanka and Andita in Paiela Census Division)
- the opening of the Porgera Vocational Centre in 1991
- access to the College of Distance Education from 1991
- introduction of the Free Education Policy in 1993
- the opening of the Paiam Independent Primary School in 1993
- an increase in district enrolments from 443 in 1986 to 1,943 students in 1993

- the planned 1994 opening of Porgera Technical High School at Paiam.

By 1994, Porgera District would have achieved the necessary mix of educational institutions to cater for most of the pre-tertiary education needs of its people: vernacular pre-schools, community schools, international standard primary school, technical high school, vocational centre and access to the College of Distance Education.

As with health, there was the difficulty of obtaining information, especially with regard to high school enrolments. The lack of census information was also a problem. Visits were made to all schools in the Porgera Census Division. As no visits were made to schools in Paiela, the following discussion deals only with Porgera Census Division.

Vernacular pre-schools

Vernacular pre-schools are commonly known by the Tok Pisin translation *Tok Ples Pri Skul*. The Enga Provincial Division of Education called its vernacular pre-school programme *Wambao Enga Pii Sikulu* (WEPS), which had been adapted to *Wambao Ipili Pii Sikulu* (WIPS) for Ipili vernacular pre-schools in Porgera District. The Enga Six Year Education plan regarded vernacular pre-schools as a component of the community school system, so WIPS in Porgera was seen to represent a contribution to the overall goal of universal primary education.

Promotion of vernacular pre-school education is based on the premise that children who first read and write in their own language achieve better results in primary education. The introduction of WIPS in Porgera was facilitated by the efforts of linguist Terry Borchard, who had studied and was fluent in the Ipili language, and supported by PJV funding. If there had been no linguist, then the introduction of WEPS would either have been delayed or would have been introduced using a dialect of the main Enga language (which did seem possible at one stage). If there had been no PJV, then there would have been no funds to produce the teaching materials.

The first school to introduce WIPS was Mungalep in 1991, followed by Apalaka in 1992 and Yuyan in 1993. Both Paiam and Tipinini were hoping to start WIPS in 1994.[6] The main problem facing the expansion of WIPS education in Porgera Census Division was the problem of finding suitable teachers, though I understand this was not such a problem in Paiela. It seems that people who had the required maturity and educational background often preferred to seek out higher paying jobs at the mine.

Community schools

Prior to 1989, there were four community schools in Porgera Census Division, all of which were church agency schools: the Lutherans had schools at Porgera and Yuyan, the Catholic Church had one at Tipinini, and the Seventh Day Adventist Church operated a school at Kairik from 1974 to 1978. The Tipinini school was closed in 1984 due to low attendance (see Pacific Agribusiness 1987, Appendix E) but re-opened in 1989. The Yuyan school opened in 1974 or 1975, but closed down in 1988 due to tribal fighting and perhaps also the effects of the Mount Kare gold rush; it re-opened for two months in 1990 then closed again until the beginning of 1992. The next school to open in Porgera Census Division was the Catholic agency school at Mungalep in 1991, followed by the government schools at Apalaka in 1992 and Paiam in 1993. In 1993, Porgera Community School became the first school in the district to have a non-teaching headmaster.

Funding for classrooms and teachers' houses for the new schools, as well as for more facilities in the existing schools (for Paiela as well as Porgera), came from the PJV's K4 million Community Facilities Grant to the PDA. Funds for teachers' salaries come from the Enga Provincial Division of Education. The PDA became committed to a heavy annual works programme to provide classrooms and teachers' houses for the schools which needed to expand to Grade 6, and this meant that it needed to concentrate its resources on improving the existing schools rather than bow to public pressure to open new schools in Porgera District.

According to the SEIS, Porgera Community School had seven staff and 210 pupils (113 males, 97 females) in 1986, while Yuyan Community School had five staff and 141 pupils (89 males, 52 females). Table 2.4 shows the overall pattern of enrolments by school grade in the six community schools operating in Porgera Census Division in May 1993, with the numbers of teachers in each grade shown in brackets after the number of pupils.

The low number of students in Grade 6 at Porgera Community School can be attributed to the Mount Kare gold rush, since 1988 would have been the Grade 1 intake for that year. The overall increase in enrolments is attributed to the growth of new schools, the increasing number of people moving to Porgera, a growing awareness by parents of the value of education, and the introduction of the free education policy in 1993. However, while we can clearly see that there had been an increase in total enrolments in schools in Porgera Census

Division from 351 in 1986 to 1480 in 1993, it was still not known what percentage of school-age children were attending school. A standard education indicator used to analyse community school enrolments is the gross enrolment rate, which is the percentage of children aged 7 to 12 enrolled in schools. Without reliable census figures, this indicator was impossible to calculate, and it was therefore impossible to assess Porgera's progress toward universal primary education.

Because there was a lot of talk that outsiders were taking up valuable space in the community schools, I asked headmasters to indicate what percentage of their students were local Porgerans. This question was complicated, especially in Tipinini, by the problem of defining what constitutes a local Porgeran, and was more difficult in those schools with no Porgeran teachers. The results were

- no outsiders in Apalaka, Mungalep or Yuyan community schools
- 31 per cent outsiders at Porgera Community School
- 16 per cent outsiders at Paiam Community School; and
- 4 per cent outsiders at Tipinini Community School.

The high percentage of outsiders in Porgera Community School is not surprising since this school was catering for children of residents of Porgera Station, as well as residents in the nearby communities.

Table 2.4 also shows that the increase in the number of teachers had not kept pace with the increase in enrolments. The SEIS reported a teacher/pupil ratio in 1986 of 1:29, compared with the overall 1993 teacher/pupil ratio of 1:44. The Enga Six Year Education plan stated that Enga Province had an overall teacher/pupil ratio of 1:31, which was below the World Bank recommended maximum of 1:35. But most Porgera schools were in excess of the World Bank recommendation in 1993. Grade 1 ratios were particularly high, indicating that these classes were little more than child minding centres. The intake of too many Grade 1 pupils reflected an inability of Boards of Management to say no to parents, and the belief that Porgera would continue to have a high wastage rate between Grades 1 and 2. The introduction of free education undoubtedly contributed to the problem. When I queried the teachers at Yuyan about the ludicrous figure of one teacher for 96 pupils, the response was that it was not so bad, because only an average of 50 pupils attended each day! There was a definite quality of education problem here.

Of the 33 teachers for 1993 (including WIPS teachers), eight were women and 25 were men. Bearing in mind the problem in defining

Table 2.4 Community school enrolments by grade in Porgera Census Division, 1993

School	WIPS	Grd 1	Grd 2	Grd 3	Grd 4	Grd 5	Grd 6	Total
Porgera	-	198 (3)	148 (3)	152 (3)	101 (3)	91 (2)	29 (1)	719 (15)
Yuyan	48 (1)	96 (1)	59 (2)	22 (1)	-	-	-	225 (5)
Tipinini	-	-	84 (2)	-	34 (1)	35 (1)	-	153 (4)
Mungalep	31 (1)	34 (1)	63 (2)	-	-	-	-	128 (4)
Apalaka	41 (1)	104 (2)	-	-	-	-	-	145 (3)
Paiam	-	110 (2)	-	-	-	-	-	110 (2)
Total	120 (3)	542 (9)	364 (9)	174 (4)	135 (4)	126 (3)	29 (1)	1480 (33)

Source: School records.

'what is a Porgeran', 27 of these teachers were non-Porgerans. The high percentage of non-Porgeran teachers meant that it was difficult to achieve the policy goal of having native speakers as Grade 1 teachers. Demand for more teacher housing could certainly have been eased if more local Porgerans became teachers. I do not know how many (if any) Porgerans were enrolled in teacher training colleges in 1993.

Table 2.5 shows the percentage of female pupils in each school grade in May 1993. The proportion of female enrolments shows a slight decline at Porgera Community School, from 46 per cent in 1986 to 42 per cent in 1993, and at Yuyan from 37 per cent to 32 per cent in the same period. But the Mungalep case shows a countervailing trend to equal or higher female enrolments. The overall 42 per cent female enrolment level compares well with the 1991 Enga provincial average of 39 per cent, but it could be argued that female enrolments needed to be improved at Yuyan and Apalaka.

Apart from the unacceptably high teacher-pupil ratios in some grades, and the lack of native speakers as Grade 1 teachers, the main problems with community schooling in Porgera in 1993 were

- Lack of curriculum materials—most schools visited had absolutely no textbooks or teachers' aids other than the WIPS reader printed by the PJV. The District Education Officer (who looked after the three districts of Porgera, Lagaip and Kandep) advised that this problem afflicted the whole province. This was particularly a problem for new schools which would, of course, have nothing left over from previous year's supplies when the system may have worked.

- Lack of community support—This was listed as a major problem by teachers at all six schools visited. It appeared to be common for parents to pay a K20 fee to the school rather than show up for community work days. The PJV's Community Relations Section had assisted schools with library books, used computer paper (conspicuous in all schools), and minor maintenance and improvements such as water supplies to some schools.
- Vandalism and tribal fighting—Mungalep School had problems with vandals damaging classrooms, and there was also an attempt to burn the school down. Yuyan School suffered severe damage to classrooms and had to be virtually rebuilt. Destruction of schools as a result of law and order problems is a main constraint to extending education in Enga Province. There has always been the possibility of similar problems in Porgera.
- School lunches—teachers said that many parents did not provide their children with lunch. Some parents gave their children money which they spent on junk food or gambling. There were no school lunch programmes in any of the schools.
- Other—problems with subsidy cheques and teachers' pay as a result of the fire in the government offices at Wabag; lack of student desks; lack of sporting facilities; teachers' dissatisfaction with conditions and salary; and the school bus issue with Porgera Community School.

Table 2.5   Female community school enrolments by grade in Porgera Census Division, 1993

School	WIPS	Grd 1	Grd 2	Grd 3	Grd 4	Grd 5	Grd 6	Total
Porgera	-	51	50	34	45	42	45	45
Yuyan	48	39	15	14	-	-	32	
Tipinini	-	-	48	-	38	23	-	40
Mungalep	58	68	50	-	-	-	-	57
Apalaka	29	38	-	-	-	-	-	36
Paiam	-	47	-	-	-	-	-	-
Total	44	47	43	31	43	36	45	42

Source: School records.

It was pointed out in the SEIS (Pacific Agribusiness 1987[2]:36) that the limited education base of the Ipili people was a constraint to their participation in the employment and business opportunities associated with the Porgera mine. The SEIS concluded that the main education need for Porgera was to improve the quantity and quality of students being prepared in the community school system for secondary and technical training. While the subsequent expansion of community school education (including WIPS) had been impressive, there was still a very definite quality-of-education problem in 1993, and there was still a need to find ways of inducing greater community participation.

In response to Kundapen Talyaga's 1979 study of educational problems in Enga Province (Runawery and Weeks 1980:5–6), the Enga Division of Education developed the Community-Based Education Policy. This policy stressed community involvement and participation. The PJV was part of the Porgera community and made significant contributions to community school education, especially in Porgera, but in other areas of Enga Province as well. Besides the Community Facilities Grant which enabled the building programme, other areas of PJV assistance included: library books, school prizes, celebrations, and assistance with school improvements such as minor maintenance needs and water supplies. But there was still a vast pool of human (as opposed to financial) resources in the mining community which could have been utilised to work with teachers and school boards of management to help improve the quality of education.

Paiam Independent Primary School

The construction of an international standard primary school by the PJV in Porgera was a condition set out in the Porgera forum agreements. Paiam Independent Primary School, which opened in 1993, was a dramatic contrast to the community schools in terms of facilities and resources. In 1993, there were three teachers for 28 students, and an impressive array of text books and teaching aids, including video and photocopying machines. This school was meant to be part of the community services which would encourage more families of expatriate mine workers to live in Porgera. However, better education is a goal of many Porgerans, and those who could afford it wanted to send their children to this school. In 1993, 13 of the 28 pupils were children of Porgeran landowners, and the proposed school expansion for 1994 was primarily to cater for the increased demand from local Porgerans. In this respect, the Independent

Primary School promised to provide the foundation for an educated élite within the local community, and thus to create another division between the 'haves' and 'have-nots' in Porgera.

High schools

Most of the Porgeran students who have gone on to high school have attended Laiagam High School. As part of their overall development goals, Porgerans wanted a high school in their own district. The desire for a local high school is a common request throughout Papua New Guinea. Besides the obvious advantages (and prestige value) of having a local high school, Porgerans were concerned about the law and order problems that frequently affected their children attending Laiagam High School. In addition, many parents felt that the Engan teachers discriminated against Porgeran students.

Porgerans were successful in their negotiations to have a local high school in Porgera, in spite of the fact that they did not have the catchment level which is normally required for this purpose. According to the Enga Six Year Education Plan, Porgera Technical High School was due to open in 1994, with Grade 7 students from Porgera and possibly other nearby areas in Enga Province such as Mulitaka. The school would offer the standard national academic subjects together with two practical subjects—possibly mechanics and electricity. The plan also indicated that this school would gradually be blocked through to Grade 12.

I was unable to obtain any figures as to the number of Porgerans actually attending high school. It should have been possible to obtain these figures, as the PJV was providing financial assistance to Porgerans for high school education. Without figures for at least 1991, 1992 and 1993, it was not possible to assess if there was still a high wastage rate from Grades 7 to 10, as previously reported in the SEIS. Another problem was the proportion of Porgeran and non-Porgeran children selected to go to high schools from Porgera and Tipinini community schools. At the end 1992, angry Porgeran parents claimed that the original selections were all outsiders, and the numbers from Porgera were subsequently increased.[7]

Porgera Vocational Centre

According to the Enga Six Year Education Plan (Ahai *et al.* 1991:90), three basic types of vocational centres have evolved in Enga

- traditional vocational centres with a 'back to the village' focus
- specialised training centres; and
- mini or pseudo-high schools.

The Porgera Vocational Centre would be an example of a specialised training centre, since it focused on mechanics and carpentry, with limited formal classes in the curriculum of the national College of Distance Education (CODE).

Enrolments increased from 16 in 1991 to 30 in 1992, and 52 in May 1993. The centre was receiving technical support from the PJV, as well as financial support from both the PJV and the PDA. In support of the basic skills training, the centre made desks for the community schools and ran a vehicle repair workshop for minor repairs and service.

The Porgera Women's Association Resource Centre was rebuilt in the vocational centre compound after the 1991 earthquake. The plan was to build a larger women's resource centre at Paiam and hand this building over to the vocational centre for home economics training. The first female students were enrolled in the vocational centre in 1993, and with the female CODE teacher formed a small sub-group within the association.

College of Distance Education

As stipulated in the Porgera forum agreements, and in order to assist those Porgeran students who either were not selected to go to high school or who did not complete high school, the CODE opened a registered study centre in Porgera in 1991. Up to the end of 1993, the CODE centre shared the facilities at the vocational centre, but was due to move from this temporary home to a newly built centre in Paiam township. This centre was providing support services to students (including the vocational centre students) who were taking Grade 7 to 10 subjects by correspondence. The centre obtained financial assistance from both the PJV and the PDA. The number of students registered with the centre increased from 23 in 1992 to 102 in mid 1993, but 53 (51 per cent) of these 1993 students were non-Porgerans. The lower percentage of Porgerans could have meant that this school was catering primarily to the needs of outsiders, but it could have meant that Porgeran Grade 6 leavers were not interested in furthering their education, or that their numbers were insufficient to fill the places available.

Tertiary education

The PJV had a scholarship programme which provided financial assistance to selected students undertaking tertiary studies. According to PJV records, three out of 30 sponsored students in 1992 were Porgerans, and only one Porgeran (out of a total 42) was being sponsored in 1993. As qualified Porgerans would have been given preference, this number indicates just how few Porgerans were undertaking tertiary studies.

Literacy and non-formal education

The provincial non-formal education function had moved from the Division of Education to the Division of Community Services and back to the Division of Education. Non-formal education focused on training programmes for youth and women and on adult literacy. In Porgera non-formal education programmes for youth and women have been undertaken through the district's youth and women's associations. The PJV Community Affairs Division has employed staff specifically to assist with these programmes. Porgeran churches have also been involved in youth training programmes.

Adult literacy has been a provincial priority, since 'over 90 per cent of the population of Enga cannot read or write' (Ahai *et al.* 1991:104). In 1991, the Adult Literacy Programme coordinated by the Porgera Women's Association began. In addition to course fees, the PJV and PDA also allocated funds to operate the programme. Besides administrative difficulties, the main problems encountered were the lack of teachers, arguments over which language to use[8] and access to buildings in which to conduct the courses. There was a need for a full time Adult Literacy Coordinator responsible to the women's association, but the difficulty of obtaining a suitably experienced Porgeran for the position suggested that it might be necessary to recruit an overseas volunteer with a Porgeran counterpart.

Women, marriage and the family

The argument here is that women are the key element to family stability, especially during periods of rapid social change. Mine development had negative impacts on the lives of local women, but paradoxically also had the potential to provide opportunities for women to gain more control of their lives and influence the course of social change. Although the United Nations proclaimed 1994 as the

International Year of the Family, the discussion in this section suggests that the family in Porgera had some serious problems in that year.

The time which Porgeran women were spending on domestic duties associated with their roles of mother, wife, food producer and tender of pigs was relatively unchanged. Meanwhile, outside influences (the steel axe, *bisnis*, education) had a significant impact on men's traditional roles. Porgeran women were therefore raising concerns that men were opting out of their traditional duties as they explored their own avenues to find the road to success. These traditional duties included heavy clearing, fencing, digging drains, house building and repairs, and care and discipline of children, especially male children.

Concerns raised by Porgeran women at formal meetings of the Porgera Women's Association, as well as in informal discussions, focused on

- the problems associated with polygyny
- deserted wives
- domestic violence
- problems of alcohol abuse and black markets
- access to family planning methods
- the need for money in an ever-growing cash economy
- the breakdown in law and order (especially the increase in rape and police violence); and
- concern for the future of their children.

Many of these concerns were similar to those raised by women in other parts of Papua New Guinea.

Women and subsistence

Women's primary economic activities still focused on the subsistence sector of the economy, with a great deal of their time spent on tending food gardens and raising pigs—though pig raising was no longer an activity for women who had adopted the Seventh Day Adventist religion. In addition, those women who had rights in areas of alluvial mining activity, or whose husbands had such rights, were accomplished gold panners. Some women also operated trade stores or engaged in informal trading activities which included the sale of home-made scones, second-hand clothes, and surplus food crops.

Women's primary traditional responsibility was food production. Subsistence agriculture was still the economic basis of Ipili society. Gold may have been the Ipili's second garden, but food was still the first garden. Not everyone in Porgera was an alluvial miner, and even for those families who did regard gold as their 'cash crop', it was still secondary in importance to subsistence agriculture. Older women especially liked the security of having and working their food gardens. It was a known source of control for them in a changing society.

Whatever the goals for rural transformation are, it is essential not to lose sight of the importance of subsistence agriculture. Trade stores and cash crops do not substitute in either the short or long-term for the value of food gardens. The problems of subsistence agriculture in the SML area have already been discussed. If the man was a wage earner, he would not necessarily give his wife the cash she needed to purchase food. Provision of food for daily meals was still viewed as a woman's duty. It was not unusual for a woman to be hit by her husband if she failed to produce a meal for him.

My own observations of food gardens in Porgera, both within and outside the SML, indicated that there was plenty of scope for improvements to subsistence agriculture in terms of variety, yields and agricultural practices. The SEIS and Robinson (1988:58) acknowledged the need for a *didimeri* (female agricultural officer) to assist primarily with the anticipated food garden problems of relocated landowners. The death of the under-qualified *didimeri* who worked first for the government and later for the PJV's Women's Division left a gap which was still waiting to be filled in 1993.

Women in employment

Women liked cash and the sense of control that went with it. Many younger women preferred to buy store food rather than work in the garden. Many women of all ages in Porgera were seeking employment. These women had even copied their menfolk and joined together to demonstrate for employment. However, while women appeared to enjoy the prospect of escaping the constant drudgery of child care and gardening, they faced similar problems to those of working women in the Western world. These problems included sexual harassment, male backlash, and child care arrangement problems.

In a predominantly male working environment, sexual harassment is almost inevitable, and was certainly reported by the PJV's female employees and those of their catering contractor, IPI-Poons. Laundry women working in bunk houses reported sexual harassment by male shift workers. There were also a few reported cases of sexual harassment of female employees, both national and expatriate, by male co-workers. Complaints of this sort were normally dealt with by the PJV's Welfare Officer or staff in the Women's Section. The male backlash for working women came from their husbands and from other male employees. For example, as a consequence of a domestic dispute, a husband might request that his wife's employment be terminated. There were also cases in which rumours were started that female laundry workers would be replaced by men.

Child care is a particular problem for working women everywhere. This has been especially true in Porgera and other areas of Papua New Guinea, where breast-feeding for one to three years is the norm. Older children can usually be taken care of at home under traditional arrangements, but babies who are being breast-fed need to be near their mothers. The centrally placed PJV creche was not successful, because the working environment was so widely dispersed, and this created difficulties of access by the mothers. The Social Development Officer dealt with problems on a case-by-case basis. The most serious problems were with the PJV's catering contractor, IPI-Poons, which employed the largest number of local women. Women feared that they would lose their jobs if they took too much time off to feed their babies. Another problem for working mothers was that of time lost when a child was sick. Going to the health centre at the government station virtually became a full-day chore. The clinic sister also reported that mothers working at the mine were not bringing their babies to the infant welfare clinics. These problems were not as serious for women employed by the government, because these women were nearer to their homes, and their failure to appear at work was not taken so seriously because public servants were seldom penalised for absenteeism.

Losing control

The breakdown of the custom requiring women to seclude themselves from men while menstruating brought women greater freedom. But the breakdown of the post-partum sex taboo brought them greater hardship. Women did not like to have children one after the other. This added to their workload. It was hard to do garden work and look after more than one child at the same time. Porgeran women appeared to be well aware of the advantages of family planning and the availability of contraceptives, but complained that access was denied by their husbands. The women in charge of family planning services at the government station would not give women contraceptives without the husbands' consent due to fears of payback. Men did not want their wives to have contraceptives because they feared that they might be promiscuous, and because men gained prestige from fathering lots of children.

Traditionally, women's influence was in the private realm, while men exerted their influence in public. This system may have been appropriate in the past because 'by remaining in private affairs and exerting indirect influence on public matters, women were sheltered from the risks of public life and left to concentrate on their primary goals—bringing up their children in safety and providing subsistence and wealth to their families' (Kyakas and Wiessner 1992:178). However, modernisation produced changes which women were unable to influence because they had no public voice. The new political, legal and economic institutions were all dominated by men. The need for women to have a public voice to influence change was the rationale behind the Porgera Women's Association. Women's associations have the potential to provide the support for women to take risks and enter the public debate. If women lose control of everyday events in their lives, not only are they further disadvantaged, but the future of the family is at risk.

Domestic violence

The subject of domestic violence as a national problem is well documented in a series of studies undertaken by the PNG Law Reform Commission (see Toft and Bonnell 1985). The stress created by rapid social change due to the development of the mine had probably increased the rate and severity of domestic violence in Porgera. This was due to men's anxiety over their own ability to cope with rapid change, women's anger over men taking new wives, and the problems related to relocation houses in polygynous marriages (see Chapter 4). While wives did hit their husbands, wife-beating was a bigger problem because it was more common and more severe. The doctors at both the government and PJV health centres reported their own concern about the number and severity of wife-beating cases. Rarely did battered men need treatment.

Women were not against domestic violence if a wife failed in her obligations—provided the beating was not too severe. When women felt aggrieved, they would provoke their husbands into hitting them. Either this would clear the air or the woman would then appear in public (enhancing the damage by not washing or tidying up in any way) to testify against unfair treatment. In marriages that were working, the husband would feel shame and compensate his wife. Women were especially concerned with alcohol-related domestic violence, as this was unpredictable and usually more severe, and they were also concerned about husbands who beat their wives in order to make them run away and thus avoid the obligation to repay bride-price.

Fighting between co-wives was common. In an extreme case, in 1992, a young Porgeran woman, who had recently become a third wife, was murdered by the jealous second wife. Fighting was also common between a wife and a woman who was felt to be in an adulterous relationship with her husband, as adultery usually led to marriage between the adulterous partners. That women appeared more often to take action against a co-wife or other woman, rather than the husband, is a reflection of women's powerlessness in society. But the incidence of domestic and sexual violence also needs to be placed in the wider cultural context where 'bouts of violence…were not only frequent in husband-wife relations, but in virtually all categories of relationships in Enga regardless of sex, age and relationship' (Kyakas and Wiessner 1992:165).

Raising children

Children are highly valued in Ipili society, as in most of Papua New Guinea. I am not aware of any customary practice of infanticide nor any recent cases of infanticide which would be an indication of stress in society. It was anticipated in the SEIS that an increase in the numbers of illegitimate children would be a problematic consequence of mine development, but this issue was not raised by the Porgera Women's Association, nor did the PJV Welfare Officer report any cases. However, problems of this kind could yet be a matter of concern in view of the reported increase in promiscuity among the younger generation.

The care of young children is generally seen as the role of women, but men also have a role in childcare, especially in the discipline of older children, and boys in particular. At a women's association meeting in October 1992, women said that, with more husbands abandoning their wives, they were worried about the discipline of their children. The general impression was that a lot of young children were very badly behaved—the most obvious example being those very young children, mostly male, who threw rocks, used obscene language, and flashed penises. My observations over a three year period were that young children of both sexes were generally left to their own devices, and were not disciplined until an adult, usually male, could no longer tolerate their behaviour, when the discipline was often over-reactive. The freedom of boys continued into adolescence, while girls soon adopted the female roles of caring for younger children and working in the gardens.

Apart from the general pattern of socialisation, the more specific factors which could have led to discipline problems included the growth of family size (too many children too closely spaced), domestic violence, alcohol abuse, and the practice of bribing children to go to school, giving in to their temper tantrums, and buying them junk food. There is also an argument that lack of discipline could be attributed to the abandonment of male initiation rights. Male initiation rights were very important in the past as a means to instil discipline and teach men the rules and responsibilities related to adulthood. The bottom line is that undisciplined children grow into undisciplined adults.

Inter-generational conflict

Although conflict between generations is not uncommon anywhere, the problem was particularly evident in the mine impact area. Areas of conflict centred around leadership, ownership of relocation houses, and distribution of mine benefits.

- Leadership conflicts were already much in evidence when people had to decide who would be their nominated representatives on the original Landowners' Negotiating Committee, and this type of conflict resurfaced with the subsequent formation of the Kaiya Landowners' Negotiating Committee (see Chapter 6). The big question was how and when should leadership be transferred to the younger generation.
- A second major area of conflict was the relocation house (see Chapter 4). Adult children of relocated landowners were demanding that they should have their own relocation house. It is normal in many societies for children to expect to live as well as or better than their parents.
- A third area of conflict was cash benefits. The substantial once-only compensation payments went to the parents. The next generation wanted its cash benefits as well. The

situation was not helped by the lack of clear decisions over the future allocation of benefits from the trust fund set up for the children of SML landowners.

At the same time, the conflict between generations was only one aspect of the overall youth problem affecting Porgera and the rest of Papua New Guinea as well.

It was the next generation of landowners (and there were many adults already) who felt that they were sold out by their parents and would therefore cause problems in the future. Add to this the lack of gardening land, unemployment, lack of discipline, and the presence of alcohol, guns and outsiders who have nothing to lose—and you had a recipe for disaster.

The Children's Trust Fund

Under the conditions of the Porgera forum agreements, 10 per cent of the total mining royalties were being paid to a trust fund for the children of the SML landowners. According to the Department of Mining and Petroleum, this fund had received K1,315,730 by the end of 1992. The whole amount had been placed in interest-bearing deposits; there had been no disbursements. As of May 1993, the following matters relating to the trust were outstanding

- the trust deed had not been signed by the Minister for Finance
- a manager for the trust had not yet been appointed
- the updated list of SML landowners' children (the beneficiaries) had not been completed
- no decision had been reached as to the form of benefits.

In May 1993, it was planned to complete updating the list of SML landowner children. The list would be published and circulated for appeals. After this, it would be up to landowners to register their children. What was not clear to me was whether the beneficiaries would also include the grandchildren of registered landowners. There were already a significant number of grandchildren in 1993.

The delay in deciding what benefits would be distributed under the trust fund was likely to compound the feelings of dissatisfaction amongst the adult children of landowners. The main benefit for which these children were agitating in 1993 was relocation-type houses. It had been suggested that the fund could be used to provide such housing for landowners' children, but if this were to be done, then the fund would soon be depleted. Another suggestion was that this fund could be used to provide international-level primary education for the landowners' children. This would be problematic as it would lead to another form of distinction between the 'haves' and 'have-nots' in Porgera society. In addition, many children could end up being excluded because of their age or scholastic ability. One thing was certain: when the time came to distribute the benefits, there would be disputes.

Law and order

The deteriorating law and order situation in Porgera was the main problem affecting the quality of life of Porgerans and the long-term viability of the mine. The 'law and order' problems in Porgera need to be seen in the national context (see Clifford, Morauta and Stuart 1984), but Enga Province as a whole has had a particularly bad reputation for lawlessness. Most of the inhabitants have been affected by tribal fighting. There have been pockets of anarchy such as the Tsak Valley. In 1991, the situation in Laiagam town became so bad that public servants abandoned it to mob rule.

In Porgera, when discussing the law and order situation, it is important to bear in mind the different perspectives of the state, the Porgeran community and the PJV.

- Most Porgerans, like most people in Papua New Guinea, are concerned with restoring harmony and patching up relations which have deteriorated, or else with being a winner in a situation of conflict. The emphasis is on restitution and compensation rather than punishment. There is also no distinction made between civil and criminal offences.
- The state is concerned with the rule of law through the formal police-court-corrections system. The state punishes those who have broken its own laws, but this may not necessarily satisfy the victim.
- The PJV wants to run its own business of mining gold with a minimum level of civil disruption and crime affecting its operations.

These perspectives can be and often are in conflict.

The justice system

In 1989, the local police detachment was housed in Panandaka. As this land was required for mine expansion, the police station moved temporarily to the government station, then to containers located at the Anawe boom gate.[9] In 1990, a new police station was opened at the Porgera government station. However, this impressive concrete building was only briefly occupied before being totally destroyed by the 1991 landslide. Police then operated out of houses on the station until the new police station at Paiam was completed later in 1992, by which time another police station had been built at Suyan.[10] Many records were lost in these moves.

The local police detachment was backed up by the mobile squad. During 1989 and 1990, the mobile squad was frequently present in Porgera, primarily to clean up criminal activity on the road between Porgera and the Western Highlands border.[11] This squad also assisted in preventing a serious tribal fight from deteriorating into a blood bath. In 1989 and 1990, the mobile squad had a reputation, with both the PJV and the more law-abiding segments of the Porgera community, of being a tough but responsible organisation.

Because of the problems facing the police, the PJV assisted with accommodation, transport, fuel and overtime pay. While the PJV had the ability to call upon police—as did anyone—the PJV did not in any way direct the police. However, community perceptions were such that any excesses of police action were blamed on the PJV. For example, in June 1991 police went to Laiagam High School to retrieve a PJV vehicle which had been 'impounded' by teachers and students. Police—both local and mobile squad—met with community resistance, and in the ensuing fracas, the police shot several high school students. In retaliation, decking on the nearby bridge was removed, thus cutting the road access into and out of Porgera. For several days there was a stand-off between the community and the police, and the whole incident was blamed on the PJV.

When the state increased its equity stake in the Porgera mine from 10 per cent to 25 per cent in 1993, the Rapid Deployment Unit (RDU) was created to protect such large 'national investments'. When the RDU arrived in Porgera, they were housed at the PJV camp in Tipinini. The community now had three different police forces to contend with—not counting the PJV's own Security Department. The local police detachment was viewed as the most benign. The mobile squad was feared or cheered depending on what action was taking place. But the RDU appeared to have absolutely no support at all from the local community. The RDU came into further disrepute when one of the men allegedly shot a Suyan landowner, and this resulted in community retaliation against the Suyan residential camp. I would argue on the side of the community, although not necessarily for the same reasons, that three different police forces were unnecessary. The state should have put its resources into strengthening the local police and the mobile squad, which could be called upon whenever the situation got out of hand.

Papua New Guinea's court system consists of the National Court, which handles most civil cases and criminal cases, the district courts, which handle summary offences, the land courts, and the village courts.[12] In Porgera there was no resident District Court Magistrate until late 1993. Some of the Provincial Affairs officers at the government station were gazetted magistrates. However, in spite of the backlog of cases which built up when the visiting magistrate failed to appear, they did not often use their powers. Once Porgera had its own district court and resident magistrate, the main priority became the improvement of the village court system. An efficient village court system should not only handle the bulk of community level disputes; it should be able to defuse situations before they become major problems, act as a force for discipline in the community, and hopefully help to prevent some tribal fights. In 1993, only the Suyan Village Court was reputed to be functioning in a satisfactory manner.

The main problems with the operation of village courts in Porgera, including Suyan Village Court, were
- lack of training for village court officials
- lack of supervision and inspection of court proceedings and decisions
- problems with financial accounting
- discrimination against women
- a preference for adjudication over mediation
- bureaucratic problems at provincial level which have obstructed the gazettal of new magistrates.

Although Village Courts are not a traditional method of dispute settlement, they were an accepted and well-used system in Porgera. Nevertheless, women were very vocal in their criticisms of victimisation in village court decisions. They did not want the courts abolished; they wanted them to respond to women's complaints. Women also demanded that female magistrates approved by the Porgera Women's Association be appointed to all village courts. This was agreed, and women were appointed, but their appointments, along with those of new male magistrates, were not gazetted because of problems at the provincial level (Porgera District Annual Report 1992).

The SEIS (Pacific Agribusiness 1987[1]:18) recommended that the village court system be strengthened by appointing 'a strong and capable Provincial Village Court Officer with the mandate to hire and fire staff, implement an effective system of supervising and training, and ensure sound financial accounting and control procedures are followed'. The Acting Assistant District Manager reported in 1992 that there had been no permanent officer to coordinate the Enga Provincial Village Court Office, thus casting doubt on the feasibility of any further recommendation for institutional strengthening at the provincial level. However, the PJV was indicating its own willingness to assist in strengthening the Porgera village court system by providing a temporary officer to work with a District Village Court Inspector appointed by the Division of Enga. The local system could also have been strengthened by the appointment of a police liaison officer, a gazetted welfare officer, a nominee from the Porgera Local Government Council and a nominee of the Porgera Women's Association.

All rural lock-ups in Enga province had been closed by 1993. The nearest correctional institution was Baisu, just outside Mount Hagen. Since Porgera already had a resident magistrate, court house, police station and police cells in 1993, there was an argument in favour of constructing a rural lock-up (in Paiam) to house minor offenders serving short sentences, who could then be made to do community work.

Tribal fighting

Tribal or inter-group fighting can be viewed as both a law and order problem and a method of conflict resolution. Prior to European intrusion, inter-group fighting was common throughout the whole of Papua New Guinea. Today it is primarily a highlands practice. Tribal fighting was harshly repressed in coastal areas by an authoritarian colonial regime. By the time the highlands were brought under the Pax Australiana, a more enlightened form of colonial rule had emerged. This led to a dramatic reduction in tribal fighting during the 1950s and 1960s. With the approach of self-government and independence in the 1970s, however, tribal fighting re-emerged as the primary method of conflict resolution.

Meggitt (1957:32) reported that, in 1957, the Ipili of Porgera were involved in continuous inter-clan feuding, even though 'the many clan fights appear to by-pass the mining claims'. By contrast, Gibbs (1977:22) observed that 'one of the changes brought by the government most appreciated by the people is the cessation of fighting, enabling them now [i.e. 1974] to move about much more freely and without fear'.

By noting the presence or absence of inter-group fighting in each census division the Clifford Report made a rough estimate of the percentage of population affected by this phenomenon (Clifford, Morauta and Stuart 1984). On this criterion, 20 per cent of PNG's total population, but 89 per cent of the people in Enga Province, were affected by tribal fighting in the early 1980s. By this criterion, it can be said that 100 per cent of Porgera Census Division's population was affected by tribal fighting in each year from 1989 to 1993.

Tribal fighting was a constant source of social disruption in Porgera. It was disruptive to the community because it resulted in deaths, injuries, and destruction of property, and because it restricted freedom of movement. It was disruptive to the mine because fighting often took place on the road, or encroached into the company's residential areas. Employees then took time off work either to participate in the fights, protect families, or flee due to fears of payback. As clashes often occurred between Porgeran and other Engan clans, and most public servants and teachers were from other parts of the province, government services were consequently interrupted. In 1993, the PJV's Community Affairs Section created a position for an officer to monitor civil unrest in the community, and to liaise with the police and kiaps for intervention and mediation.

As tribal fighting was so pervasive, I felt this was an area worthy of investigation. Tribal fighting was supposed to be reported in the monthly 'Situation Reports' submitted by each district office, but no such reports had been filed in Porgera since 1985 due to lack of directives from Provincial Headquarters (Jeffrey Puge, pers. comm.). I therefore attempted to compile basic information on fights from 1988 to mid 1993 by asking people who had knowledge of these fights— *kiaps*, lands and community relations officers for example.[13]

Porgeran tribal fights differ significantly from those in neighbouring Enga-speaking areas in that they are of shorter duration and involve comparatively little damage to property. This can be attributed to lack of manpower, because it takes a lot of warriors to create the devastation seen after Engan wars. Furthermore, the cognatic kinship system in Porgera would tend to dilute clan loyalties in fights (Pacific Agribusiness 1987[1]:18; Burton 1991:12). But the impact of outsiders on Porgeran fighting was evident in the Kairik fight of 1992–93. This was an intra-clan fight in which each group had Engan allies, and the result was a fight of lengthy duration and destruction. Alcohol and motor vehicle accidents were new triggers for fighting. In addition, the gun had finally arrived in Porgera. This was inevitable, as guns were so pervasive in tribal fighting in other areas of Enga (and the highlands in general). While I did observe 'a gun' in one fight in Panandaka in 1993, I do not know if anyone had already been injured or killed by one in a local clan fight.

Compensation was the normal way to achieve a reconciliation between the warring parties. Cash could lead to an inflation in compensation payments and groups could opt out of compensation by saying that it was against their religion (if they belonged to the Apostolic or Seventh Day Adventist churches); but the biggest problem was that the increase in the actual number of fights, combined with the introduction of 'the gun', may have meant that the number of deaths and injuries outstripped a group's capacity to pay. At a meeting with women of the Maip-Mulitaka Women's Association, the women complained that all their efforts were going to produce sweet potato to raise pigs for compensation payments.

Crime

One problem in analysing any trends in crime is the lack of any annual crime statistics for Porgera before 1992 (see Table 2.6).[14] Even the 1992 figures may underestimate the number of cases reported to the police, as there was a reference in the Annual Report to a 'torn' Occurrence Book. There was also the usual problem of trying to determine how much crime was reported to the police. Police attributed the low arrest rate to victims preferring compensation.

The reported wilful murders do not include deaths in tribal fighting. The three murders recorded in 1992 were those of a young woman by a co-wife, the pack rape and murder of a young woman after a disco, and the murder of a man during compensation negotiations. I am unsure if the co-wife was convicted or still awaiting trial in 1993. There were no convictions for the other two murders.

As is true world-wide, it was difficult to document whether the incidence of rape was increasing or not. However, Porgeran women felt that it was increasing in Porgera. As the victim received no justice under the legal system, rape was often not reported to the police. Restitution was achieved by compensation and reputedly through the village court, even though this offence is outside this court's jurisdiction. Pack rape is a recent and unfortunately common practice in many parts of Papua New Guinea, not just the highlands. However, until the two vicious pack rapes of 1990, this practice was not common in Porgera.

There were three types of arson committed in Porgera: police arson, arson in tribal fights, and payback arson. Most arson from 1989 to 1993, in terms of the total number of houses burned, had been done by the police. In one case, the police burned and looted approximately 39 houses in the Mungalep area after the official opening of the Porgera mine on 20 October 1990. In late 1993, the police burned over 300 houses at Paiam in retaliation for the killing of a fellow policeman (Laurie Martin, pers. comm.). Arson was not a feature of tribal fighting until the Kairik fight in early 1993.

Incidents of theft ranged from armed robbery to minor thefts of anything that was left unattended for the briefest moment. The two largest robberies in Porgera were the 1990 armed robbery of the

Table 2.6   Porgera crime statistics, 1992

Indictable offences	Reported	Arrests
Armed robbery	2	0
Wilful murder	3	4
Arson	4	0
Attempted robbery	3	0
Break and enter and stealing	9	0
Attempted murder	1	1
Rape	5	4
Carnal knowledge	2	2
Grievous bodily harm	4	4
Indecent assault	2	0
Wounding	6	3
Summary offences		
Common assault	102	44
Stealing (minor)	49	21
Fighting	19	21
Tribal fighting	3	0
Drunk	1	1
Drunk & disorderly	2	2
Threatening behaviour	28	3
Adultery	2	0
Escape	10	9

Source: Porgera District Annual Report, 1992.

Westpac bank agency and the 1990 New Year's Day riot and looting of the IPI Supa Store. Armed robbery and hijacking of vehicles with goods for the PJV and Porgera stores was less common in 1992–93 than in 1989–90. However, the PJV, banks and stores were not the only victims of theft; it was pervasive in the community and was even common within families. Women carried the family bank passbooks in their bilums as it was not safe to leave them at home, and even then women often had these passbooks stolen. The 1992 figure of 49 reported 'minor' stealing offences indicates that most thefts were either unrecorded or unreported. Minor theft charges were also heard in the village courts.

Riots, roadblocks and demonstrations

This is another area in which it proved difficult to obtain information. As with tribal fighting, there were no Situation Reports which might mention major riots and demonstrations. The PJV's Community Affairs and Security section reports only mentioned those events which had or could have had an impact on mine operations. Incidents which might be noteworthy in more peaceful areas of the country (for example riotous behaviour at the Lands Office or minor roadblocks) were accepted as part of daily life in Porgera.

Mob action and violence was common at Porgera Station, especially on pay days. Roadblocks were another common method of airing grievances. Most roadblocks in Porgera were directed at the mine. This was frequently the case during the indecent haste of construction, when foreign contractors overstepped agreed land boundaries. Many grievances could have been sorted out first through discussion. While I witnessed some pretty scary mob action, all the roadblocks I encountered were relatively peaceful events. The object was to air a grievance, not to engage in combat, but this in no way condones what was usually an illegal action.

Examples of serious riots which took place in Porgera include
- the looting of IPI store on New Year's Day in 1991
- the riot stemming from the union strike at the mine in May 1991
- the attack on the mining camp at Suyan on the night of 14–15 October 1992.

The only surprising thing about this serious attack on Suyan was that it had not happened sooner. It was an event waiting for a trigger. In a place of known violence and with grievances against the mine, it was not strategically sound to house employees so far from the mine site. When trouble occurred, mine employees either stayed in camp or ran the gauntlet. Even with all the new security arrangements which now give Suyan the appearance and ambience of a prison, it would be hard to say that the risk of such an attack has been removed.[15] There are plenty of Porgerans with grievances against the mine and vast numbers of idle outsiders ready to fuel these grievances or join in demonstrations. The rent-a-crowd mob have nothing to lose.

Outsiders

A squatter is a person who settles on land without authorisation. As most non-Porgerans residing in Porgera have had landowner permission to reside, it is more accurate to say that Porgera has had an 'outsider problem'. While there are no census data to indicate just how many outsiders were living in the Porgera Census Division during the period of this study, there was agreement by all (the Porgeran landowners, the provincial government officers in Porgera, and the PJV) that the numbers were considerable. It also appeared that most of the outsiders were western Ipili people from the Paiela Census Division, Enga-speaking people from the Maip-Mulitaka, Kera-Lagaip and Wage census divisions of Enga Province, and Huli people from the Tari Census Division of the Southern Highlands Province. People from all these areas had traditional links with the Ipili of Porgera. The Ipili granted permission to outsiders to reside for reasons of culture and commercial gain. Relatives and families of the person obtaining residence then moved in, and this led to a chain migration problem.

A distinction must be made between the more permanent outsiders who resided in Porgera and the considerable number of temporary outsiders who came to Porgera during the fortnightly pay day period, known locally as the 'thank you market'. Six provinces have highway access to Porgera: Morobe, Madang, Eastern Highlands, Simbu, Western Highlands and Southern Highlands. While the highway provided easy access to Porgera, it also meant that people could easily return to their homes. It is quite possible that Porgera would have had even more outsiders and a larger 'squatter problem' if there was no highway. A programme to reduce the number of outsiders in the Special Mining Lease was actually undertaken by the PJV in their capacity as the leaseholders. The two most positive features of this programme were landowner support and lack of violence.

The permanent and temporary outsiders had different reasons for coming to Porgera. Many permanent outsiders came to Porgera for quality of life factors: employment possibilities, access to health and education facilities, and even to reside in a more peaceful place. Temporary outsiders came for economic gains, which included selling goods at pay day markets, obtaining part of the wages of relatives or friends, and prostitution. Many came simply for the excitement, and these formed the bulk of the ever-ready rent-a-crowd that joined in the fights and riotous behaviour which became a standard feature of pay day. As previously mentioned, the social and environmental problems caused by excessive numbers included overcrowding, shortage of land for food gardens, lack of firewood, and pollution of creeks and rivers (see Chapter 5). As outsiders could return to their own land and communities, they had little to lose on their own account, but might gain by joining forces with Porgerans and encouraging them to take action over real or perceived grievances.

Unemployment

Unemployment has been a major issue in Porgera. It was the cause of an unknown number of demonstrations, mostly peaceful, some of which were staged by local women. The mine and its contractors were the major employers in Porgera. Employment preference was given to Porgerans but, due to the lack of education in the community, most employed Porgerans were in unskilled or semi-skilled positions. Many Porgerans were resentful at the number of outsiders employed by the mine. However, given the education base at Porgera, it would be many years before there would be enough qualified and experienced Porgerans to occupy skilled and senior positions in the mine work force. There were very few wage employment opportunities in Porgera besides those offered by the PJV and its contractors. Some Porgerans were involved in alluvial mining and business activities, but most Porgeran-owned businesses were spin-offs from the mine (see Chapter 7). In 1993, there was virtually no agricultural base in the district other than a few small-scale coffee and vegetable growers, though the government had already set up an agricultural base camp at Tipinini for coffee and vegetable extension programmes.

All this pointed to large numbers of unemployed or under-employed people living in a valley which was very much geared towards the life-styles of a cash economy. Easy money from the Mount Kare gold rush, and from PJV and government land compensation, meant that people's expectations for a reasonable wage were definitely too high from 1988 to 1991. Add grievances and mix with rent-a-crowd, and you had a recipe for civil unrest.

Alcohol and drug abuse

Money made at Mount Kare led to an increase in alcohol-related problems in Porgera. In response to this, the Enga Provincial Government banned both the sale of alcohol and its importation into Porgera in late 1988, with the sole exception of the restricted club licence at the mining camp. In 1989, the escalating law and order problems in Enga Province led to a province-wide ban on the sale and importation of alcoholic beverages.[16] While there were pressures to ban alcohol, there were pressures to remove the ban, once it was in place, due to loss of revenue by the provincial government and the inability of the police to control black markets. Alcohol black marketing was common in Porgera due to the wealth of the population. Large compensation payouts were generally followed by periods of alcoholic haze. There were also indications that the local black market was well organised.

Alcohol abuse was primarily a male problem in Porgera. The Porgera Women's Association, like its counterparts throughout Papua New Guinea, frequently had alcohol-related problems on its agenda. Women in Porgera knew the who, how and where of alcohol black marketing, but did not wish to report this information to the police for fear their houses would be burnt.[17] The women's main concerns regarding alcohol abuse were the resulting incidents of domestic violence, loss of family income, motor vehicle accidents, and the numbers of children and adolescents who were learning to drink with their male relatives. While prohibition leads to black markets, the alcohol-related problems in Porgera would probably have been much worse if alcohol had been sold in legal outlets. In 1993, the Enga and Porgera women's associations both wanted the alcohol ban to remain in place throughout the province.

In 1993, there was only one recorded case of someone growing marijuana in Porgera, and this was ironically on the government agricultural station. However, marijuana was easy to obtain and was thought to be imported into Porgera along with the fortnightly influx of people on pay days.

Prostitution and promiscuity

Obtaining any specific information on the subject of prostitution was a real problem. There were reports of two female prostitutes operating from an Alipis disco in 1987, as well as reports of prostitutes operating in the gold fields of Mount Kare. I heard many stories of Porgeran men spending Mount Kare and compensation money on the good life in Mount Hagen, Port Moresby, Cairns and the Philippines. There were also a few stories of Porgeran women soliciting in Mount Hagen. Prostitution in Porgera itself appeared to be primarily a problem caused by the pay day influx of outsiders. There were unconfirmed reports of prostitution being conducted out of one or two houses in Porgera government station.

Concerns expressed by women did not focus on prostitution per se, but on the incidence of adultery, the possibility of contracting AIDS from unfaithful husbands, and the increasingly promiscuous behaviour of young people. Adultery was a major issue with women because it usually led to marriage. My impression was that more men were committing adultery than women, and that the increase in adultery was correlated with the influx of wealth from Mount Kare and mine compensation payments. Adultery was not only socially disruptive because of its association with polygyny, but also because it led to domestic violence and an increased risk of sexually transmitted diseases. As we have seen, domestic violence was a serious social problem in its own right, and one that could not be easily overcome, given the overall level of violence in the community.

Other socially disruptive factors

Three other causes of social disruption may also be mentioned here: quarrels over land compensation, the incidence of gambling, and the conduct of local 'discos'. In order for construction of the mine to begin, the PJV needed to acquire land and compensate the owners for the temporary or permanent loss of land use and for improvements to the land—mainly food gardens, economic trees, and buildings. Investigations by PJV's lands officers resulted in disputes over land boundaries and the rights to receive the compensation—whether in the form of cash payments or relocation houses. This was a major source of social disruption in the SML in 1989, and in Suyan and Kairik in 1990.

Unlike alcohol consumption, gambling was an activity widely practised by both sexes. High stake gambling was common after compensation payments. It was also common for children to gamble. The most common form of gambling was card games, although snooker and darts were also quite popular.[18] The Porgera Women's Association expressed concern that some women were gambling to such an extent that they were neglecting their children. This appeared to be a new problem in Porgera, which was associated with the recent inflow of cash. My own observations of card games in Porgera indicated that there was less cash involved in 1993 than in 1989-90, though when I remarked on this, one woman pointed out that the players hid the paper money when I came around. The President of the Enga Women's Association, Scholla Warai, reported that many women living in Wabag town were spending a lot of time gambling, and consequently neglecting their children and household duties.

It was (and still is) common in many parts of Papua New Guinea for a community to raise funds by charging admission to dances held in a fenced-off area. In some parts of the country these dances to raise money have been called 'six to sixes' (i.e. dusk to dawn), but today the more common name is 'disco'. A major change in the conduct of discos in Porgera was that they were no longer supervised community fund-raising events, but a form of private business where security arrangements were designed to protect the property of the owner, rather than to ensure communally acceptable forms of behaviour. As with alcohol, there was nothing inherently wrong with discos; it was the activities and behaviours associated with them that caused problems and community concern. Discos were as popular with young people in Porgera as they are world wide. The problems in Porgera were black market alcohol, marijuana, prostitution, and the fear that attendance would lead young people into promiscuous behaviour—not to mention the problem of noise pollution. A disco was blamed for the dreadful pack rape and murder of a young girl in October 1992. The problem was that in Porgera, with the increased number of outsiders and the general breakdown of family discipline, it was virtually impossible to obtain an acceptable level of supervision and security to ensure that discos were both fun and socially acceptable.

Institutional strengthening

In the period covered by this study, there had been a disproportionate amount of energy and resources directed towards works programmes in Porgera to the neglect of quality of life issues. This was understandable, as Porgera was one of the least developed districts in Enga Province. But once many of the infrastructure demands had been met, the time had come for institutions to direct their resources and energies to the following quality of life investments

- establishing peace and good order in the community—a fundamental prerequisite for social and economic development
- providing more education, formal, non-formal and informal
- improving the health status of the community by concentrating on preventive rather than curative measures
- improving income-earning opportunities for the majority and not the few, while ensuring that immediate economic gains would not be achieved at the expense of future generations
- improving the status of women so they could participate in, and benefit from, development.

National and provincial government

The national government's mineral revenues are supposed to be directed towards development in various social and economic sectors. However, as Jackson (1993:169) comments in his review of the Ok Tedi mining project

> ...the hope that mining would kickstart more desirable and appropriate forms of development around the country has clearly been disappointed. In the twenty years since BCL opened there are very few indications that general development levels in the country have shown anything more than sluggish, partial growth. Agricultural performance, admittedly in the face of almost continually declining world prices, has been particularly abysmal. Like almost all other developing countries heavily dependent on metal exports, the PNG government has not been able to utilise mining revenues to raise productivity elsewhere in the country.

This suggests that the national government is unlikely to have the political will or institutional capacity to assist Enga Province to maximise the benefits that can be obtained from having a world class, profitable mine within its boundaries.

The main financial benefits of the project to the Enga Provincial Government have been the royalties paid on mine production and a Special Support Grant from the national government. Royalties initially represented 1.25 per cent of the export value of the mine's output.[19] These were paid by the PJV to the national Department of Mining and Petroleum, and the provincial government then received 77 per cent of the total, while the remaining 23 per cent went to: the SML landowners (8 per cent), the PDA's community development fund (5 per cent), and the 'Landowners' Children's Trust Account' (10 per cent). In addition, the national government has agreed to pay the provincial government a Special Support Grant which represents 1 per cent of the export value of the mine's output. According to the Porgera forum agreements, Special Support Grant expenditures are subject to national government approval and are supposed to be accountable on a quarterly basis.

According to the Department of Mining and Petroleum, the provincial government had received K6,665,000 from the Special Support Grant and K10,154,229 from mining royalties by the end of 1992. I was unable to find out how this K16 million had been used.[20] This highlights three problems

- the lack of accountability for public monies
- institutional incapacity to design and implement infrastructure construction projects; and
- Engan attitudes to mine benefits.

Many angry Engan people were complaining that they had received no benefits from the PJV. This attitude was understandable. The provincial government's failure to direct the above K16 million to infrastructure projects in Laiagam, Kandep, Wabag, Wapenamanda and Kompiam districts placed the PJV in a difficult situation. In order for the PJV to secure road access through Enga province, Engans needed to perceive that they were receiving benefits from the PJV. The PJV's response was firstly to increase its public relations and community development assistance to areas outside Porgera District, and then to introduce the Resource Development Tax Credit Scheme (later known as the Infrastructure Tax Credit Scheme), as an arrangement between itself and the national government, under which it could deduct the cost of infrastructure construction projects up to the value of 0.75 per cent of gross income from its corporate tax liability.

Lack of accountability and corruption have been allegations frequently made of both the national government and various provincial governments. The main difference between the targets of these accusations is that the national government has had the power to suspend provincial governments. The Enga Provincial Government was suspended twice for financial mismanagement in the decade preceding this study. The problem with suspending provincial governments, and replacing the elected provincial politicians with a caretaker administrator, is that this rarely did anything to improve the performance of the provincial public service. The effectiveness of public servants in the Department of Enga did not improve, despite the efforts at institutional strengthening under the province's integrated rural development project, called Enga Yaaka Lasemana, which operated for most of the 1980s.[21]

Problems facing the Enga public service included

- lack of middle management skills to get things done, which was exacerbated by the problem of attracting skilled public servants to work in Enga
- tribal fighting, which not only prevented the delivery of services and destroyed infrastructure, but also became an excuse for public servants, especially extension staff, to fail to perform their duties
- buck-passing between the national and provincial government, the opportunities for which were further increased when functions were decentralised to the district level
- an excessive number of policies and policy changes
- regional divisions between eastern and western parts of the province; and
- poor staff morale.

Deficiencies in the public service were recognised, but the proposed remedies had not made much difference

- divisions were restructured, and functions decentralised to the district level, without the staff and resources required to make the system work[22]
- staff were reshuffled without the means or the will to get rid of 'dead wood'
- conferences, workshops and planning exercises became an end unto themselves.

The experience of integrated rural development projects in Enga and other provinces (East Sepik, Southern Highlands, Milne Bay) suggests that sustainable institutional strengthening was not achieved because these projects operated alongside of, instead of being integrated into, the provincial public service, and because expatriate contract officers were placed in line positions in order to achieve immediate results.

The improving performance of the public service in Porgera itself (known as the Division of Porgera) was reflected in the Annual Reports. Had it not been for the presence of the mine, it is doubtful whether there would have been any improvements, and arguable that there might even have been a further decline. Most probably, the road connecting Porgera to Laiagam would have become untrafficable, leading to a further deterioration of services. While there had been significant improvements in health, education and agricultural extension staffing, other rural extension services were still almost non-existent. Many of the significant improvements in Porgera could be credited to the efforts of the PDA rather than the provincial government. Nevertheless, Division of Porgera staff, with assistance from the PDA and the PJV, had the potential to strengthen other institutions to be models for the rest of Enga Province, specifically: the local government councils, the village court system, and government extension programmes.

The Porgera Development Authority

The PDA was formed in 1989 as a fourth level of government between the provincial government and the two local government councils in Porgera District. The PDA's general functions, as specified in its own legislation, were to

- control, manage and administer the Porgera District
- ensure the welfare of its residents
- assist the local government councils in carrying out functions within the district
- maintain the Kairik airstrip
- receive and distribute royalties from the provincial government
- administer the spending of monies under the PJV's Community Facilities Grant (K4 million by 1993)
- advise on liquor licensing matters in Porgera District; and
- assist the Provincial Town planning Board in planning any township in Porgera District.

The rationale for creating a fourth level of government was to overcome the bureaucratic constraints of local government legislation in order to get things done, and to ensure that both local government council areas received their due share of mine-related benefits. In the short term, the PDA was an effective institution for getting things done. The PDA demonstrated accountability for the money it received.[23] The PDA was responsible for the building and upgrading of community schools, aid posts, recreation facilities, minor roads and bridges, as well as the development of Paiam township. However, the formation of the PDA compounded the institutional weakness of both Porgera and Paiela-Hewa local government councils.

The Porgera Local Government Council

The development of provincial governments weakened the local government system. The focus of centralisation merely moved from Port Moresby to provincial capitals, while the quantity and quality of services to rural areas declined. By 1993, this outcome had been officially recognised by the national government with its launching of the Village Services Programme. Although this programme appeared to be specifically aimed at revitalising local or community government councils, it also seemed to make some provision for by-passing these bodies.

Following the creation of the PDA, the activities of the Porgera Local Government Council were mainly confined to the operation of garbage collection contracts at Porgera Station, Suyan and the mine site, the construction and maintenance of market facilities, and the cleaning of Porgera town. In addition, the council was receiving the village court fines and using this money to upgrade village court facilities. But local councils have the potential for engaging in a wider range of activities. The 1992 Porgera District Annual Report indicated that the Porgera council had an interest in both law and order and public health issues. Since 1990, it had passed the following rules

- Litter Rule 1990
- Offensive Weapon Carrying Rule 1990
- Animal Keeping Rule 1990
- Fighting in Public Rule 1990
- Pig Trespass Rule 1990
- Street Selling Rule 1990
- Aerodrome Trespass Rule 1990
- Tax Rule 1991
- Disco Control Rule 1991.

However the council had problems with documentation and gazettal of the rules, and it is not clear from the Annual Report which rules, if any, had been gazetted. Even if all rules were gazetted, there was still the problem of finding the manpower to enforce them.

In 1993, the Porgera council had new council chambers at Paiam, indicating perhaps that the town itself would come under the council's jurisdiction. However, the council did not have adequate staff or finance to undertake its existing functions, even after its works function had been taken over by the PDA. The council needed more permanent staff to manage its affairs and programmes, and some additional temporary staff to tackle outstanding administrative and organisational problems, as well as any new proposed activities.

The Porgera Landowners' Association and Community Issues Committee

According to the SEIS (Pacific Agribusiness 1987[2]:12), 'the Porgera Landowners' Association [PLA] was formed in January 1986 to represent clans owning land within the SML area, but has since been weakened by conflict between "true" landowners and invited guests who subsequently gained control of the executive for political purposes'. Because of this problem, the Landowners' Negotiating Committee was formed, in early 1987, specifically to negotiate the compensation and relocation agreements for the SML. The SEIS suggested that 'such single purpose groups are likely to succumb to conflicting purposes once the immediate aim is fulfilled'. In fact, after the agreements were negotiated and signed, the Negotiating Committee continued to meet, and became a successful forum for debating issues and grievances between the PJV and the landowners. The committee then expanded to include the original 23 members and their alternates, plus the nine local councillors who took part in the Development forum and signed the Mining Development Contract. This expanded group was renamed the Community Issues Committee (CIC). This committee was still meeting regularly with the PJV in 1993, and had grown into a responsible and effective group, though this did not mean that the two parties were always in agreement.

Meanwhile, the PLA—which still represented the Porgeran landowners at the quarterly review meetings coordinated by the Department of Mining and Petroleum—was suffering (at least until 1992) from a lack of credibility due to organisational problems. According to its chairman, the PLA only became a registered organisation in 1991 (Nixon Mangape, pers. comm.). In 1992, it became a more professional organisation, and began producing written documents relating to its concerns and demands.

While I am still unclear as to the structure and membership of the PLA, I assume that it was supposed to represent the interests of all landowners in the Porgera Census Division, not just the SML. In 1993, it appeared that the PLA and the CIC were really one and the same group. In 1992–93, the same person was chairman of both groups, and many of the PLA executives were attending CIC meetings. Issues debated with the PJV were often the same issues presented to the national government at the quarterly review meetings. Therefore, the CIC could be viewed as the unofficial forum for debate, and the PLA as the official body which monitored progress on the conditions of the Porgera forum agreements, as well as the other concerns of Porgeran landowners. This appeared to be a very satisfactory arrangement.

The Christian churches

The Christian churches in Papua New Guinea have always had an important role in social development. This has included mission-run schools and health services, youth and women's programmes. In addition, all churches bring the basic message of peace and preach against socially disruptive influences such as polygamy, tribal fighting and adultery. In 1962, after Porgera was de-restricted, four Christian denominations entered the valley: Apostolic, Roman Catholic, Seventh Day Adventist and Lutheran. These remain the four main churches in the Porgera District. Gibbs (1977:23) wrote that in 1974 'mission bodies exert a considerable influence, though this is truer in the Paiela valley than in Porgera'. Interviews with church leaders in Porgera indicated that this situation still existed in 1993.

The Apostolic Church was a strong, peaceful influence in the community until the split in its membership in 1992. The breakaway church, led by a couple of Apostolic pastors from Kandep, was called the Apostolic Pentecostal Church of PNG, while the parent church was called the Christian Apostolic Fellowship, and still belonged to the worldwide body of Apostolics. In 1993, this division was causing problems in the Porgera area—especially in Paiam, Kulapi and Anawe—but the influence of the breakaway church had apparently not yet extended to Paiela. One result of the conflict was a court case over who should conduct services at the newly built Paiam Apostolic Church and the closure of the literacy classes at Paiam and Anawe. According to Pastor Patimo Kolape, there were about 1,000 active Apostolic church members in the Porgera District in 1993, and about another 1,000 who had been baptised but were no longer attending services.

The Lutheran Church came into Porgera District in 1962, and acquired leases at Mungalep, Yuyan, Yendekale and Kolombi (Paiela). The conflict in the Lutheran church in Enga had not affected Porgera, as only the Maramuni church was represented in the district. In 1993, the church had three agency community schools at Yuyan, Porgera Station and Takopa (Paiela). According to Pastor Pes Kiwale, there were between 750 and 950 active church members in the Porgera District. The Roman Catholic Church was based at Mungalep, and was running three community schools at Mungalep, Tipinini and Kolombe (Paiela). According to Father Peter, there were about 2,000 active church members in the district, and the membership was stronger in the Paiela area than in Porgera Census Division itself. The Seventh Day Adventist Church was based at Yendekale. According to Pastor Lambu, there were about 2,000 active members in 1993, and the Adventists had been actively recruiting new members since 1992.

All churches appeared to have gained strength since 1989. However, according to some church leaders, the 1988 Mount Kare gold rush had a very negative impact on their activities. Church leaders also agreed that weekly church attendance and other church activities were more common among women than men. This difference was explained by the fact that men were practising polygamy, which is against the principles of all four churches, and were involved in compensation practices which were contrary to the principles of the Seventh Day Adventist and Apostolic churches. All four churches had very good programmes for youth and women in other parts of Papua New Guinea, but these programmes were very weak in the Porgera District, possibly because of the lack of an educated congregation to implement community programmes.

The Porgera Women's Association

The Porgera District Women's Association, generally known as the Porgera Women's Association (PWA) or Ipili Wanda Yame, was formed on 18 October 1989. The basis for the association was the small group activities under the PJV's Women's Relocation Programme in the SML and the small number of women's groups which already existed in the district. The association started out with six member groups, but this had increased to 36 by July 1992. Besides the village women's groups (wanda yame), there were separate groups representing Porgera and Paiela government stations, and one group for women employees working at the mine, while the girls attending the CODE centre had also formed a group and joined the association. Many, but not all, of the member groups were church-based groups. Church-based groups were encouraged because these groups generally have greater strength, or greater potential for strength, as they are based on and supported by existing church programmes.

The PWA was an incorporated association managed by a nine-woman executive or management committee which met monthly. General meetings were held monthly for ten months, with a two-month break over the Christmas period. The association had been recognised and supported by the PJV, the Division of Porgera, the PDA, and the Porgera Local Government Council. It was also a member of the Enga Council of Women.

The initial success of the PWA can be attributed to the social disruption in the community caused by both the Mount Kare gold rush and mining development at Porgera itself. Local women had many problems or issues of common concern. In addition, Porgera society was fluid and flexible in the face of change, and since there had never been any previous attempt to form a district-level women's council in Porgera, there were no historical problems to be overcome. The association also had the support of a few leading Porgeran men who prevented any organised male backlash.

The primary purpose and function of a district-level women's association was to give women the leadership skills and public voice which would enable them to participate in decision making, and eliminate discrimination against half the population, in a world populated by an increasing number of non-traditional, male-dominated institutions. Where rapid social change is taking place, as it was in Porgera, a strong women's association is necessary to ensure that women are not further disadvantaged by male decision-makers. In Porgera, the newly created institutions included the PLA, the CIC, the PDA, the Porgera Allied Workers Association, and of course the PJV itself. These were additions to the existing non-traditional institutions, like the provincial government, the local government councils, and the village courts.

A second function of the PWA was to promote relevant formal, non-formal and informal education programmes to meet the needs of women, their families and the wider community. A third function was to identify and promote economic activities—improving subsistence agriculture, business skills and income-generating opportunities for women.

The President of the PWA was the elected women's representative on the PDA.[24] The first project undertaken by the PWA was the successful lobby of the PDA to construct a Women's Resource Centre. Women wanted a building of their own for the association's activities, as well as for prestige. This resource centre was constructed by the PDA using funds from the PJV's Community Facilities Grant. It took one year to progress from project approval to occupancy in mid November 1990. The centre was officially opened on 8 March 1991, as part of the association's Women's Day activities, and was dismantled in May 1991 to prevent its total destruction by the Porgera landslide. The PDA rebuilt the centre next to the existing classrooms at the vocational centre. The resource centre, a modified relocation house, was now too small for the association's needs. The District Manager suggested that, when Paiam town was built, a new and larger Women's Resource Centre should be located there, and the present centre could then be turned over to the vocational centre as a home economics building.

Programmes and projects organised by the PWA from October 1989 to May 1993 included

- International Women's Day celebrations in 1990 and 1991
- lobbying the PDA for the appointment of women as village court magistrates
- a 'Women and Law Day' on 2 October 1991
- the Porgera literacy project
- women's leadership and skills courses
- business awareness and book-keeping courses
- a screen printing project
- an ore sample bag-making business
- a second-hand clothing business
- poultry and vegetable projects; and
- an artefact business.

Some of these programmes and projects were on-going in 1993, and some were one-off affairs. Some were highly successful, while some had problems.[25]

The Porgera Paiela Youth Association

The Porgera Paiela Youth Association (PPYA) was formed on 28 August 1989. Over the next four years, its affiliation grew from eleven to 51 member groups, approximately half of which were church-based groups, and 12 of which were based in Paiela Census Division. The PPYA was specifically formed as an independent youth association outside of the National Youth Movement Programme (NYMP) and the Enga Youth Council. In 1989, the Enga Provincial Youth Council was experiencing many problems, and was dominated by 'grey-bearded' youth—a fact which supported the suspicion that most member groups were in fact not youth groups at all, but family business groups registering with the NYMP in order to access money under the latter's grant scheme. This grant scheme encouraged a 'handout mentality' and an atmosphere of conflict and competition, as opposed to cooperation, between member groups. In addition, there were many groups, especially in the Tipinini area, which had been ripped off by investing in the now defunct National Youth Development Fund which was part of the NYMP.

Youth associations are more complex than women's associations. The first problem is defining just what the term 'youth' means. The 'adolescence' definition of youth is the period between childhood and acceptance of the full responsibilities of adulthood, but this becomes problematic when one considers the early age of marriage in Porgera. When one hears references to the 'youth problem' in Papua New Guinea, the reference is normally to unemployed, out of school, males between the ages of 16 and 25. A rigid definition of youth simply is not possible if one is trying to develop youth programmes which are integrated into, rather than separate from, the community. In Porgera this problem was tackled by defining 'youth' as people between the ages of 13 and 25. Anyone older was classified as an 'adviser'. In order to register with the PPYA, youth groups had to have more 'youth' members than 'adviser' members.

The second problem is appeal. For example: in areas where women's concerns tend to focus on their roles as mothers and wives, older teenage girls may feel they have more in common with women's groups. At the same time, very 'naughty' male youth are unlikely to join youth groups, while older male 'youth' who are married have a different agenda to younger teenagers. Youth associations are also more vulnerable than women's associations to being manipulated for political purposes.

In order to discourage the 'handout mentality' syndrome associated with grants to youth groups, a Youth Contract Scheme was initiated by the PJV. Under this scheme, youth groups registered with the PPYA undertook labour contracts to earn money. For some reason, this programme lapsed in 1992, but was being revitalised at the time of the present study.

Youth and women's groups often have money-making projects. The PJV's Youth Coordinator reported that in 1993 17 youth groups had vegetable projects, 50 had poultry (meat bird) projects, 12 were involved with trade stores, and three with tyre services. There were often unrealistic expectations as to the outcomes of these projects. At best, they offered skill training and a fund-raising source for group activities; at worst, they failed due to lack of knowledge and support or misuse of project funds by a member of the group. The members of the PPYA also wanted a project to give them a 'name'. They decided on a *didiman* (agricultural supply) store. This was funded by the PDA, and had a government business development officer attached to the project. By 1993, the store, which was located in Porgera market, had expanded to include a bookstore, as well as the sale of agricultural supplies.

Youth training courses to mid 1993 had concentrated on sporting skills (basketball, volleyball, badminton and table tennis), business management skills, and leadership. In 1990, the association organised a law and order rally at Porgera Station, but this was not very successful for a variety of reasons, which included heavy rain. Youth groups and the PPYA were very effective as organisers of the Independence Day celebrations in Porgera, which included a Youth Show. Both the PPYA and the PWA had extensive social networks which had tremendous potential for extension work.

PJV's Community Affairs Division

The primary function of the Community Affairs Division was to handle all matters relating to relationships between the PJV and landowners in Porgera, as well as the wider community in Enga Province and in the vicinity of the Hides transmission line. In early 1989, the division consisted of three separate but closely related sections—Community relations, Lands, and Business Development. These three sections were gradually being strengthened and brought up to full divisional status on a par with the other two divisions— Production and Administration. The elevation of the 'people side' of mining was due to the strong leadership and capabilities of the Community Affairs Manager, Noel Walters. The process was probably also facilitated by the closure of the Bougainville mine in mid 1989, which sent shivers around the mining community, and by the law and order problems in Porgera and along the highway to Lae, which was the lifeline of the mine. In early 1989, the company's efforts had been concentrated on land investigation and acquisition, relocation and business development. With the notable exception of business development, which had an office in Wabag, all programmes were aimed at the Porgera Valley. The hijacking of a truck loaded with mine equipment in 1990, near the Kera bridge in Laiagam District, triggered the beginning of a wider community relations programme in Enga Province, and later in the Tari District around the Hides-Porgera power transmission line.

By mid 1993, the Community Affairs Division had a staff of about 85 working in the following sections

- Lands and relocation
- Community relations—Porgera
- Community relations—other (i.e. the rest of Enga Province and the transmission line)
- Business development: Porgera and Wabag
- Social development and women's affairs
- Youth and recreation (i.e. community level as opposed to site services for PJV employees)
- Media unit.

Local community relations staff were recruited to work in their own home areas, for example Porgera, Laiagam, Sirunki, Wabag and Tari.

There is a growing awareness that the lands, community relations and business development functions are an integral component of modern mining development in Papua New Guinea. However, many senior staff in this field (and not just in the PJV) have felt that they are viewed as a necessary evil—heavily supported when there are problems, but ignored and under-resourced at other times. This is to some degree understandable, as expatriate mine developers are in the business of mining—this is their area of training and expertise. Weaknesses in the government system have forced mining companies to undertake what are traditionally government activities—the most notable being land investigation, land acquisition and business development. Other activity areas, such as welfare services and community development programmes, were gradually added as the need was identified. The reality is that a strong Community Affairs Division staffed with experienced field officers is critical for the short, medium and long-term viability of the mine.

One problem affecting the Community Affairs Division in 1993 was inadequate and inappropriate office facilities, with its sections divided between two locations, thus making coordination between staff more difficult. The division's future was also under a cloud because an increase in production costs was forcing the senior management to look for savings in the non-mine production areas. Future concerns also included the sensitive issue of localisation. There would be a need for strong expatriate representation in the Community Affairs Division, though not necessarily in the top position, throughout the life of the mine. If Community Affairs is totally localised there is a danger of senior mine management becoming isolated from the needs, concerns and attitudes in the community. This would have an adverse impact both on the community and on mining operations—as appears to have been the case in Bougainville.

Notes

1   I am grateful to Glenn Banks for pointing out the general economic characteristics for each stage of this model.
2   The PJV had requested the allocation of 48 residential blocks at Paiam as part of its Home Ownership Programme. This option would most likely be taken up by Porgeran and possibly by Engan employees.
3   For example, it was estimated that K500,000 per annum was required for staff salaries alone, and this figure did not include Item 10 funds needed for hiring cleaning staff.
4   These figures do not include deaths soon after arrival of which the cause was unclear, nor bodies brought in after death. Nor do they include the significant number of Porgeran deaths due to road accidents, tribal fights and murders.
5   Dr Kramer reported that in the African model, one confirmed AIDS case equals 350 HIV positive. If the African model is applicable to Papua New Guinea, then that would indicate a pool of at least 700 HIV positive persons in the Laiagam area by 1993.
6   The reason given for the absence of WIPS at Porgera Community School was that this school was catering for non-Ipili speaking children from Porgera Station. However, my own visit to the school in May 1993 revealed that an estimated 77 per cent of Grade 1 students were Ipili-speakers.
7   I was told that seven of 12 selected from Tipinini Community School were outsiders.
8   The women wanted Tok Pisin literacy as Porgera had so many non-Ipili speakers, while educationists wanted Ipili literacy as most women did not speak Tok Pisin. A compromise was being initiated in 1993.
9   At this time, the boom gate was in operation to control movements into and out of the SML.
10 The Suyan station was the first building to be completed in the PJV

compound.

11 The Suyan station was the first building to be completed in the PJV compound. The worst area for armed holdups and hijacking was the Kera River area near Laiagam.

12 Village courts were established in 1973 to deal with minor offences and customary disputes. Village court decisions can be appealed in a district court.

13 The task proved to be more time-consuming than I expected, and I cannot say that my information is complete.

14 The 1991 Annual Report did contain some crime statistics, but they were patchy.

15 The cost of the attack in 1992—for losses, repairs and upgrading of the facility—was reputed to be K1 million.

16 The PDA retained the right to maintain this ban if it were to be lifted by the Enga Provincial Government, but it did not have the power to permit sales and importation during a provincial government ban.

17 Women in Association meetings also alleged that some police were involved with black market alcohol activities—at least on the consumption end.

18 Snooker tables were common in the larger trade stores, and local children had begun making mini-snooker tables where marbles were used in place of snooker balls.

19 The royalty rate has since been raised to 2 per cent of export value.

20 By contrast, the records concerning the 23 per cent share of royalties paid to landowners and community institutions are readily available for public scrutiny.

21 In 1995, the national parliament passed a new Organic Law on Provincial Governments and Local-Level Governments which radically transformed the whole system of provincial government. The impact of these reforms is beyond the scope of this study.

22 The Department of Enga was restructured twice between 1989 and 1993.

23 Sources of revenue for the PDA included a Special Support Grant from the provincial government, Community Facilities Grant from the PJV, and tied grants from both the provincial and national governments.

24 There was only one woman on the CIC, and none on the PLA executive. I was tempted to suggest that there should be more, but I did not hear this demand from the PWA.

25 One problem that had never been successfully resolved was the status of women's groups in Paiela Census Division. There was no Paielan woman on the PWA Management Committee, and there was poor attendance by Paielan members at the general meetings because of the area's remoteness from Porgera. Paielan women indicated that they would like an association of their own.

3

The economic impact of the mine

Glenn Banks

A common observation from around mining projects in Papua New Guinea is that the local communities become stratified as 'different members of the local community will experience the different aspects of the development process in different forms and degrees, and the process as a whole will give rise to new forms of inequality, division and conflict within the community' (Filer 1992:6). This observation influenced the focus of the fieldwork reported in this chapter, which aimed to identify some of the inequalities developing within the Porgeran community.

The objectives of this initial piece of fieldwork were defined as

- collection and analysis of information from all available documentary sources (especially mining company records and local business records) relevant to construction of a model of the local economy
- design, testing and refinement of household survey instruments which measured local patterns of income and expenditure and other relevant variables, plus tabulation and analysis of data collected by these methods
- design, testing and refinement of additional methods of collecting information at the level of the household, for example diaries

- direct observation and open-ended questioning of local informants in respect of transactions which occurred at critical or nodal points in the local economy, such as the market places on pay fortnights.

The primary task of this fieldwork was thus to establish a set of baseline data, and a system for collecting measures of economic change, with the intention of constructing a 'model' of the workings of the Porgeran economy.[1]

Methodology

Economies, even local ones, are complex, dynamic entities, and so their modelling and monitoring requires the use of a variety of methods which can provide information on the mechanics of their different elements. This chapter is largely based on six weeks of fieldwork conducted in Porgera in November and December 1992. In the case of this portion of fieldwork, the need for a variety of methods was doubly important, as one of the objectives was the testing of these different methods. Questionnaires, interviews and the analysis of company records were used as part of a wider effort to build up baseline data against which future changes could be measured.

The contribution of the Porgera Joint Venture (PJV) to local employment levels and wage incomes was calculated for the whole period in which records had been kept. This meant making a monthly record of the levels of Porgeran employment at the mine from early 1990 (when the records began) to the end of November 1992 (when the fieldwork began), and then taking a random sample of local employees and using the value of their wages for the first 11 months of 1992 to calculate the total local annual, monthly and fortnightly wage contribution of the company. Two problems were encountered with this approach

- there was some doubt amongst local community members and company staff alike as to whether all the 'Porgerans' employed were in fact Porgerans, and representatives of both sides were taking steps to resolve this question
- the high local employee turnover rate may have affected the validity of using a random sample of employees to calculate the total wage contribution of the PJV.

Neither of these factors is thought to have had a significant effect on the results.

The PJV Business Development Office records were analysed to try and establish the value of local goods and services purchased by the company. The supply of services was relatively easy to establish, as the bulk had been let by contracts recorded in the quarterly reports submitted by the company to the government. There were a number of smaller contracts (predominantly labour only) for which records were less accessible, but total values were still available. The value of goods locally supplied to the company was harder to establish, mainly because these were low-value items provided at irregular intervals. The PJV Business Development Office also had records of a trade store survey carried out in early 1991, which are discussed below.

The company records relating to compensation were analysed in order to calculate the amounts of cash injected into the local community from this source. A problem encountered here was that, while there were detailed records of each individual payment for the most recent years, there were no aggregate figures for annual compensation payments since the start of construction. The figures that were available represented internal company transactions, and included the cost of items such as relocation houses and even some wage payments. Wherever possible, I excluded all but cash payments made to local people, but in some cases it was impossible to determine exactly what the itemised figures represented and, as a result, my own figures may err on the side of underestimating the amount of compensation actually received by Porgerans.

Department of Enga royalty payment records at Porgera Station were also examined. An attempt was made to get figures from the Porgeran branch of the PNG Banking Corporation (the only alluvial gold mining in Porgera) relating to the levels of deposits at various dates, but no response was forthcoming.

Questionnaires were utilised to determine both the significance of the PJV contribution to the local economy and the way in which money circulated within it. Three separate questionnaires were developed for this purpose. The first questionnaire focused on households and their assets. This included demographic questions relating to the make-up of the respondent's household the previous night, and examined household assets, sources of income, contributions to traditional exchange, and trips to various places. The objective was to provide some basic economic data on the local communities around the mine and to establish a baseline of quantitative measures against which future changes could be measured. Wherever possible, this questionnaire built on earlier surveys which had been carried out in the area.

Four distinct areas were targeted with this survey, and these were chosen to represent four differently impacted communities. Apalaka and Yarik were relocated communities within the Special Mining Lease (SML). Mungalep was just outside the SML and was relatively out of the way, having previously been a centre for alluvial mining. Anawe was also just outside the SML, but this 'community' was rather less marginalised, since it was located between the mine and the government station. Tipinini was the least 'impacted' of the four communities, being located ten kilometres down the valley from the township and mine (see Map 1.1). A fifth sample was made up of PJV Porgeran employees, as it was felt that daytime visits to the different communities might miss employees at work.

The original plan had been to visit each of these communities and interview people inside their own homes. Very early on, it became apparent that this was unrealistic as people tended not to be in their homes during the daytime. Instead, it was found necessary to interview people in the central areas within these communities, where they tended to congregate on our arrival. As a result, the survey samples were not random in the statistical sense, but they do generally represent a cross-section of the community. Whenever possible, interviewers carried out the interviews in private, taking their subjects away to a quiet corner. However, this was not always possible. Interviews typically lasted around 15 minutes. Since Susanne Bonnell was engaged in a parallel round of interviews with local women (see Chapter 4), and since the interviewers in this economic study were all males, it was decided to focus largely (but not exclusively) on male respondents.[2]

The second questionnaire focused on the recall of income and expenditure categories for the previous fortnight, as well as basic demographic information. For reasons discussed below, the sample used for this questionnaire was different from (and larger than) that for the household survey. The objective here was to understand both sources of income and patterns of spending, and hence the circulation of money within the community. Originally, it had been hoped to follow up the household survey with weekly or fortnightly visits to determine income and expenditure patterns. However, given the changes that were made to the household survey method, this proved impractical. Instead, an attempt was made to cover all the areas in the valley, including those in the household survey. Basic demographic questions were included in this questionnaire, to allow a comparison of this sample with that of the household survey. A sample of the crowd at the government station one pay Wednesday was also surveyed.

The third questionnaire was directed at the sellers of goods and produce at either the markets or along the roadside. The intention was to record the goods being sold, the origin of both the seller and the goods, and an estimate of the average daily income of the seller. All the major markets were surveyed at least once, and the main market (Yanjakale) several times, including two pay Wednesdays.

Unstructured interviews were carried out with company and government workers, and other individuals (such as Father Phil Gibbs), to gain information on particular aspects of the local economy. Thus, the role of women in the economy, the workings of the Infrastructure Tax Credit Scheme, the contribution of commercial agriculture, and the role of the Porgera Development Authority (PDA) were addressed in this way. A series of semi-structured interviews was also carried out with the recipients of large, recent compensation payments made by the company in order to establish what had happened to the money. As will be seen below, 12 payments accounted for around 50 per cent of the K3 million paid in compensation during 1992. This obviously represented a large proportion of the money that the company injected into the local economy.

Finally, a search was carried out of all literature relating to the pre-mine Porgera Valley. This included the early patrol reports, the anthropological studies of Meggitt and Gibbs, and the reports commissioned by the company as part of its Social and Economic Impact Study (SEIS). The objective was to build a picture of the pre-mine economy against which the current situation could be compared.

Validity

Social surveys, questionnaires, and any other research which depends on information from individuals have a widely acknowledged blind spot—much of the information collected is inaccurate. There are three main reasons for this—respondents cannot remember accurately, they deliberately mislead, or they misunderstand the intent of the questions being asked.

In relation to the first, few people can remember exactly their expenditure patterns for the last two weeks. The problem is exacerbated when asking about income for the previous 12 months (see Overfield 1993:24). In the case of our own household survey, however, the bulk of the questions related to large, very irregular payments such as compensation, royalties and traditional exchange, with the implication that these were more likely to be remembered with a fair degree of accuracy.

Previous work in Porgera (Meggitt 1957; Gibbs 1977; Pacific Agribusiness 1987) has made much of the secrecy of the Ipili. In addition, the PJV, the mine, and money in general had become very political topics in the survey area, and people may have been presenting figures to match their particular view of the changes that were occurring in the area. For these and other reasons, respondents may have deliberately provided inaccurate information. Against this possibility, we have the comment of Jackson (1987) in respect of his earlier social survey work in the area—where 'respondents appear to have been unexpectedly frank' when discussing household assets. In our surveys, we found that people were usually only too willing to discuss personal financial matters with the interviewers, and certainly keen to air their grievances.

Another potential problem was the misunderstanding of the questions being asked. This does appear to have occurred with some of the information, particularly in regard to 'profits' from businesses, and with older respondents. In most cases, however, the interviewers felt that they had few 'understanding' problems with their interviewees.

For much of the data collected, direct questioning of individuals was the only practical method available. In some cases, it was possible to cross-check the survey data against figures from other sources. As we shall see, the aggregate survey figures appear to be remarkably close to figures obtained by other means. This gives greater weight to the other figures from the survey. Figures on alluvial gold mining balances (total personal accounts, rather than individual balances) would have been useful, but the PNG Banking Corporation branch at Porgera, while not averse to the idea, did not provide access to the information.

Several small design problems were discovered during the use of the survey questionnaires. This was particularly the case with the market survey, which should have gone into more detail on both the interviewee (with more information on their length of stay in Porgera, whether they were male or female, who they were staying with, etc.), and the goods being sold. In the case of the last, it would have been useful to have listed the value and the quantity of goods that the sellers had with them for sale. This would have given a more reliable estimate of the value of daily sales. The demographics pages of the household survey could have been simplified somewhat, and extended to allow for more names to be included, even though details of up to 22 family members were recorded by the interviewers. In the income and expenditure survey, specific questions about expenditure on alcohol would also have been useful, given the level of anecdotal evidence about both the price and quantity of alcohol in the area.[3]

Finally, the methods of sampling used for the surveys were not random, reflecting the practicalities of working around Porgera. Biases may have crept in, particularly those associated with using relatively young male interviewers. In some cases (though certainly not the majority), there was an element of self-selection on the part of the respondents. All the areas surveyed were accessible by road, which again may have introduced an element of bias into the sample, although it appears that most people in the valley were within easy walking distance of a road.

The pre-mine economy

The Ipili of the Porgera Valley have a relatively short history of European contact, but during this period they have had almost continuous exposure to the gold economy. It is now thought that the Fox brothers, on an (unauthorised) expedition in 1934 down the Lagaip Valley seeking gold and other minerals, were the first Europeans to enter the Porgera Valley. However, it is likely that they crossed the Porgera River at a low level, just above the junction with the Lagaip, and thus missed the bulk of the population in the valley (Chris Ballard, pers. comm.).

The first documented contact occurred during the 1938–39 Hagen–Sepik patrol, though the interim patrol report, somewhat prophetically, mentions the 'Poredigar' only in the context of mineral resources. Black examined 'the area very closely and ascertained that his gold discovery was of very little value and had no commercial possibilities' (Taylor 1971:43). H.J. Ward, an Australian Bureau of Mineral Resources geologist, located the source of the gold and mapped mineralised areas on the east side of Waruwari in 1943 (Handley and Henry 1990).

Meggitt (1957) describes the subsequent history of contact in the valley, with the first of the gold claims being staked in 1946 on the upper Porgera, near Mungalep, by Joe Searson. A small 'rush' followed in 1948, with about half a dozen prospectors entering the area (with Administration permission), though none seriously worked their claims. Soon after, an Administration geologist and a party of Bulolo Gold Dredging Company officers surveyed the valley, but decided that there was insufficient gold to warrant large-scale commercial activity. A patrol post was manned at Mungalep during 1948–49 to ensure the prospectors' safety, but this was withdrawn in 1949. There was a break between 1949 and 1952, when the area was only visited a couple of times by patrols. In 1952, the establishment of a permanent patrol post at Laiagam meant more regular Administration visits (twice a year), and a permanent post was re-established in the area in 1961. Searson transferred his leases on the Kogai (Kakai) and Porgera rivers to Jim Taylor in 1955, and Taylor ran them on a tribute system for many years (Pacific Agribusiness 1987[1]:6). Missions were allowed into the area in 1962, when it was de-restricted, and four moved in immediately (Gibbs 1977).

Placer Pacific and Mount Isa Mines (MIM) first entered the area in the mid 1960s, and the latter, with Ada Explorations Pty Ltd, put two adits into Waruwari in 1970. MIM acquired Searson's leases in 1973, and operated a medium-scale sluicing operation which ran at a loss until 1985, when the leases were transferred to a trust for the PJV (Pacific Agribusiness 1987[1]:7). The PJV consortium carried out extensive exploration work on the Porgera lode from the late 1970s. However, it was not until October 1985 that the high-grade zone was discovered and a sizeable mine became a viable prospect.

It is important to note that local labour was used from the beginning, first by the individual miners (often on a tribute system), and subsequently on a larger scale by the companies. For example, in 1974, MIM alone employed between sixty and one hundred local men. In addition, occupation fees were paid to the local landowners on the mining leases. This meant a fairly continuous supply of trade goods and cash to the local community for over thirty years. Smalley (1983:4) noted that

> Joe Searson introduced the people to a cash economy. They were paid cash with which goods were purchased at the local tradestore owned by Jim Taylor. The people soon developed a taste for Western products.

Gibbs (1977) recorded that, during 1974, up to A$20,000 a month was paid into the local economy, with A$10,000 paid in a single week at one point. By his estimate, the annual total was made up of

- A$4,500 in annual occupation fees paid by MIM
- A$3,500 earnt by small-scale miners on the claims of MIM and Taylor
- A$1,200 in fortnightly wages from MIM
- A$500 in compensation paid by government and mission for damage to pandanus
- A$200 in monthly wages for mission workers.

Three studies which describe aspects of the local economy were carried out in the Porgera area during the mid 1980s. These can be used to build up a picture of the pre-mine environment and allow comparison with the more recent situation. The first of these was the Department of Enga's 'Subsistence Systems of Enga Province' study, carried out by Paul Wohlt between 1982 and 1986 (Wohlt 1986). This was primarily directed at subsistence agriculture, though it also covered some socioeconomic measures. It is useful as a comparison with the current study, because it also involved sampling households in different parts of the Porgera Valley. In total, 47 households (279 residents) in Porgera were sampled, ten each from Paiam, Pandami and Yanjakale, eight from Tipinini, and nine from Yuyan.

The second study was coordinated by Richard Jackson, and involved a series of social surveys in the Porgera Valley for the PJV in 1986–87 (see Jackson 1987).[4] Like the Wohlt report, the Jackson study included a number of questionnaire surveys in different parts of the valley. The actual numbers of households surveyed varied in each of the different surveys, though ten was the target number. Five separate areas were covered—Paiam, Mungalep, Suyan, Anawe and Alipis. The SEIS utilised some of this earlier work, and described the economy of the area in some detail. Much of the material in that report can be used for comparative purposes.

In summarising these studies, four points are emphasised. First, the opportunities presented by the presence of gold in the valley (alluvial mining and employment with the miners) had been utilised by some Porgerans for over forty years. This had led to a gradual shift away from dependence on subsistence activities—gold was a 'second garden' for some Porgerans before the PJV began operations. Second, and balancing this, the bulk of the population were still dependent on the subsistence sector for food and housing. Related to this were the inequalities in access to cash-earning opportunities within Porgera, for only some areas had access to the gold. Third, the scant data available confirms the anecdotal evidence that consumption patterns in Porgera have long focused on food and alcohol, rather than investment or consumer goods. Finally, local business aspirations tended to be relatively modest, primarily directed to the establishment of family-based businesses such as trade stores and transport.

The picture given by these studies of the pre-mine Porgeran economy is generally one in which subsistence agriculture was still the predominant activity and major source of livelihood. However, the impact of at least forty years of contact with the gold economy was evident. The gold economy, both for alluvial miners and wage employees, was virtually the only cash-earning opportunity available to the local Porgerans. In 1986, it was estimated that local incomes from alluvial gold came to at least K1 million per annum (Pacific Agribusiness 1987[1]:39). A time budget survey reported in Jackson (1987) showed that, at Mungalep and Alipis, male and female respondents spent 12–14 per cent of their time (excluding absences and sleeping) engaged in alluvial mining. The maximum reported paid employment (amongst males) was 14 per cent for Paiam and Alipis, and averaged 9 per cent for the five sites. Although it is not specified, the bulk of this employment was likely to have been with the PJV, the only alternatives being the missions and the government, or some other limited opportunities with local businesses.

These figures compare with averages of 15 per cent for males and 31 per cent for females engaged in gardening, bush work and tending pigs, primarily subsistence activities. In summary, the SEIS and Jackson's report give the impression that Porgeran males, at least, while still heavily dependent on the subsistence sector, were spending almost as much time on cash-earning activities as they were on subsistence (44 per cent of their time on cash earning, 56 per cent on subsistence).

Given the importance of the gold economy noted in both the SEIS and Jackson's study, it is perhaps surprising that Porgera, the major source of gold in Enga, does not stand out from the rest of the province economically in the findings from Wohlt's (1986) study. Only one respondent reported (a possible) income from sale of gold, and the (possible) contribution of gold to household income was well below the provincial average (0.4 per cent compared to 1.8 per cent). As sale of gold was included in the 'other' category, it is hard to be definitive; yet these findings point to a far less significant role for alluvial mining. The contribution of wages to household income in Porgera was marginally greater than the provincial average, with a greater proportion of wage-earners (4 per cent of residents compared to 2.5 per cent) and lower average earnings (K20 per wage-earner compared to K32). In total, the implied annual per capita cash income for Porgera of K81 was less than the provincial average of K87. Likewise, the survey of non-traditional economic indicators reported in Wohlt's study shows little difference between Porgera and the province as a whole, with Porgera generally coming in behind the provincial averages.

A possible reason for the discrepancy between the Wohlt and Jackson findings is that Wohlt's study was targeted at 'ordinary' Enga farming households and specifically excluded urban areas, rural non-village areas (such as aid posts, schools), successful businessmen or large-scale commercial ventures. In contrast, the Jackson study included a representative sample in areas already affected by mining and exploration activity. Both suffer from the small sample size used in the different areas, which could also account for the differences in their findings.

The SEIS made the following comments in relation to the impact of earnings from gold.

> The gold economy reverberates through Ipili society. People often equate gold with consumption...Tradestores symbolise the wealth and consumption made possible by gold...Cash is now very much a part of traditional payments...Gold-induced inflation is apparent in most aspects of daily life...Cash has greatly weakened traditional leadership in Ipili society...

> From school-age children who are cashing in gold at tradestores to buy luxury food and drink, to the adults who are gambling, drinking and discoing, there is heavy consumption financed by a finite asset. When asked about this, many people seem both aware and worried (Pacific Agribusiness 1987[1]:40).

The report also commented on the consumption patterns 'creating wealth for a growing Ipili élite'—the gold buyers and trade store owners. They noted an 'untapped desire for secure investments' and widespread hoarding of gold. In 1974, Gibbs had also noted that the availability of cash from gold was promoting a switch from dependence on garden produce to food bought at trade stores, with 5,000 pounds (2.3 tonnes) of foodstuffs and 50 cartons of beer being brought in each week by plane (Gibbs 1977:22).

Business activity in Porgera was limited before the start of the mine. Trade stores were common. A PJV survey in 1987 found 143 established trade stores in the Porgera Valley (including Muritaka)—

93 still operating and 50 which had closed. This amounted to one trade store for every ten families (Pacific Agribusiness 1987). Wohlt (1986) records a frequency of one trade store per 16.7 households for Porgera, compared to one trade store per 5.2 households found for Enga as a whole. The SEIS found that, apart from Ipili Porgera Investments (IPI), business activity in Porgera was limited to small-scale activities, including gold buying and sawmilling, and most of the numerous business groups which had been formed in the area had, for one reason or another, failed. This had left many Porgerans viewing such activities with suspicion, and contributed to gold hoarding. In spite of this, *bisnis*, along with employment, were the two most sought-after aspects of mine development.

From the Jackson survey, and from the general comments in the SEIS, it is clear that different parts of the Porgera Valley have had uneven access to cash-earning opportunities. Initially, Yuyan and Mungalep, being closest to the alluvial areas, were the focus of the cash economy, and people in these communities became relatively more wealthy than people elsewhere in the valley. Mungalep's dominant position was reinforced by the presence of the mission, then fell as Yuyan took over as the gold-buying centre. From the early 1980s, Alipis became more important, being the site of intense exploration. Jackson notes that independent gold panning may have been the principal reason for the greater accumulation of wealth by families in Mungalep and Alipis, and that inequality of assets appeared to be a well-established feature of life in Porgera. Certainly, the results of the Jackson survey point to significant differences between the various communities covered.

Similarly, all the studies noted the different cash-earning opportunities available to men and women, and the consequent marginalising of women from the cash economy. Alluvial mining was one lucrative activity where women (and children) could become involved.

The main points to be taken from the above review of material on the pre-mine economy are

- The area had been a significant gold producer since the 1950s, and Porgerans had thus had a relatively long exposure to cash and the gold economy. In some areas, significant amounts of cash had been earned by the local communities. The PJV was therefore not suddenly introducing money into a cashless society—Porgerans had being dealing in cash for many years.

- For as long as Porgerans had been earning cash, there had been opportunities for them to spend it quickly—food, drink and gambling have a history in Porgera that goes back longer than the influence of the missions.
- Aspirations in Porgera focused strongly on *bisnis*—generally trade stores, public motor vehicles (PMVs) and machinery—in spite of several recent disappointments.
- Variations in access to cash-earning activities were well entrenched in the valley, in terms of both gender and regional differences. The focus of these activities in the cash economy had shifted several times. Inequality (and jealousy) were well established before the arrival of the PJV.

The Porgeran economic base in 1992

One way to approach the analysis of the Porgeran economy in 1992, and the one adopted here, is by breaking down the various input and output components of the economy to gain an idea of their relative contributions and the broad-scale flows within the community. Vail (1995) carried out a similar exercise for the distribution of monies from the Mount Kare gold rush. When this is combined with the household-level data collected, a good understanding of the workings of the local economy can be obtained.[5]

A convenient and measurable starting point for analysis of the cash economy is the range of inputs into the system. At Porgera, the PJV was clearly the engine of the local economy, with direct payments of wages and occupation fees, compensation, donations, and royalty payments, and indirect contributions through business contracts to local Porgeran companies and individuals, and through the support provided for the PDA. The figures given below, despite their apparent precision, are nevertheless approximate. They do, however, give an indication of the relative importance of the various types of inputs.

Compensation[6]

Landowners were paid by the company for loss of land, for damage to land or improvements (including 'economic plants'), and for various other losses (such as livestock killed by vehicles, various kinds of nuisance, and the loss of alluvial earnings). Annual occupation fees paid to SML and LMP (Lease for Mining Purposes) landowners are also covered under the heading 'compensation'. Rates paid were in accordance with a schedule negotiated between the PJV and the major landowning clans of the SML, which was agreed on 31 January 1988.

Strictly speaking, compensation payments were not a benefit of the mine, but represented reimbursement for costs incurred by the recipients due to damage caused by the company. Compensation payments could also represent a shift from the subsistence sector to the cash economy on the part of the recipient, since the cash could be used as seed capital to establish trade stores or other businesses.

One feature of the compensation payment process at Porgera which distinguished it from the Ok Tedi situation was that the assessment, negotiation, administration and payment process itself was carried out by PJV employees on Department of Enga letterhead, rather than by the Department of Enga itself. The practical effect of this had been a much more rapid response to landowner claims at Porgera than at Ok Tedi (John Burton, pers. comm.).

Compensation registers, detailing the amount of each compensation claim paid, had been kept by the PJV since August 1987. In total, the PJV had paid 6,605 compensation claims totalling K25.9 million between August 1987 and the end of December 1992. It is important to note, however, that each individual claim was usually distributed among a number of recipients at the payment stage. That is to say, each payment form usually had a list of recipients receiving differing amounts from the payments. For large payments, or where the area affected involved several families, the list could be extensive—up to sixty people. On the other hand, there were a number of individuals who featured prominently amongst the lists of recipients, usually collecting a substantial proportion of the payments. This made it very difficult to determine just how many people had received PJV compensation, although it appeared that the majority of Porgerans within or close to the SML or the LMPs would have received at least some cash over this five-year period.

Figure 3.1 provides a breakdown of the payments made by quarter for the period 1987–92. The pattern matches the stages of development of the mine—large amounts are associated with the construction phases of the plant site, the Anawe spoil, the relocation roads and houses, Kairik airstrip, the Hides transmission line, Suyan, the open pit expansion, and the waste dumps. The implications of these variations for the local economy are very significant—when combined with irregular royalty payments, it is clear that short-lived periods of 'boom' were frequently followed by relatively lean times. When these

Figure 3.1   PJV compensation payments by quarter, 1987–92

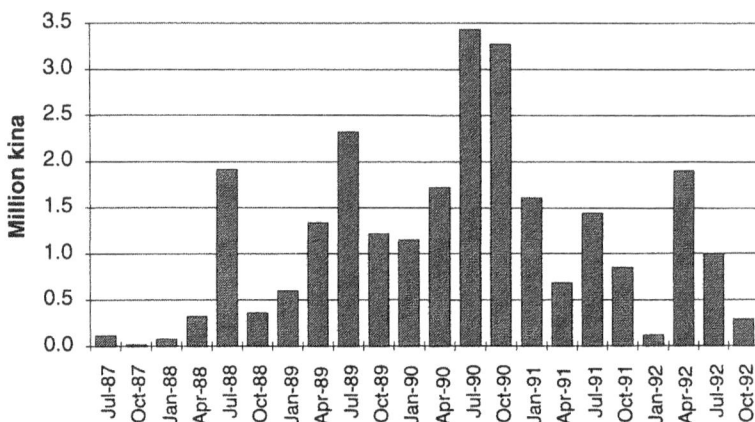

Source: PJV/Department of Enga records.

Table 3.1   PJV compensation payments made during 1992 by type

Type of compensation	Number of payments	Total amount paid (kina)
Lands General Compensation	107	187,298.60
Kairik area	11	34,028.20
Suyan area	10	9,689.00
Maiapam area	31	31,172.60
Hides Line	5	6,878.00
Open pit compensation	152	1,331,707.20
Northern waste dump compensation	76	431,476.20
Highway compensation	27	8,206.30
Pangalita limestone compensation	6	10,270.00
Pangalita limestone royalty	9	26,304.00
Waile Creek Rd and dam compensation	3	39,351.40
Starter dump 'C' compensation	5	787,510.00
Paiela Bypass Rd compensation	66	162,576.20
PA 60 compensation	4	1,904.90
PA 860 compensation	10	16,833.30
SML occupation fees 1989	20	34,842.60
SML occupation fees 1991–92	20	61,187.90
Hides Power Line occupation fees 1992	61	94,450.38
Other occupation fees 1989–92	142	33,668.80
Total	785	3,309,356.18

Source: PJV/Department of Enga records.

temporal variations are broken down by location, the pattern is one of a dynamic, continuously changing flux, with different parts of the valley experiencing large cash inflows at different times.

Table 3.1 provides a breakdown of compensation by area and type of payment in 1992. It is important to note that 'one-off' payments for 'improvements' and areas of bush made up the bulk of these payments. This had been the case for each year following the start of construction. The implication was that once the mine and its waste dumps were fully established, compensation would drop dramatically as a source of income for the valley.

The remaining big compensation payments would have been for the lower Porgera and Kaiya river systems, which were expected to be made in 1994, and some ongoing additions to the open-pit and waste dumps. It was expected that the value of compensation would stabilise at around K700,000 per annum after this, comprising general compensation, occupation fees, and ongoing payments linked to volumes of tailings and incompetent waste rock placed in the Anjolek and Anawe failing dumps. Landowners in the Kaiya and lower Porgera would also have additional compensation-derived income from the trust funds set up to manage the compensation paid for the loss of alluvial gold in these areas. While these payments would provide a reasonably regular source of income for a limited number of landowners in one or two communities, the real 'boom years' of compensation were almost over.

Porgeran wage income from the PJV

Employment records started late in 1989, with the exception that the origin of Operations staff was not reported regularly until July 1990—the explanation for a statistical 'hollow' in Porgeran employment in early and mid 1990 (see Figure 3.2).

Since I do not have direct figures for the total wage income received by Porgerans, I have estimated this by multiplying figures for the average numbers of Porgeran employees over the year by an estimate of the average wages paid to them. In 1992, a random sample of 50 of the PJV Operations staff between January and November 1992 had an average income of K6,925 per annum. Making the assumption that wage levels had grown at 10 per cent a year, through wage increases and increasing skill levels within the local workforce, Table 3.2 sets out my calculations for previous years, and gives an approximation of the total value of Porgeran wage income (after tax).

Figure 3.2   Porgeran and total PJV employment, 1989–92

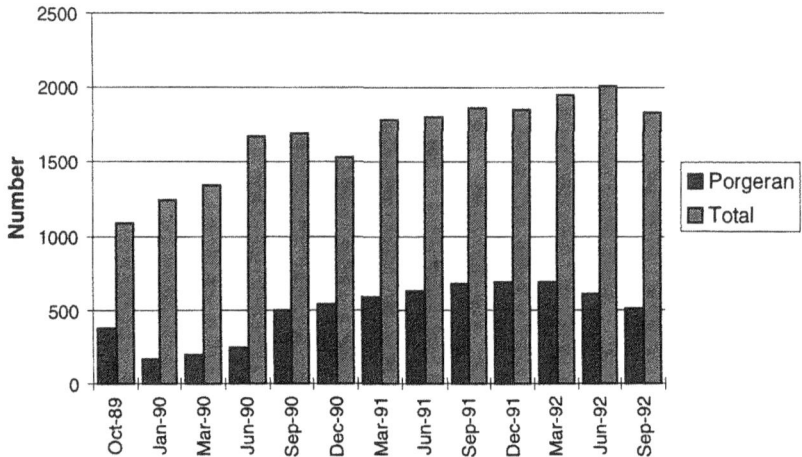

Source: PJV records.

Within the Porgera Valley, employment was relatively evenly spread, as shown in Table 3.3, though the company acknowledged that their records, based on information provided by the employees themselves, might not be completely accurate.

The figures for the sample of 50 PJV employees for 1992 show a high employee turnover rate, with 18 of the sample having being employed for less than the full 11 months. Table 3.4 shows that, of the total workforce at 18 November 1992, over 65 per cent had been with the company for less than two years. These figures undoubtedly over-estimate the turnover of staff, as a number of employees had been re-employed several times. The implication is, however, that few Porgeran staff were realising the benefits (promotion, pay rises and so on) of long-term service. This is important, as it casts doubt on the ability of the company to meet local expectations in regard to the localisation of senior positions within the company.[7]

In addition to the formal employment figures cited above, there were a large number of casual labourers employed for short periods who do not appear in these tables. These included people employed on small road maintenance and upgrade contracts for the road between Porgera and Wabag, contracts for the construction of new gardens for relocation (worth over K600,000, all to locals), and labour-only contracts let through the Community Affairs Division (over K10,000 for the September–December 1992 quarter). In total these would have contributed up to K10,000 a month to the local economy.[8]

A small survey of non-Porgeran PJV employees (both PNG nationals and expatriates) revealed, as expected, that these employees did not spend money in the local economy while on site. Even the few families on site (16 at December 1992) did the bulk of their shopping at Mount Hagen on a monthly basis, and thus made no significant contribution to the local economy.

Royalties

Under the agreements between the national and provincial governments and the SML landowners signed in 1989, 23 per cent of the royalties from the mine were to go to landowners in the Porgera Valley. This was to be split three ways—8 per cent to SML landowners, 5 per cent to the Porgera Development Authority, and 10 per cent to an investment fund set up for the children of SML landowners.[9] The direct royalties were paid by the company to the national government, and the landowner share was then redistributed by the Department of Enga. This process meant that the quarterly payments were often several months late. For example, the second quarter 1992 payment was made in late November 1992. Payments were divided amongst SML landowners on the basis of the proportion of the lease area they owned. Payments were made to 192 nominated SML representatives, either in cash or by cheque. The only exception to this was the January 1992 payment of K40,470.77, which was used to send a delegation to Port Moresby for discussions with the Prime Minister. The exact amount paid each quarter varied depending on the value of gold produced, with a maximum quarterly payment of K143,710.58 for the third quarter of 1991.

All the sources of income discussed above can be added to show the total cash benefits to the community arising from the mine. More than K10 million a year made its way into the community in the peak years of compensation payouts during the construction phase. Depending on future compensation assessments and Porgeran participation in the PJV workforce, the annual flow was likely to settle at K6–8 million a year during the operation phase (Table 3.5).

Table 3.2   Wages paid to Porgeran employees, 1989–92 (estimated)

Year	Employees (average)	Average wage (kina)	Total wages (million kina)
1989	285	5,263	1.50
1990	488	5,717	2.79
1991	639	6,371	4.07
1992	585	6,925	4.06

Source: PJV records.

Table 3.3   Distribution of PJV employment within the Porgera Valley

Village name	Employees
Apalaka/Yarik	46
Yokolama	13
Kulapi	24
Anawe	39
Mungalep	38
Yuyan	41
Politika	27
Yanjakale	22
Suyan	31
Paiam	47
Kairik	25
Tipinini	33

Source: PJV records.

Table 3.4   Porgeran PJV employees by length of service as of 18 November 1992

Start year	Service	Employees	(per cent)
1992	<1 year	151	(31.9)
1991	1 year	168	(35.5)
1990	2 years	79	(16.7)
1989	3 years	53	(11.2)
1988	4 years	16	(3.4)
1987	5 years	3	(0.6)
1986 or earlier	>6 years	3	(0.6)
Total		473	(100.0)

Source: PJV records.

Business contracts

The role and contribution of PJV business contracts to the economy was a controversial topic at both the local and national level. Unlike the compensation, wages and royalties discussed above, they were not direct cash payments made to the community, although they tended to be discussed in these terms. The local community repeatedly questioned the figures presented by the PJV at meetings with the government, on the basis that these over-emphasised the value of business contracts for Porgerans. These figures included joint ventures between Porgeran companies and national or international companies, and community representatives argued that the bulk of the profits from these (generally) large joint ventures did not accrue to the community.

Table 3.6 shows the breakdown of contracts by origin compiled from PJV Quarterly Reports to the Department of Trade and Industry. This shows that national companies (including joint ventures) won over half of the construction contracts, while the size of the Porgeran share (K27.96 million to September 1992) is also significant. For the operations contracts, which were generally ongoing (unlike the construction contracts), Engan contractors (including joint ventures) had picked up the greatest share to date, with the Porgeran share again being significant (K6.59 million). On a per capita basis, the contracts were worth K3,455 for Ipili speakers against K180 for other Engans. As with the labour figures, there are also a number of small contracts which were not included in the formal figures. The PJV Quarterly Report for the period to September 1992 noted that K191,774 was expended on plant contracting, but it is not clear whether this was included in the above contracts, or what proportion was accounted for by Porgeran contractors.

The figures given in Table 3.6 are for work completed to date. The estimated value of committed costs on Porgeran contracts current in September 1992 was K8.08 million. When combined with the value of work to date from the above table (K34.55 million), the total value of contracts awarded to Porgeran companies (including joint ventures) totalled K42.63 million. This was the figure publicised by the company and criticised by some of the landowners, as they believed that the big Porgeran contracts included here were all joint ventures, with the profits going mainly to the other partners. However, because profits from contracts are generally a small component of their total value (between 6 and 10 per cent was likely in the Porgeran setting), a large

Table 3.5 Cash inputs into the local economy originating with the PJV, 1989–92 (kina)

Year	Wages	Compensation	Royalties	Total
1989	1,499,977	3,444,228	-	4,944,205
1990	2,794,589	7,725,918	-	10,520,507
1991	4,072,651	8,769,395	279,703	13,131,748
1992	4,056,713	3,309,356	483,464	7,849,533
Total	12,423,930	23,248,897	763,167	36,445,993

Source: PJV/Department of Enga records.

Table 3.6 Value of contracts by origin of contractors, 1990–92 (million kina)

Construction	1990	1991	1992 (to Sept)	Cumulative
Porgera	13.71	10.14	4.11	27.96
Enga	19.92	10.86	2.36	33.14
Other PNG	52.29	34.77	13.20	100.26
Overseas	10.48	1.98	1.96	14.42
Sub-total	96.40	57.75	21.63	175.78
Operations				
Porgera	0.46	2.33	3.80	6.59
Enga	0.32	1.02	10.29	11.63
Other PNG	0.07	1.75	6.17	7.99
Overseas	0.18	0.10	2.73	3.01
Sub-total	1.03	5.20	22.99	29.22

Source: PJV records.

proportion of the value of these contracts, in particular through local wages, probably did accrue to local interests. Although it is impossible to put a figure on this, my survey of the larger local businesses (discussed below) gives some idea of the contribution of PJV-related work to the local economy.

Indirect and secondary sources of income

The PDA was established under the Mining Development Contract, using K4 million from the PJV's Community Facilities Grant. Ongoing income included an annual K0.5 million unconditional grant from the Enga provincial government, and a 5 per cent share of mineral royalties. In 1992, spending in the Porgera area was approximately

K3.5 million. The bulk of this was spent on infrastructure development—roads, community schools and aid posts. The PDA employed 20 Porgerans in primarily unskilled positions.

Donations from the PJV to schools, organisations and individuals were worth well over K100,000 a year. However, their impact on the Porgeran economy was limited for two reasons: they were largely to groups or individuals outside Porgera, and they were usually earmarked for goods or services from outside Porgera, so their value very quickly left the Porgera area. Thus, while they served an important community and public relations role, their local economic impact was minimal.

The Infrastructure Tax Credit Scheme, which was instituted during 1992, was largely focused on projects outside Porgera. The scheme enabled the PJV to get tax deductions from the national government for infrastructure projects which it funded within Enga Province, as approved by the provincial government. In 1992, around K250,000 of this funding had been spent in Porgera, with another K900,000 worth of projects planned for the local area—K80,000 for the College of Distance Education, K400,000 for road sealing near Paiam, and a K400,000 contribution to the Porgera–Paiela road.

A final source of money for the local economy was alluvial gold earnings. Although it is very difficult to put a figure on this, 13 (15 per cent) of the 87 households we interviewed in Apalaka/Yarik, Mungalep and Anawe reported earnings from alluvial mining over the previous 12 months. Average reported earnings were K1,400. Given that there were approximately 1,200 households in the whole valley (John Burton, pers. comm.), there were probably 900 households in the upper part of the valley with potential access to the alluvial areas. On this basis, it was likely that current production was still worth K189,000 per annum.

Circulation

Once the direct cash payments from the company entered the local community, the money was used for a number of purposes. It could be invested (inside or outside Porgera), used for consumption, or for traditional exchange purposes. The results of the household survey and the income and expenditure survey give some indication of the extent of these alternative uses.

The household survey covered 122 households, concentrated in four areas. The demographics of the sample are described statistically in Table 3.7. Of note in the table are the lower household size in Tipinini compared to the rest of the valley, the higher proportion of Porgeran born people in Apalaka than elsewhere, the relatively consistent proportion of children in the households (between 39 and 46 per cent), and the consistent male bias in the sex ratio. On the basis of these figures, the following trends can be inferred.

- The SML area had a higher proportion of people of Porgeran origin, probably as a result of the relocation agreement negotiated between the SML landowners and the PJV, which largely excluded non-Porgerans from relocation areas.
- There had been a movement of people within the valley towards the mine area, borne out by the fact that Apalaka and Mungalep both had higher proportions of households with 'other relatives' staying with them (41 and 44 per cent respectively, compared to 26 per cent for Tipinini).
- The male/female ratio may have been a result of the influx of males to the valley in search of employment and other benefits, or it may reflect the under-reporting of females as a result of the predominantly male-male interviews carried out (though under-reporting of children does not appear to have occurred). A greater number of males is the reverse of what one would expect in a polygamous society.[10]

From previous studies of the Porgeran population (John Burton, pers. comm.), it appears that the sample was demographically representative of a cross-section of the population. On this basis, the results of the household survey can be treated as a 10 per cent sample of the whole population (given that there are approximately 1,200 households in the valley).

Table 3.7   Household survey statistics, 1992

Location	Total h'holds	Relocated h'holds	Total persons	Mean h'hold	Mean no. of children	M/F ratio	% with wantoks	% born in Porgera
Apalaka	32	23	228	7.1	2.9	120:100	40.6	93.0
Mungalep	23	8	177	7.7	3.7	130:100	43.5	81.4
Anawe	24	7	164	6.8	2.7	135:100	33.0	72.0
Tipinini	35	0	198	5.7	2.6	133:100	26.5	84.6
Total	122	41	832	6.8	3.0	125:100	36.4	82.9

Source: Porgera household survey.

The income and expenditure survey involved interviewing 231 individuals aged over 16 years, and questioning them as to sources of income and patterns of expenditure over the previous two weeks. The aim was to carry out as many of these interviews as possible, and, as a result, the demographic section of the questionnaire was kept small. The sample included 180 individuals who lived permanently in Porgera (or 3 per cent of the adult Porgeran population), and 51 who, for one reason or another, were visiting. The latter group included some national PJV employees, but most were individuals who had come from other parts of the highlands and were interviewed at the government station on a pay Wednesday. This combination of interviews was intended to show how much money the permanent residents contributed to the local economy, and whether the 'visitors' carried significant amounts out of the area. There were 129 Porgeran-born people in this sample, and 99 who were born elsewhere; there were 198 males and 32 females; and there were 144 household heads as against 86 non-household heads.[11] The average household size reported was 7.96, slightly higher than in the household survey.

Sources of income

Sources of income for the local population can be determined from a mixture of the household and income and expenditure survey results. Table 3.8 shows the distribution of income from various sources reported in the household interviews. Given that the sample represented around 10 per cent of the population (122 households surveyed from an estimated 1,200 households), the validity of the PJV payments reported in the interviews could be cross-checked with the amounts documented in the company and government records. The PJV's figures for compensation payments (which included occupation fees) came to around K3 million, while a scaled-up estimate from the compensation payments and occupation fees reported in the interviews amounted to K2.49 million. Likewise, the documented royalty payments for 1992 came to K483,463, while the interview findings would suggest a total of K413,080. These approximations lend a similar level of confidence to the other survey findings.

There are some anomalies in the data (for example, all those who received royalties should presumably also have received occupation fees), but these are unlikely to affect the overall figures, given the sample size. The picture that emerges from Table 3.8 is largely what one would expect: people in Apalaka received the bulk of the royalties, compensation and occupation fees, while those in Tipinini receive none. The latter engaged in more sales of produce (though incomes from this source appeared to be low), while involvement in business was relatively evenly spread throughout the valley.[12]

Figures 3.3 and 3.4 show the sources of fortnightly income and their value, as revealed by the income and expenditure survey. Several points are worthy of note.

- Wantoks (outside the household) were the most common source of income, although Figure 3.4 shows that this source of income was very small in monetary terms. For 54 (23.4 per cent) of the sample, income from household members or other *wantoks* was the only source of income.

- PJV wages, the second most common source of income, accounted for 34 per cent of the value of income, the highest from any source. The role of PJV inputs (in this case wages) in driving the local economy is again highlighted, as they were virtually the only money entering the system from outside—all the other sources relied on redistribution (even 'other wages', as discussed below).

- Sales of goods and produce, and money from other members of the household, were the third and fourth most common sources of money in the previous two weeks, accounting for 15 and 12 per cent respectively. However, the value of both these sources was relatively small, just 9 and 4 per cent respectively.

- Forty-one individuals (17.7 per cent) reported no income for the previous two weeks, and another 25 (10.8 per cent) reported less than K10.

- There were great inequalities in income across the sample, with the top 10 per cent of the sample earning 58.8 per cent of the income, and the bottom 50 per cent earning just 2 per cent of the income.

Significantly for the purposes of the economic modelling exercise, there was a total of K200 reported for alluvial gold earnings, K209 reported for compensation (though respondents did not specify if this was PJV compensation), and K451 reported for royalty payments. Given that the sample was approximately 3 per cent of the adult population in the valley, these equate to total annual figures of K173,333 for alluvial gold, K181,133 for compensation, and K390,866 for royalties. Both the alluvial gold earnings and the royalty payments

Table 3.8   Sources of income by value (in kina) and number of recipients, 1992

Income source	Apalaka (32)	Mungalep (23)	Anawe (24)	Tipinini (35)	Various (8)	Total (122)
Royalties	30,500 (25)	2,048 (8)	6,400 (6)	-	2,360 (4)	41,308 (43)
Occupation fees	4,979 (20)	1,170 (5)	1,645 (4)	-	660 (4)	8,454 (33)
PJV compensation	167,500 (16)	3,300 (4)	12,900 (5)	3,050 (2)	54,500 (5)	241,250 (32)
Cash cropping	570 (5)	3,180 (10)	834 (9)	1,240 (15)	230 (2)	6,054 (41)
Alluvial mining	3,350 (6)	7,200 (4)	7,040 (2)	-	560 (2)	18,150 (14)
No. in business	7	8	4	7	4	30

Source: Porgera household survey.

Figure 3.3   Numbers of individuals reporting income from different sources, 1992 (N = 231)

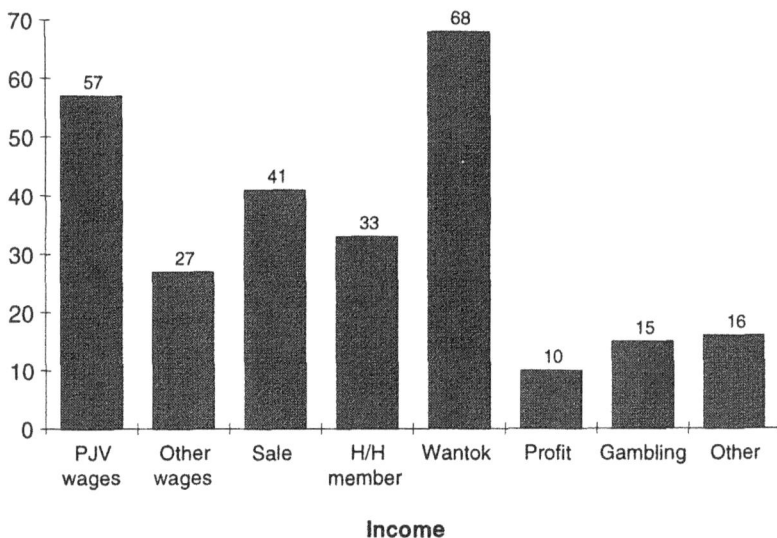

Income

Source: Porgera income and expenditure survey.

Figure 3.4   Value of fortnightly income sources, 1992 (total K42,395)

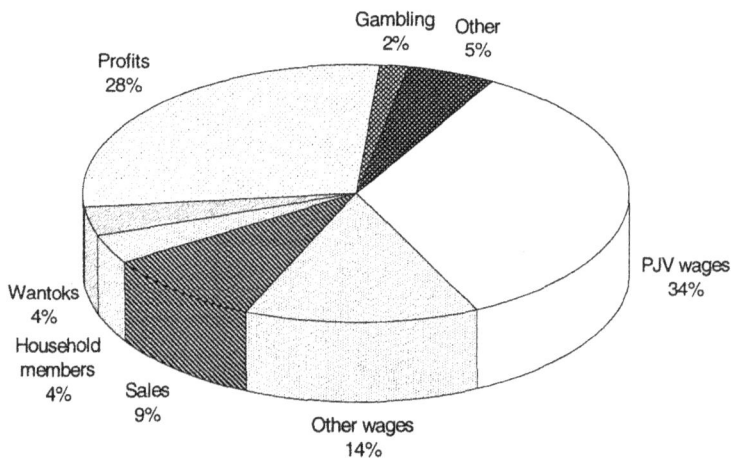

Source: Porgera income and expenditure survey.

correspond well with the figures calculated earlier. The compensation figure, however, is well short of the annual total of approximately K3 million for 1992. This relative absence of PJV compensation payments in the sample is not surprising, given the small number of payments which had been made (631 for the first 11 months of 1992). The additional K2.8 million in compensation would have been equivalent to about K14 per adult per fortnight.

Average fortnightly income reported in the income and expenditure survey was K183.53 per adult. When the figure for PJV compensation is added to this average, adult income rises to K197.53 per fortnight. By highlands standards, this figure is very high, and can be directly attributed to the presence of the mine. However, as previously noted, the income distribution was highly skewed. Clearly, the presence of the company had greatly increased cash incomes for a minority of the local population, while the bulk were still dependent on the subsistence sector and on relatives for their survival.

Expenditure patterns

Expenditure patterns were addressed through both the household and income and expenditure surveys. The household survey questioned respondents on household assets, investments, and contributions to traditional exchange ceremonies. Table 3.9 shows the distribution of respondents in the different areas reporting ownership of various items, and for comparison, the figures found by Jackson (1987) and Wohlt (1986). The latest figures show no increase (even a slight decrease) over Jackson's figures, but a definite increase over those presented by Wohlt.

The latest figures do not show the pattern which might have been expected within the valley, with those who have received the bulk of the compensation and other direct benefits having a greater number of material items. Apalaka only showed a significantly higher score in the case of watch ownership. Thus, while the distribution of income was unequal, this did not manifest itself in the obvious material status of householders. Clearly, levelling factors were at work. Exactly what these were and how they operated is open to further inquiry. Cultural traits could, in part, be responsible, with customary obligations to redistribute compensation and other income among family and *wantoks*. Likewise, people may have been unwilling to invest in material items which they knew would have demands for use placed on them by relatives. A high attrition rate may also have been partly responsible for the results. For most items (excluding cars and videos), even Tipinini ranked alongside the other areas.

Table 3.10 shows the pattern of investments (largely passbooks and IPI shares) held by people within the areas covered in the household survey. The value of investments per household matches the expected pattern, with Apalaka having the highest score. However, it is worth noting that Mungalep was only a short way behind, which may have represented a legacy of the alluvial mining boom, and that the figure for Tipinini was higher than that for Anawe, the former having a

Table 3.9   Percentage of households with particular assets, 1992

	Lamp	Sewing machine	Radio	Car	Video	Watch
This study (1992)						
Apalaka	44	9	34	19	3	44
Mungalep	42	17	42	4	8	21
Anawe	57	17	48	26	4	26
Tipinini	37	9	46	-	-	26
Various	75	50	63	25	25	50
Jackson (1986–87)						
Alipis	n.a.	20	60	50	n.a.	40
Anawe	n.a.	10	40	20	n.a.	40
Mungalep	n.a.	40	80	60	n.a.	40
Suyan	n.a.	-	40	-	n.a.	40
Wohlt (1986)	-	6	8	-	n.a.	4

Source: Porgera household survey.

Table 3.10   Patterns of household investment, 1992

Area	Total value (kina)	Value per households	Per cent households with investment
Apalaka	104,220	3,256.88	50.0
Mungalep	69,310	3,150.45	54.6
Anawe	12,410	517.08	29.2
Tipinini	24,250	692.86	60.0
Various	6,852	856.50	50.0
Total	217,042	1,779.03	50.0

Source: Porgera household survey.

greater number of people with lower value investments against the latter's smaller number with larger investments.

One other surprising feature of these figures is a lack of correlation, at the household level, between cash benefits from the mine (compensation and royalties) and levels of investment—with a very low correlation coefficient (r) of 0.09. This poses two further questions: what happened to the compensation payments, and where did the investors get their funds? The answer to the second question may be related to the Mount Kare gold rush, or to earlier compensation payments which were not recorded by this survey, either because interviewers did not go far enough with their questions or because respondents were unwilling to reveal the payments. But the answer to the first question is partially answered by another part of the household survey, which asked about contributions to traditional exchange (brideprice, compensation) in the last 12 months, as well as to national election expenses. Table 3.11 shows that people living closer to the mine spent more money on both types of contribution, and that Tipinini spent much less than the rest. This is not surprising, as one might expect greater demands to be placed on those who had received cash from the mine. The relationship between cash benefits received and cash contributions made (r = 0.26) was closer than with levels of household investment, though it was still not statistically significant. On the other hand, the proportion of house-holds engaged in such contributions was much the same in all four areas.

Expenditure patterns revealed by the income and expenditure survey are illustrated in Figures 3.5 and 3.6.

Table 3.11   Cash contributions to national elections and traditional exchange, 1992 (kina)

Area	Total value of contributions	Value per household	Per cent households contributing
Apalaka	70,500	2203.13	62.5
Mungalep	68,840	3129.01	63.6
Anawe	78,320	3263.33	62.5
Tipinini	11,903	340.09	57.1
Various	39,163	4895.38	87.5
Total	268,666	2202.18	63.1

Source: Porgera household survey.

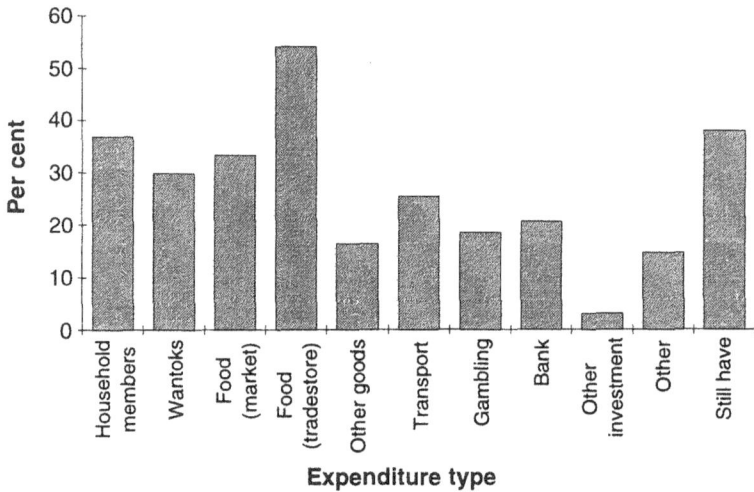

Figure 3.5   Number of people reporting expenditure by category, 1992

Source: Porgera income and expenditure survey.

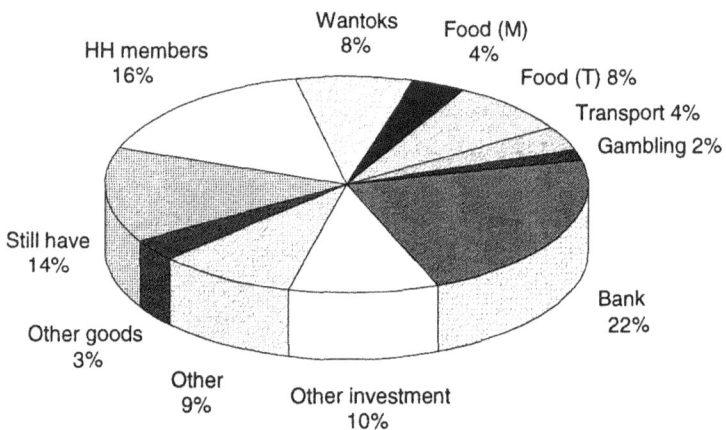

Figure 3.6   Expenditure patterns by value, 1992

Source: Porgera income and expenditure survey.

- Taken together, household members and other *wantoks* were very significant expenditure sinks, accounting for almost a quarter of all reported expenditure by category and by value: 37 per cent of the sample had given money to household members, and 30 per cent to other *wantoks*.
- Over 50 per cent of the sample had bought food at a trade store, and a third had bought food at the local markets. Such purchases accounted for 12 per cent of the total expenditure.
- Almost 20 per cent of the sample reported gambling in the previous two weeks, though this accounted for just 2 per cent of the total expenditure, while 21 per cent reported that they had invested money in the alluvial gold mining, accounting for 22 per cent of total expenditure.

Compensation funds

A series of interviews was carried out with known recipients of 20 large compensation payments made during 1992, in order to try and establish if there were any general patterns in their use of the money. In total, these payments accounted for almost 60 per cent of the compensation paid during that year. During the interviews, several of the respondents also gave details of how they had spent earlier payments, while some actually denied having received any payments in 1992. All but one of those interviewed distributed the bulk of their payments to family members (up to 80 per cent in one case), retaining amounts which ranged from K15,000 to K165,000. This redistribution, based on cultural expectations, presumably reduced the funds available for investment, rather than immediate consumption. A significant (though unquantified) proportion of this redistribution was directed to 'wantoks' living outside Porgera—mainly in the neighbouring Paiela area or in Southern Highlands Province.

Of the money which they retained, most recipients had invested some in a range of businesses—there were at least five trade stores and PMVs, three contracting businesses, a sawmill, a signwriting business, and a service station. Most of these required a minimum investment of K10,000–15,000. Most of those interviewed also stated that they had invested some of their cash in the alluvial gold mining, and one still held the whole of his payment in this form (mainly in interest-bearing deposits). Five had purchased vehicles (one had bought two), and most had contributed to campaign funds for *wantoks* during the 1992 national election.

Several interviewees stated that they believed the other members of their family had used their share of the payments for consumption: 'they drank their money in Tari, Hagen and Moresby', 'men spent their money on prostitution, sleeping in hotels in Hagen and drinking alcohol in Tari', 'the others consumed their money in beer and women', and 'others spent their money on vehicles that are now run-down, and on brideprice for more wives, and on alcohol—they have spent it all'. Only three of those interviewed admitted to practicing this kind of consumption themselves—'I ate them up', as one put it.[13]

From this set of responses, we may derive an approximate picture of the way in which the compensation money was used.

- 10–15 per cent was invested with alluvial gold mining
- 25–30 per cent was invested in local businesses
- 10–15 per cent was consumed by the primary recipient (including vehicles, brideprice, etc.); and
- 40–55 per cent was redistributed, of which 75–80 per cent was consumed.

With the redistribution and consumption, our primary concern was with how much of this money left Porgera. Consumption primarily involved buying goods originating outside Porgera, although a small proportion was retained (as profit) when purchases were made within the area. Much of the redistributed money passed through several pairs of hands, following traditional obligation networks, and was eventually consumed or passed out of the area.

Given the assumption that smaller amounts are more likely to be used for consumption than for investment, it is thus possible to estimate the final use made of the total compensation funds (K23 million) which had so far been paid by the PJV

- 5–10 per cent (between K1.625 million and K2.3 million) had been invested with alluvial gold mining
- 20–25 per cent (between K4.6 million and K5.75 million) had been invested in local business; and
- 65–75 per cent (between K14.95 million and K17.25 million) had been consumed directly, redistributed and consumed, or redistributed to relatives outside Porgera.

The estimate of alluvial gold mining deposits corresponds closely with the figure of K2.1 million derived from the household survey.

Local businesses

Directly or indirectly, the PJV had certainly stimulated local business development in the Porgera area. In general, these businesses depended either on trade generated by PJV inputs (wages, compensation and royalties), or on direct dealings with the PJV. As an indication of the latter, PJV figures for April 1990 show there were an additional 354 Porgerans employed by contractors to the mining company.[14] Assuming that wages for local contractors would have been lower than those offered by the PJV—say an average of K3,500 per annum—this would have amounted to K1.2 million annually.

Five of the largest businesses in Porgera were investigated in terms of their role in the Porgeran economy, their current levels of employment, and their dependence on the PJV.

- Ipili Porgera Investments is the company formed in 1983 to act as an umbrella company through which local landowners could take advantage of the opportunities offered by the mine. Shareholding in the company was reserved exclusively for Porgerans, but the exact details of the shareholding were not obtained. After a period of serious financial difficulties, IPI had been reduced to a core of four activities: the IPI Supa Store in Porgera, the Mountain Lodge accommodation, some plant hire to the PJV (which was leased to Kulapi Holdings), and a 30 per cent share of the IPI/Poons Joint Venture. Employment in 1992 (excluding Poons) was around 80, with over half of these being Porgerans. The Supa Store was the largest store in Porgera, and acted as a wholesaler for many of the smaller trade stores. Turnover was reputedly up to K10,000 on pay Wednesdays, and the store carried around K400,000 in stock.

- The IPI/Poons Joint Venture won the tender for the supply of catering services to the PJV camps in mid 1992. Employment totalled 229 in December 1992, 121 of these being Porgeran. The value of the three-year contract was in excess of K1 million. Figures provided by Poons show that the bulk of their supplies were sourced through PNG companies. K17,000 was spent on local vegetable supplies during 1992, though this figure includes some supplies from other parts of Enga. K30,000 was spent on Australian sourced goods, around 10 per cent of the total.

- Kulapi Holdings was owned and managed by Yanis Polopa and family, local Porgerans who began operations in 1989. Initially, Kulapi was involved in plant hire contracts for the PJV, and then expanded into freight (again for the PJV) and servicing of heavy vehicles (through Porgera Motors). More recent diversifications had included a fuel depot, a mechanical spare parts retail section, investment in Port Moresby real estate, a building and civil works section, and helicopter services (with a leased helicopter). The company had 120 employees at the end of 1992, including 39 Porgerans. Turnover for 1991 was K1.5 million, increasing to a projected K5.5 million for 1992.
- The Porgera Bakery was a (50/50) joint venture between a local business group and Golding and Company of Australia. The company began as a gold-refining business in 1988, and became a bakery in 1990. Due to alleged misappropriation and the deportation of the Australian partner, the local partners were trying to establish full ownership in 1992. In that year, 17 Porgerans and six non-Porgerans were employed. Goods were sold throughout the valley, and efforts were being made to extend supply to other parts of Enga and to the Southern Highlands.
- Kumbi Enterprises was registered in 1989 by an expatriate married to a local Porgeran woman. The primary activity of the company was a laundry service for the PJV, and for this they employed 23 staff, 19 of them Porgerans. Kumbi had an associated company, Porgera Catering, which supplied catering services to the PJV Tipinini camp, and employed another ten people, eight of them Porgeran.

In total, these five businesses employed 308 Porgerans and a substantial number of non-Porgerans who lived permanently in the valley (unlike the PJV's non-Porgeran employees). In addition, the PDA employed 20 Porgerans and 20 non-Porgerans, and other government departments accounted for approximately 20 additional staff. On a conservative estimate, these people would have accounted for at least K100,000 a fortnight in wages, or another K2.6 million per year in total. Much of this income, however, represented the redistribution of money initially spent by the PJV.[15]

In addition to these large businesses, small business appeared to be flourishing in Porgera. A count revealed almost 150 operating trade stores in the valley, excluding Yuyan and Tipinini. The bulk of these were owner-operated, and most served a socio-cultural function in addition to an economic one—indeed, several owners told us they were not running their stores for the money. Turnover ranged from a few kina a day for smaller operations up to several thousand kina a day for the IPI Supa Store. Of those surveyed (around thirty), the average daily turnover was approximately K100. Many of the smaller ones, however, were only open two or three days per fortnight, so a more realistic figure may be K350 per week, giving a total annual turnover for the valley of K2.5 million. This approximates the figure from the income and expenditure survey. A more comprehensive survey by the PJV Business Development Office in early 1991 found 103 stores with an average turnover of K622 per week, or a total annual turnover of K3.3 million. This higher figure ties in with the anecdotal evidence that trade store owners felt people were buying less in 1992 than they had done in the past. This could have been due to increasing competition (due to a greater number of stores), or to the substantially lower amount of compensation money entering the local economy, or simply a romantic view of the past.

A quick survey of owners indicated that soft drinks, tinned fish, rice, coffee, sugar and cigarettes were the biggest sellers. Some of the more sophisticated stores also offered hot food. All trade store goods were imported from Mount Hagen, Lae or Port Moresby, and the markup on prices at Porgera was high—in most cases at least 100 per cent over the cost of similar goods in Lae or Port Moresby. This meant that half of the value of sales was the wholesale cost, and on average a further 25 per cent represented transport costs for the store owner. Both these cost components were lost to Porgera when the store owner restocked. Most of the other 25 per cent (the profit) tended to be spent on consumer goods, food from trade stores, and meeting demands from family members and *wantoks*.

The markets were another form of small-scale business activity of some importance in the area. Surveys were carried out of sellers at both the main Yanjakale market at Porgera Station, and several of the smaller markets in the area. In total, 116 sellers were interviewed. Average reported daily income was K62.90, ranging between K5 and K400. On pay Wednesdays, it was not uncommon to have 200 sellers at the main markets, and another 200 spread across the other half-dozen markets in the valley. If we assume that these Wednesday markets accounted for around half of the total market activity for the fortnight, then the total value of market sales must have been around K1.3 million a year, which also agrees with the figure obtained from the income and expenditure survey. Of the sellers interviewed, 25 per cent were local Porgerans, almost 60 per cent were from other parts of Enga, and the remainder came from as far away as Goroka and Tari. The average reported daily sales of Porgerans (K30) were less than those of non-Porgerans (K73), so these sales must have represented a direct leakage of at least K1 million from the local economy.

Even less formal activities included roadside sellers (usually betelnut, cigarettes and greens), small-scale petrol sales (30 seen between Karik and Anawe Police Station), firewood sellers, 'bakeries' (selling deep fried flour balls for 10–20 toea a piece), poultry sellers (buying chicks from Mount Hagen and selling 8–10 weeks later for K10–12), and the cooking and sale of 'lambflaps'.

All of the above activities—from redistribution to trade store and market sales—point to a very low multiplier effect, with little capital accumulation in the Porgera Valley, as money was shifted rapidly out to other parts of the province and the country. It must be stressed that this is likely to occur in any remote area with a limited population base. However, the effect was highlighted at Porgera due to the large amounts of money which had been injected into the economy over a short period of time.

Conclusions

This review of the Porgeran economy in 1992 points to significant continuities with the pre-mine situation. This is not to say that nothing had changed in the area: clearly the value of cash inputs had increased significantly. However, many features of the local economy had seen little change since the start of production. The bulk of the population was still dependent on the subsistence sector for survival; consumption patterns were still focused on food, drink and gambling; bisnis aspirations were still dominated by trade stores, PMVs and machinery; and there were still significant patterns of inequality within the valley.

Although the surveys focused primarily on male household heads, significant gender differences showed up in the income and expenditure survey. Average female income for the fortnight was K60, compared to just over K200 for males. The primary source of income for women was sale of goods and produce (38 per cent of the total), with over 50 per cent of women reporting sales ranging between K5 and K300 for the fortnight. Eight per cent of male income came from the same source. Money from household members was more important for women than men (16 and 3 per cent of income respectively), while PJV wages and business profits accounted for 3 and zero per cent for women, compared to 36 and 29 per cent respectively for males. There were few differences in terms of expenditure patterns, the most significant being a smaller proportion being banked by women (23 per cent against 9 per cent), and a larger proportion still being held (31 per cent against 13 per cent).

As previously noted, differences in access to cash earning opportunities were established in the Porgera Valley prior to the arrival of the PJV. As early as 1948, people in the lower part of the valley had the advantage of access to alluvial gold, and Mungalep and particularly Yuyan developed as major centres of the local cash economy. Jackson (1987) found that households in Mungalep and Alipis had significantly greater values of possessions than those in Anawe and Suyan, and attributed this to the emphasis on independent gold panning in these communities. Our own surveys shows that, since the arrival of the PJV, the focus had shifted further up the valley and was now centred on the SML. This came out most clearly in the household survey: Apalaka had received over 70 per cent of compensation and the bulk of other direct PJV payments, while Tipinini had received virtually none. On the other hand, there was no simple relationship between the amount of compensation received and household assets, investments, or contributions to traditional exchange obligations. Clearly, Tipinini was lagging behind the other parts of the valley in terms of cash earning opportunities, but its residents appeared to make good use of the smaller incomes to which they had access. It is also important to note that, although there were significant differences between the various communities surveyed, there were more marked differences within each of these communities. In other words, inequality was greater at the level of the individual or household than at the level of the community.

Another feature of the local economy was the marked fluctuations in inputs over time, dominated by those sourced with the PJV. Compensation payments peaked in 1991 at K8.77 million, but were more than K5 million down from this peak in 1992. The records for 1992 also show that roughly half the compensation for the year was paid in the three-month period from May to July. Royalties were being paid approximately each quarter, while business contracts were awarded on an irregular basis. The most visible fluctuation was the fortnightly payment of PJV wages, which injected over K100,000 into the economy on a regular basis. For two or three days a fortnight, this drew people to the area from other parts of Enga, and stimulated market and trade store activity. These patterns were significant for the long-term development prospects of the local economy, because the irregular variations made forward planning difficult.

Notes

1   This chapter is concerned primarily with the economy of the Porgera Valley, though reference is occasionally made to contributions at the provincial, regional and national levels.
2   These interviews were largely carried out by Ben Imbun and five male students from the University of Papua New Guinea, in either Enga or Tok Pisin.
3   One of the more successful businessmen interviewed as part of this survey reported alcohol sales of K1,500 in the past fortnight.
4   Unfortunately, Jackson's report was not sighted until the fieldwork for this chapter was already under way, which was too late to directly influence the methodology used, though there is no major inconsistency between the two.
5   This section deals almost exclusively with the cash economy at Porgera, in keeping with the objectives of this stage of fieldwork and the methodology adopted. See Chapter 5 for discussion of the subsistence and non-cash economy around the mine.
6   This section includes reference to some data collected during my second trip to Porgera in June 1993, when I was able to complete the records of compensation payments made in 1992, and to consult the detailed compensation registers and code books for the whole period from 1987 to the end of 1992. These sources had their own problems—illegibility, clerical errors and alterations—but were a better source than the aggregated records which I had consulted during my first field trip (see Banks 1993).
7   A similar situation existed at Ok Tedi (Jackson 1993).
8   Employment created by the PJV through local contractors was also significant, but this is discussed in the subsequent section on business contracts.
9   The Porgera SML Landowners' Children's Investment Fund was set up to administer the 10 per cent share of the royalties which were to go to the children of the SML landowners. By the end of 1992, the value of this share was around K1 million, and the fund was expecting to start paying out benefits to 7–18 year olds in 1995 (with some small payouts during 1993 and 1994 to 19–21 year olds).
10 The number of polygamous households was greatest at Apalaka (five, or 15.6 per cent), and averaged 8 per cent across the valley.

11 These figures do not add up to 231 because the occasional survey form omitted the relevant information.
12 No figures were collected on business turnover or profitability in this survey (see Chapter 7 for further discussion).
13 The focus on consumption of gold money has parallels in Clark's (1993) account of Huli involvement in the Mount Kare gold rush, and may have occurred for similar cultural reasons.
14 Figures had not been kept by the company since that date.
15 Direct purchase of Porgeran goods by the PJV was minimal, reflecting both the specialised needs of the mine and the lack of local suppliers. However, the September 1992 Business Development Office's quarterly report noted that 32 per cent of purchases made by the warehouse were sourced from within Papua New Guinea.

4

The landowner relocation programme

Susanne Bonnell

The history of relocation

In order to construct the mine, the Porgera Joint Venture (PJV) had to relocate landowners living in the area of proposed mining activity and provide these landowners with improved housing. The Relocation Agreement was negotiated directly between the landowners and the PJV as part of the total compensation package programme. The Porgera relocation programmes was of a massive scale unprecedented in Papua New Guinea's mining history. In 1988, those planning for relocation never envisaged just how massive it would be. The original number of families planned for relocation grew progressively from 230 to 420. Relocation houses and new villages were the most visible change to Porgeran lifestyle brought about by the development of the mine. By the time the fieldwork for this chapter was undertaken, more relocation was being planned for the new Kaiya Lease for Mining Purposes (LMP) (see Chapter 7). It then looked as if something like 600 relocation houses would have been built by the end of 1994. This new relocation programme should have benefited from the experience gained in the previous programmes. But the sheer size of the relocation programme complicated the foreseen and unforeseen consequences of planned change. The landowners who negotiated a better lifestyle for themselves now had to deal, not only with the jealousies of the 'have-nots', but also the judgments of their children and grandchildren. And for the PJV, relocation was a bit like grabbing the tiger by the tail. The PJV had to take hold, it could not let go, and the eventual outcome was uncertain.

Background

The Social and Economic Impact Study (SEIS) for the Porgera project recommended that relocation should be kept to a minimum as 'the relocation of people under other mining developments in PNG has inevitably resulted in considerable misunderstanding, conflict and social hardship' (Pacific Agribusiness 1987[1]:92; see also Jackson 1987). This was certainly the case with Bougainville, the only landowner relocation programme which had been undertaken by a mining project at this time. But relocation was unavoidable in Porgera because, unlike Ok Tedi or Misima, a large number of people were living in the area proposed for mine development.

The SEIS recommended the 'design of the mine infrastructure and operations so as to minimise relocation of families', and that 'those families unavoidably relocated be supplied by the PJV with housing equal to or better than their existing housing, with an upper limit established by negotiation between the PJV and community representatives, with government arbitration if necessary' (Pacific Agribusiness 1987[2]:39). Both Jackson's 1987 report and the SEIS recommended that Alipis village be assisted to develop into 'an informal Melanesian mining community'. Other than that, the reports left the mechanics of the inevitable relocation unresolved.

Placer duly contracted Fritz Robinson, who had been part of the SEIS study team, to undertake an in-depth relocation study which began in January 1988 and lasted six weeks.[1] Robinson's study was based on the assumption that a relocation programme, in which people moved house but remained on their own land, was preferable to a resettlement programme, which would have meant moving people onto purchased or leased land. The relocation option was seen to be less socially disruptive, and its feasibility in the Porgera context was enhanced by the cognatic kinship system of the Ipili, which provided considerable flexibility for people to find alternative land on which to build their new houses.

Robinson's study included a survey of existing houses on and near the proposed plant site area, the proposed open pit area, and Alipis village. He also surveyed land and gardens in Yarik, Olonga and

Timorope. Besides meeting with male landowners, he met with women's groups to ascertain their opinions and needs. The latter was probably a first for the mining industry. The comprehensive report included details of plans with costings of various house design options; relocation areas; compensation arrangements; and the physical aspects of relocation, including garden contracts, rations and infrastructure needs. The main deficiency in this study was the author's estimate that only 230 families would need to be relocated. This was due to

- changes in mine development plans which Robinson had not been aware of
- an increase in the number of eligible persons previously omitted from the lists compiled by clan leaders; and
- failure to consider the relocation of Alipis village because the land on which it was situated was not needed for mine development.[2]

Nevertheless, Robinson's report provided the framework for Placer's negotiations with the landowners for the relocation agreement.

Negotiations

Placer employees Dave Moorhouse and Graham Hogg set up the Landowners' Negotiating Committee (LNC) in early 1987 for landowners of the clans and sub-clans within the Special Mining Lease (SML). This committee was composed of 23 representatives of the clans and sub-clans and their agreed alternates.[3] The LNC was originally set up to negotiate the Compensation Agreement which was concluded at the end of January 1988, and it then went on to negotiate the Relocation Agreement. Involvement of the LNC was critical in the negotiations, and the members soon developed in confidence as the negotiations continued. Vic Botts' laconic comment (Davis Film and Video 1990) that the Porgerans were accomplished negotiators rather understates the aggression, intimidation and chaos of the negotiation process. The LNC had the capacity to stop proceedings, but did not do so because they wanted the mine. Many Porgerans perceived the mine to be their only possible chance to catch up with the rest of Papua New Guinea after years of neglect. In addition, there was also an element of personal greed in the negotiations from some landowners seeking additional benefits. Despite disagreements which were often violent, both parties always returned to the negotiating table.

The establishment of criteria for eligibility to receive a relocation house was the most contentious subject of negotiation between the two sides. An arbitrary decision had to be made which was acceptable to the company and to Ipili culture. The outcome is best summarised by Robinson (1991), who was not only responsible for the relocation study, but also for implementing the relocation programme itself.

Some of the criteria for inclusion in the relocation programme included:

1. A residential status of longer than 3 years (originally 5 years).
2. Inclusion in one of the seven clans on the SML.
3. The presence of a 'habitable' house.
4. One relocation house per head of family.
5. Only married people to be eligible.

These apparently simple criteria were not simple in practice. There were a number of different perceptions operating. Someone who had been living with relatives in Paiela or Tari, but who had visited the SML (and perhaps stayed a month or two) considered themselves fully eligible.

Inclusion in one of the clans in the genealogy books said nothing about residential status. In several cases genuine members of the clan were not in the genealogies. There were a significant number in the *epo atene*—invited guest—group. These people have the rights to garden and build houses and to participate in most of the life and actions of the clan. But they are not part of the clan by blood, and do not appear in the genealogies. There are individuals in this group who have lived and worked with the clan for 15 years or more.

The 'habitable' house was very difficult to determine. The way houses developed is either purpose built as a dwelling (which is not a problem); or developed from a garden house (or in some cases a piggery), which is a problem. What begins as a garden house can end as a major family residence. This often happened.

For six months preceding the relocation another of the several waves of immigration occurred. Many of the garden houses and piggeries became occupied by relatives and were upgraded and made habitable.

During the survey which determined eligibility for relocation, the average household size was 13. Wiessner's figure for Wabag in the Central Enga is 5 per household.

Various other anomalies appeared: widows who have remarried outsiders, abandoned women and children, unmarried men and women of nearly marriageable age who suddenly declared themselves married, and unmarried men and women of middle age who had a well-established household.

When these anomalies appeared and continued to appear, decisions were made quickly and in consultation with the Landowners' Negotiating Committee...I suspect up to 8 relocation packages should not have been given to the individuals concerned.

The long term *Epo Atenes* were included for full relocation if they had been resident for 10 years or more. Shorter terms were given lesser benefits.

Another problem to overcome was that of the design of the relocation house. Robinson felt the men would have been just as happy with the cash, but the PJV viewed the relocation house as a family benefit. Robinson's research had shown that most people lived in houses between 25 and 32 square metres in area. Most people to be relocated lived in bush material houses, but some lived in houses partially or totally made of permanent materials. In addition, some houses in Alipis had electricity. There was a need to find a compromise between the style of Frank Faulkner's house on the government station, which was the preference of the LNC, and a semi-bush material house suggested by the PJV.[4] The LNC insisted on electrical wiring and running water, and many members also requested six bedrooms. The LNC and PJV finally came to an agreement for a four-bedroom house with a total living area of 42 square metres and sidings made of 'V' crimp aluminium as protection against fire and theft (see Map 4.1). An internal shower was optional.

Village trade stores were another major issue. There were 42 trade stores in Alipis alone. These stores varied from small bush material buildings selling a limited variety of goods to quite large buildings made of permanent materials. The larger trade stores carried a wide variety of goods, including frozen meat, often had a snooker table, and had huge turnovers. Owners wanted compensation for loss of trade while these stores were being moved and/or rebuilt. The outcome was that trade store owners either received compensation in cash or their stores were moved and rebuilt to the same or higher standard. There was no compensation for loss of trade.

With the exception of Alipis village, most Porgerans lived in small hamlets or homesteads. This settlement pattern tends to lower social stress due to the distance between neighbours. However, the cluster

Figure 4.1 Porgera relocation house plan

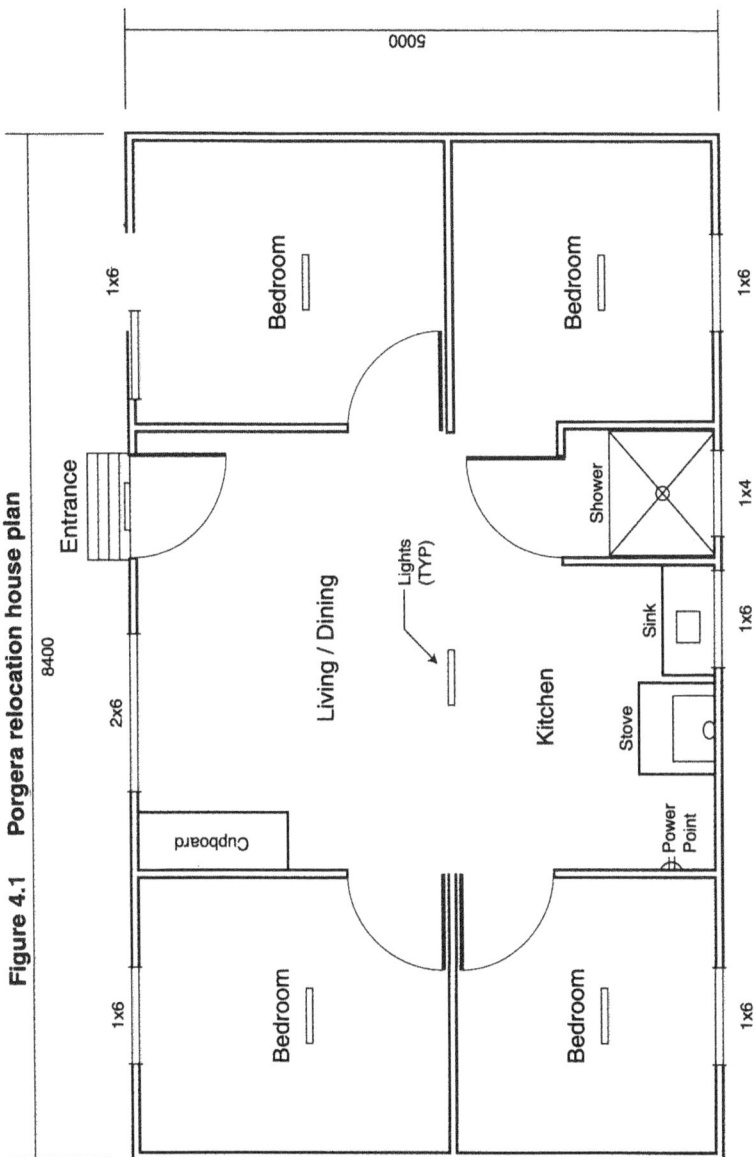

Source: Bonnell, S., 1994. *Dilemmas of Development: social change in Porgera, 1989–1993,* Porgera Social Monitoring Programme Report 2, Subada Consulting Pty Ltd for Porgera Joint Venture, Thornlands (QLD).

settlement pattern had attractions to both landowners and the PJV. From the people's viewpoint, clusters or villages would mean better services and utilities. From the PJV's viewpoint, this reduced the cost of building a large number of houses. In the end, the two parties agreed to focus on the creation of new villages within the boundaries of the SML at Apalaka, Kulapi, Yarik, Olonga and Timorope, with the PJV providing access roads and services.

The Relocation Agreement

The Relocation Agreement for the SML between Placer (PNG) Pty Ltd (on behalf of the Porgera Joint Venture) and Landowner Agents of the Tieni, Waiwa, Tuanda, Pulumaini, Angalaini, Mamai and Anga clans of Porgera was signed in September 1988. Some of the main points in the agreement were

- 'The PJV and the Landowners have agreed that if the mine is developed the PJV will in addition to making payments under the Compensation Agreement make certain payments and grant certain benefits to assist in the relocation of those landowners whose rights of residence or occupation are affected by the development of the mine. This payment represents a once only event to residents affected by the developments. No further payments for relocation will be considered' (p.2).
- 'The PJV agrees to pay compensation for hardship and disturbance as follows: to the head of each family of Re-Located Landowners One thousand Kina (K1,000); and to the head of each family of Epo Atene Residents Five hundred kina (K500)' (p.3).[5]
- Construct housing to the standard of attached plan (see Figure 4.1).
- 'Seek Elcom's agreement to provide assistance or funding to erect a standard Elcom pole and transformer where the houses in the new locations are clustered near enough to transmission lines to make this feasible' (p.4).[6]
- 'Construct a road from Yokolama to Apalaka and an access road linking the Pulumaini new location with the Anawe by-pass road: and to maintain them in a trafficable condition' (p.4).
- 'Clear small, flat areas adjacent to housing clusters in new locations for use as community meeting places' (p.4).

- 'Provide professional geotechnical officer to inspect, and advise on the stability of house sites in order to minimise any future problems from landslide damage' (p.4).
- 'Relocate two churches and provide one relocation house for each to be used by the respective pastors' (p.5).
- 'Relocate two aid posts and provide one relocation house for each to be used by the respective Government Health worker, subject to government approval' (p.5).

The PJV was not obliged to

- 'Maintain or repair houses other than failure caused by poor workmanship or materials for the first six months' (p.5); or
- 'To pay for the connection of individual houses to the power supply or for the supply of power to such houses' (p.5).

With regard to rations

- During the period of relocation the PJV agrees to provide rations to relocated landowners if necessary as follows: 'Such rations will be in accordance with prescribed Government scales; Rations will be delivered weekly to a representative of each family at a designated point...' (p.6).
- 'The supply of rations will commence on the date the family no longer has access to traditional garden land and shall continue until the food gardens in the new locations are ready to harvest or for a maximum period of nine (9) months' (p.6).[7]

Similar relocation agreements were later negotiated between the PJV and landowners for the Suyan Townsite and Kairik Airstrip. The Suyan townsite was a lease for mining purposes outside the SML, while Kairik was a state land purchase. While the state paid the Kairik landowners for the land, the PJV paid for all improvements at the same rate of compensation as for land within the SML, and provided relocation houses in the same way as for the SML and Suyan landowners. This action was felt by some to be a dangerous precedent for future state land purchases.

The PJV entered into a relocation agreement before they knew the extent of the ore deposit, and faced the dilemma of committing large amounts of money before they had a mining agreement. Construction of the relocation houses began in late 1988. The first 49 houses, most of which were in Kulapi, were ready for occupancy in February 1989, with an additional 71 houses under construction. By the time the SML was issued in May 1989, nearly 120 families had already been relocated.

The move

In view of the anticipated social disruption caused by mine development, especially to women and the family, Robinson (1988:7) recommended in his report that a female social worker be based in Porgera. Although this was originally envisioned to be a government position, mine management agreed to hire a temporary consultant to assist initially with the settling-in process of the relocation families, especially the women. I arrived in February to take up this position during the week in which the first families were moving into their new homes.

The relocation programme consisted of lands and relocation staff assisting families with the physical move, relocation staff purchasing and distributing rations to households, and the social development staff visiting each household to assist with settling in. Programmes to relocate landowners were coordinated from the chaotic Yokolama Lands Office complex, which more often than not resembled a fighting zone. High decibel arguments, physical fights and threatening behaviour were centred around grievances concerning compensation payments and relocation houses.

Social development staff visited each house as soon as possible after the owners moved in. The programme was primarily aimed at assisting women with the adjustments. Most of the families relocated had never lived in permanent material houses before, and needed advice on use, care and maintenance of the relocation house and its contents; this included demonstrations on operation and care of the stove, cleaning S-bend of sink, care of mattresses, how to clean floors, and so on. In addition, the house was checked for any construction faults, and those found were referred to the construction contractors. This was also a time to discuss any other concerns brought up by the women.[8] Settling-in visits were followed up with workshops. These workshops were conducted in one house with occupants from nearby houses attending. Workshops covered house care, hygiene, consumer awareness plus general discussion on any matters women raised. These workshops formed the basis for starting women's groups and the Porgera Women's Association.

Three relocation villages were built within the SML boundaries. The first was Kulapi/Area 6 (on Pulumaini and Angalaini clan land), followed by Yarik/Timorope/Olonga (on Tieni clan land), and in 1990 the first houses were constructed at Apalaka (on Tuanda and Waiwa clan land). Construction at Suyan began in 1990, and at Kairik in 1991.

Besides the relocation villages, houses were constructed on or near existing roads, either scattered among existing houses or in small extended family clusters. In mid 1993, relocation houses were located along the Yokolama-Panandaka-Mungalep-Kakendaka road on Mamai and Angalaini clan land, and along the Wendegonga-Anawe-Poare section of road to Porgera Station on Pulumaini and Anga clan land. From Porgera Station, houses were located on the road between Suyan and Kairik and between Suyan and Ingau. A few houses were constructed off-road, the most notable being the single house across the Kaiya River.

The impact of relocation

My own relocation survey was conducted between January and May 1993. By this time, many relocation houses, especially those in Kulapi and Yarik, had been occupied for about four years. The purpose of this survey was to observe the condition of the relocation houses and to find out what changes had taken place in the lives of the people who had been relocated. The survey was aimed primarily at getting the women's viewpoint. Mogom Tili and More Aliana, PJV Community Affairs staff who also lived in relocation houses, assisted me with the interviews. Mogom, More and I had worked together for nearly three years with most of the people interviewed, and we were able to reflect with the women on the changes that had taken place. In spite of explanations, I am sure that people I interviewed still considered me to be a PJV employee, and this may have affected some of their replies.

The survey sample

As of January 1993, 420 relocation houses had been built. Out of this total, one house was destroyed in 1989 during a family dispute, and two houses at Kairik were burned down early in 1993 during tribal fighting. The relocation survey covered 96 houses in all the main cluster areas except Mungalep and Kairik (see Table 4.1). This represents 23 per cent of the total number of relocation houses constructed. Mungalep and Kairik were not surveyed due to tribal fighting in these areas during the survey period.

The number of people (actual residents) living in relocation houses ranged from two to twenty, with an overall average of 8.1 persons per house. This would indicate that approximately 3,400 people were relocated (i.e. 8.1 people times 420 houses). John Burton (pers. comm.) estimated that there were approximately 7,000 Porgerans in the

Table 4.1   Relocation survey sample, 1993

Location	Houses	Persons	Mean h/h size	Range of h/h size
Kulapi	24	204	8.5	2–16
Anawe	15	111	7.4	3–11
Suyan	11	97	8.8	2–11
Apalaka	15	120	8.0	3–10
Yarik	21	148	7.0	3–13
Olonga	10	99	9.9	5–20
Total	96	779	8.1	2–20

Source: Relocation survey data.

Porgera Census Division in 1993, which would suggest that about half of them were living in relocation houses. However, my survey did not attempt to differentiate between 'Porgeran' and 'non-Porgeran' residents. Many of the landowners, male and female, were married to non-Porgerans, and their children might also have been married to non-Porgerans, and the relatives of these non-Porgerans might also have been living in the relocation houses. Therefore, it is probably more accurate to say that somewhere around one-third of 'Porgerans' were living in relocation houses in 1993.

Settlement patterns

Prior to relocation, most Porgerans (with the notable exception of Alipis village) lived in scattered family hamlets. The preferred relocation option was cluster-style living. This option was preferred by the landowners because the company agreed to construct access roads and supply electricity connection points to clustered settlements. The option was also preferred by the company because it would simplify the logistics of constructing the relocation houses. Some people, however, did opt for living outside the main cluster areas. The reasons for this included personal preference and the fact that some people were obliged to settle on land to which they had traditional rights.

The result of the people's decision to have their houses built in cluster areas was the creation of new villages. Many people during the survey said that they liked this new style living pattern because they felt more secure living close to other clan members. On the other hand, the creation of new villages created new problems. These problems (as discussed below) include rubbish disposal, firewood availability, easy access to food garden land, toilets, and so on. Most of these problems were compounded by the influx of non-Porgeran relatives.

Overcrowding

It was difficult to come up with a criterion for defining overcrowding. One option to define overcrowding is to use the average number of people per house prior to relocation. In his 1988 study, Robinson found the average household size to be six, and he used this number for all the planning options for relocation, which included house size, rations, etc. However, the relocation houses were larger than the average pre-existing houses—42 square metres as opposed to 25–32 square metres. Therefore, a second option is to use the average of two people per bedroom, or eight people per house, which was the average number of occupants in the survey. A third option, suggested by Robin Hide (pers. comm.), was to find out how many houses had more than twice the number of occupants that were originally envisaged, i.e. more than 12 people per house. Table 4.2 shows the level of 'overcrowding' on each of these three criteria.

Other factors in the definition of overcrowding would be adult/child ratios and the relationships between the people living in the house. One example of overcrowding was an unhappy household with 12 occupants: the husband, his first wife and their six children; the recent young second wife whom the first wife disliked; and the oldest daughter's husband and their two children. Customarily, a man would have separate houses for wives who did not get along, and married children would also have separate houses, all in the same compound. If custom had been followed, there would probably have been only seven people in this house.

Table 4.2   Number of relocation houses with more than 12, 8 or 6 residents

Location	Houses	Over 12 (%)	Over 8 (%)	Over 6 (%)
Kulapi	24	3 (12.5)	12 (50.0)	16 (66.6)
Anawe	15	0 (00.0)	4 (26.7)	10 (66.6)
Suyan	11	2 (18.1)	6 (54.5)	10 (90.9)
Apalaka	15	1 (06.7)	7 (46.7)	11 (73.3)
Yarik	21	1 (04.8)	6 (28.6)	12 (57.1)
Olonga	10	3 (30.0)	4 (40.0)	8 (80.0)
Total	96	10 (10.4)	39 (40.6)	67 (69.8)

Source: Relocation survey data.

Another example of overcrowding was a house with 20 occupants: the owner and his family plus the owner's brother and his family, who were not entitled to a relocation house. A third example was a household with 16 people: the owner and his wife and children, plus two children from a previous marriage and four non-Porgeran relatives.

These examples illustrate the main causes of overcrowding

- polygamy, especially the case of men who had taken new wives since moving into relocation houses
- Porgeran relatives moving in because they felt they were entitled to relocation houses
- non-Porgeran relatives moving in to gain the advantages of living near the mine
- married children continuing to live with parents because they wanted relocation houses of their own.

The effects of this overcrowding were family disputes, wear and tear on the house itself, plus the damage caused during these disputes. It was also a strain on already limited water resources and food gardening land. There were possible health consequences from communicable diseases.

Condition of houses

The way that the houses were maintained was itself a reliable indication of the people's attitude to a new way of living, and the relative success of the relocation programme. The houses were generally well looked after, especially when one considers the ratio between the total area of the house and the number of people living in it.

On the survey form, I gave each house a subjective rating of either excellent, good, fair or poor. 'Excellent' was for an outstanding example of cleanliness and care for the house and its surroundings. 'Good' meant the house was above average, very clean and well looked after. Houses with a 'fair' rating could have done with an improvement in housekeeping. The 'poor' rating was for houses which were basically uninhabitable due to filth or damage or both.

There was some criticism, especially in the Community Issues Committee meetings, that the relocation houses were too small—that they were 'matchboxes'. This was certainly a valid complaint for the 40 per cent of households with more than eight occupants. However, all but one of the women interviewed liked the new houses, and this was reflected in the care they were taking of them. If the people did not like the houses, they would have destroyed them or not cared for them. The demand for relocation houses by those who did not qualify, as well as the adult children of those who did, indicates that the relocation house was definitely the status symbol of Porgera.

The following is a list of the reasons which women gave for liking their relocation houses, in order of their relative frequency. Many women gave more than one reason.

Good stove, no smoke and saucepans are clean	56
Water inside the house	51
No lice, fleas or cockroaches	14
No rats	10
Electricity	10
Easy to clean	7
Shower inside the house	7
We sleep well	6
The houses last a long time	6
We have good beds and furniture	4
We do not get sick, we are healthier	4
Lots of space, 4 bedrooms	2
They look nice	2

Another advantage of the relocation houses that many women mentioned was that they no longer had to carry heavy loads of firewood. This confused me at first, until I realised that they had no firewood to carry because they were buying it. There were very few negative responses, but they are noteworthy.

The house is too small for more than one wife	1
The bush material houses are warmer	2

Table 4.3   Condition of relocation houses

Location	Excellent	Good	Fair	Poor	Total
Kulapi	0	7	17	0	24
Anawe	1	7	6	1	15
Suyan	1	9	1	0	11
Apalaka	0	8	7	0	15
Yarik	4	10	7	0	21
Olonga	1	7	2	0	10
Total	7	48	40	1	96

Source: Relocation survey data.

A *haus kapa* (permanent materials house)
is no good if you do not have money   2

Many house owners had made extensive and interesting alterations to the basic relocation house design. The most common change was the addition of a veranda, which was usually covered and sometimes enclosed to make additional rooms. Other alterations noted were the removal of internal walls to make fewer, but larger rooms, the addition of a septic toilet, and a larger concrete shower block. Nearly all owners had built a bush material kitchen (*haus kuk*) near their relocation house. This was encouraged by relocation staff for the following reasons

- older people and sick people were more comfortable sleeping in more traditional style houses, with the open fire on the floor
- it was a good place to house excess visitors or unruly children
- at times, it was more appropriate for cooking
- it was handy during domestic disputes.

In the house of an old couple, the husband said he preferred to sleep in the *haus kuk*, but his wife said she preferred to sleep in the relocation house. The matter of the *haus kuk* is best summed up by one woman who said that she liked both houses—the relocation house was good for sleeping, and the *haus kuk* was good to sit in and tell stories.

Four years after house occupancy, the lino on the floor was beginning to show some signs of wear and tear, but otherwise the houses still appeared to be structurally sound. As previously mentioned, the PJV had no responsibility for maintaining relocation houses under the terms of the Relocation Agreement. The rationale behind this was not just the convenience and cost savings to the company, but also because it would encourage self reliance. The problem was the lack of any custom or history of maintaining traditional houses—one merely lived in a house until it fell down, and then built a new one. The concept of preventive maintenance was hard to get across, as was the problem of gaining the skills and access to materials needed for repairs.

Owners appeared to have no problem in accepting responsibility for specific damage caused by people, such as the broken louvres and flywire often caused by owners who had lost or misplaced their keys. But they were not inclined to accept responsibility for damage caused by landslips or routine wear and tear. Despite the Relocation Agreement, PJV Community Affairs relocation staff were assisting landowners with maintenance needs, for example providing materials for minor repairs, referring home owners to local plumbers and carpenters, and replacing rotten timber on tank stands (a contractor fault discovered long after the six-month deadline had passed).[9] Furthermore, any landslip problems were being referred to the PJV's geotechnical staff for investigation. The dilemma was in trying to find the balance between developing a sense of home owner responsibility and assisting owners with maintenance problems as they developed over time.

Water supply

It appeared that the 500-gallon water tanks connected to the relocation houses were adequate for no more than three rain-free days for small families, and required daily rain for larger families. This problem was recognised during the first dry spell in Porgera in 1989. It was a constant issue with the women, who were the primary users of water, and was raised with the PJV Site Manager during a meeting of the Porgera Women's Association in July 1991. Later, this issue was raised by the men during a Community Issues Committee meeting.

New style houses and increased income for buying clothes, bedding and improved personal hygiene made the Ipili more intensive users of water than they had been before relocation and compensation. Other factors compounding this problem were

- overcrowding
- traditional alternative water sources affected by mine development and the influx of outsiders
- obligations to relatives who did not have tanks
- stealing of water
- tanks filling up with silt
- leaking taps
- no cultural history of water conservation; and
- people just used more water because it was there.

The size of the water tank was a point lost amongst the various trade-offs made in the negotiations over the relocation house design. While it is certainly arguable that the water tanks were too small, the results of the survey in Table 4.4 show that an unreasonable number of people were using them, especially when compared with the number of occupants recorded in Table 4.2.

Many relocation house owners were providing water for other people who lived nearby or in their homestead. Most of these were outsiders, with the notable exception of Olonga, where the owners were providing water primarily to other sub-clan members who were

Table 4.4	Numbers of people using water tanks			
Location	Houses	Users	Average users/ house	Range of users/ house
Kulapi	24	277	11.5	2–21
Anawe	15	215	14.3	3–39
Suyan*	11	121	13.4	3–23
Apalaka	15	129	8.6	3–13
Yarik	21	178	8.5	3–17
Olonga	10	125	12.5	5–20
Total	96	1,045	11.1	2–39

Note: *Figures for Suyan are for nine houses. Two houses had tanks that were damaged beyond use.
Source: Relocation survey data.

not eligible for relocation houses. With the benefit of hindsight, it may have been better to install 1,000 gallon tanks with the relocation houses, but access to a safe, clean water supply was not just an issue for people in relocation houses; it was a widespread concern throughout the valley.[10]

Food gardens

The loss of land for food gardening purposes was recognised as a probable negative consequence of mine development by several experts. A 1986 garden survey (Jackson 1987:B-1) showed an average of four gardens per household, ranging from a low of 2.8 gardens per household in Suyan up to 5.2 gardens per household in Alipis.[11] Robinson's 1988 survey also indicated an average of four gardens per household, with an average household size of six persons (no details of household size had been given in Jackson's study). In the 1993 relocation survey, I asked household occupants how many sweet potato gardens they had. The results shown in Table 4.5 indicate a significant decrease in the number of gardens since 1988. In Yarik, there was a distinct difference between the number of food gardens belonging to the Tieni Wuape and the Tieni Waingalo households, with an average of 1.6 gardens per household and 8 gardens per household respectively. The one household with 25 gardens was a one-off case which I cannot explain.

Even though I made no attempt to measure the total area of the gardens reported by each household, the decrease from an average of

Table 4.5   Number of food gardens per relocated household

Location	Houses	Gardens	Average gdns/ house	Range of gdns/ house
Kulapi	24	28	1.2	0–2
Anawe	15	18	1.2	0–4
Suyan	11	21	1.9	0–6
Apalaka	15	34	2.3	1–10
Yarik	21	83	4.0	0–25
Olonga	10	21	2.1	0–5
Total	96	205	2.1	0–25

Source: Relocation survey data.

of four to two gardens per household, as well as the reported 15 households with no food gardens at all, indicated the need for further investigation.

- How many families actually did not have enough land for food gardening due to loss of land from mine development?
- How many families had alternate land they could use, but not within reasonable access of their relocation houses?
- How many women were not gardening by choice because they had adequate income to meet their present needs?
- How many women were not gardening because their husbands were not clearing, fencing and draining new garden land?
- What was the effect of garden land shortage on the traditional fallow system?

Reduction in the number of food gardens was a concern because food gardens were the economic base of Ipili society. Removal of this economic base created a situation of economic dependency and problematic relationships between the landowners and the mining company, especially when combined with unmet employment expectations. This had already happened on occasions, especially with the Pulumaini landowners at Kulapi. There was certainly nothing to indicate any alternatives for the majority of landowners, other than to return to a subsistence lifestyle when the mine finally closed or if they were unemployed. Yet women who were not gardening were not passing their skills on to their daughters. With a projected further mine life of approximately 15 years (in 1993), this could mean a generation losing its gardening skills. Furthermore, food gardens were the main area of control that women had in society, and their loss could have negative consequences for the family.

With regard to food garden land, the people of Kulapi were disadvantaged compared to the other relocation areas (see Chapter 5). The people of Kulapi had to clear primary rainforest to make their new gardens. Soil was poor, with a high water table, and there was excessive leaf mould with a high nitrogen content. This, combined with the comparatively high altitude, inhibited the formation of tubers in sweet potatoes. When this problem was recognised in early 1989, experts from the national Department of Agriculture and Livestock were brought in to make recommendations. It was felt that time would cure the problems of excessive nitrogen and draining of the soil, but improved agricultural practices would be the only way to improve soil fertility. In the meantime, a programme was initiated to grow potatoes as a substitute staple crop. From September 1989 to April 1991, free seed potatoes and fertiliser were distributed under a programme supervised by the Women's Section of the PJV. The programme was suspended because of the increasing numbers of outsiders requesting seed, and because a few women who had persevered with their sweet potato finally had gardens that were producing tubers. It was also recommended in 1989 (and periodically re-recommended) by relocation staff that the PJV release unused Pulumaini land in the SML to Kulapi landowners for gardening purposes.[12] The PJV had already paid compensation for the use of this land, and there was concern that, if the PJV needed to use this land in the future, there would be further compensation demands by landowners.

The creation of the Anjolek dump site and excision of the Kaiya LMP also threatened to have a negative impact on the availability of gardening land. During the survey, several women in Apalaka and Yarik expressed their concern about losing their remaining garden land to the expansion of the mine. This included

- loss of land due to the Kaiya LMP surveying
- fear of increased landslides due to mining activities
- possible loss of land if the mine expanded to the ridge behind and above Yarik; and
- loss of access to their gardens which lay on the other side of the proposed Anjolek dump site (see Chapter 6).

Rubbish disposal

While most houses in the relocation areas and their immediate surrounds were tidy and free of rubbish, this was not the case for trade stores, public areas, or tracks leading to the houses. People were encouraged to build rubbish pits as part of the relocation programme, and there was extensive extension work on the 'effluence of affluence' problem, but any improvements were short-lived. Kulapi village was even the target of a special improvement programme, mounted by the PJV's Community Affairs Division, in which the community was provided with centrally located rubbish bins, but these were still being dumped in the bush.

The main problems with rubbish disposal throughout Porgera, and not just in the relocation areas, were

- people not perceiving rubbish to be a problem
- the local government council's inability or lack of will to enforce council rules pertaining to rubbish disposal
- the new clustered settlement pattern which made rubbish more visible; and
- increased affluence which produced more rubbish than in the past.

Some people were using rubbish pits which they had dug themselves, but most threw their rubbish in the bush or in creeks, and most of this rubbish, unlike that of the past, was not biodegradable. Only two people interviewed during my relocation survey (one man in Apalaka and one woman in Yarik) perceived rubbish in the community as a problem, and both suggested that the PJV arrange for rubbish collection.

Toilets

The relocation house came with a pit toilet built on a cement slab, enclosed by a moveable steel shed. In the first 49 houses, the shed was not moveable, but the design was subsequently changed. Pits were shallow in construction due to the high water table. The actual hole in the cement slab was quite small, and while this ensured that children did not drop in, it did make hygiene a bit difficult. Toilets did not come with a lid for the hole, but many people constructed lids as recommended during the relocation settling-in programme.

The theory behind the relocatable slab and shed was that when the pit was full, the owner would then dig a new pit and move the slab and shed. The results of my survey, as shown in Table 4.6, indicate that this was not happening. Out of the 96 households in the survey, 37

Table 4.6   Toilet facilities of relocation houses

Location	New pit	Old pit	Dug out	Blocked	Flush	None	Total
Kulapi	4	1	14	4	1	0	24
Anawe	8	5	0	1	0	1	15
Suyan	3	4	0	3	0	1	11
Apalaka	7	2	3	2	0	1	15
Yarik	9	4	7	0	0	1	21
Olonga	6	2	1	1	0	0	10
Total	37	18	25	11	1	4	96

Source: Relocation survey data.

(38.5 per cent) were actually using a new pit; 18 were still using the old pit in its original form;[13] 25 were using a 'dug out' version of the old pit, in which the owner had dug a hole beneath the latrine and poured water in to flush out the pit;[14] and 11 were no longer able to use the old pit because it was blocked, but the owners were not interested in constructing a new one (Table 4.6). In one case, the owner had installed a septic flush toilet in the house. In four cases, there were simply no toilet facilities at all. One person reported to me that he got rid of his toilet because his neighbours' children were using it and soiling the area.

Firewood availability

As a result of the influx of outsiders into Porgera, and the new clustered settlement patterns, there were very obvious areas of deforestation in the Porgera Valley. This had led to a shortage of firewood and building materials. As indicated in Table 4.7, many people in the main relocation areas were beginning to feel the effects of the shortage of firewood in 1993. This was obvious in the houses which used to have a lot of firewood stored underneath. Four years previously, when I began the relocation work, the stoves were in constant use, but during this later survey, I found that most of the stoves were cold, suggesting a marked decline in the frequency of use. People were now buying firewood at Kulapi (Waile Creek road area), Paiam, Kairik, Tipinini, and as far away as Tumudan and Mulitaka. While this would have provided some additional income for the people in those areas, it was tough on those people who had to buy firewood but did not have an income earner in the family. One woman actually said the relocation houses were cold.[15]

Electricity

Jackson (1987) reported that electricity was an anticipated benefit of mine development, and indeed the provision of electricity to relocation areas was a major consideration in the negotiations for both the Relocation Agreement and the Porgera Development Forum agreement between the landowners and the national government.[16] At the time of my survey, the national Electricity Commission was only just starting to connect relocation houses to electricity generated from the Hides gas plant. Houses in Kulapi had not yet been connected, but 26 of the 46 houses visited in Yarik, Olonga, Timorope and Apalaka had been.[17]

Prior to electricity connection, landowners protested—at times violently—that they wanted the connection and electricity supply to be free. However, once connection was underway and the first electricity bills were received, this became rather a dead issue. The initial connection fee was K80, which included a K20 deposit. If only lights were being used, the cost was about K5 per month. The accounts shown to me during the survey were as follows: K19.40 for 74 days; K12.75 for 90 days; K11.68 for 81 days; K12.72 for 90 days; K14.08 for 90 days; and K55 for 90 days (but this last house had security lights, a TV-video, and connection to a chicken project). Kerosene cost between 50t and K1 per bottle, and the women said that they were using one or two bottles a night for lamps, which would have meant a monthly expenditure of K15–30. The advantages of electricity were obvious to all. Besides the cost factor, other reasons people gave for liking

Table 4.7   Availability of firewood in relocation houses

Location	Enough	Short supply	Must buy	Total
Kulapi	12	11	1	24
Anawe	2	3	10	15
Suyan	11	0	0	11
Apalaka	4	9	2	15
Yarik	1	4	16	21
Olonga	0	1	9	10
Total	30	28	38	96

Source: Relocation survey data.

electricity were its cleanliness and the convenience of having light at night whenever they felt like it. On the other hand, a few people still expressed concern about finding the money to pay their electricity account. The first overdue account notices were about to be issued, and if there were many defaulters, there would probably have been a resurgence in the demand for the PJV to foot the bills.

Electricity could mean a quantum leap in consumerism. As electricity had only recently been connected, and only to Apalaka and Yarik, the results of the survey were rather inconclusive on this score. Many women appeared happy just to have electric lights. Some expressed interest in purchasing washing machines and electric cookers, and this would be related to the lack of firewood in the area.

Problems and concerns

The problems and concerns listed below, in order of stated frequency, were those of the women interviewed during the survey. The numbers do not add up to 96 because women often had more than one concern. It is also interesting to note that many of the women who listed tank water as one of the primary benefits of living in the relocation house also listed lack of water as their main concern.

Concerned about food gardens	33
No work or no money	27
Concerned about water	26
Want electricity	18
Lack of firewood	15
Concerned about children's future (in housing or employment)	12
Just worried about the future	6
Worried about the possibility of landslides	5
Concerned about outsiders stealing	5
Concerned about drinking and gambling	4

Other concerns mentioned by three or less women included

It is hard living in Yarik

How do we fix things if our husbands have left us?

It is too crowded

Miss the old house (life?)

Water used to taste better (than tank water)

The clinic fees are too high

Worried about new sicknesses (AIDS).

One of the problems that came out strongly in the survey was the conflict between parents and children. Older children were putting pressure on their parents by bringing their spouses to live with them in the relocation houses. The children wanted their own relocation houses, and were accusing their parents of selling them short when they entered into the relocation agreement. Many women said that their big worry was, 'Where are our children going to live?' This was expressed as part of their concern for the children's future in the survey form, as well as in informal meetings with groups of women in the relocation areas. Some women were very concerned that their sons were idle, and all they did all day long was drink and play cards. The problem of idle, unemployed youth, who felt they had been left out of all the benefits of compensation and relocation that their parents received, was considered by some to be near the explosive point. Some people I spoke to thought it was quite possible that in the near future some relocation houses in Kulapi and Mungalep would be destroyed by angry children.

Many women in Kulapi were very concerned and anxious about the future. They were concerned about how long the mine was going to operate, was the PJV going to stay or go, would they ever be able to go back to their land. It was suggested by one prominent Porgeran landowner that this concern was related to the 'fly-in/fly-out' issue. He said that, because the company was not bringing the families of employees to live in Porgera, people were worried that the mine wasn't going to last a long time. Another explanation of this anxiety could be related to the 'end of the world' beliefs that crop up from time to time in Ipili culture. Perhaps the most logical explanation is that, because the women's expectations were not met, they were merely wondering 'What next?' It should be pointed out that not everyone was in a state of anxiety. Residents of 12 houses in the survey said they had no problems and were happy with their new lives.

The dilemma of the relocation house

It could be said that the relocation programme was too successful. The objective of the relocation programme was to move landowners from the area of proposed mining activities, and to provide these landowners with an improved house as part of the total compensation package. The result was that the relocation houses provided a dramatic improvement in the standard of living for a large number of people. The improved standard of living for owners of relocation houses then created new problems. People who did not get relocation houses were jealous of those who did. Children of parents who had relocation houses were demanding that they too be provided with relocation houses. The relocation houses locked people who were previously more mobile into their new places of residence. The newly created relocation villages, with increasing population density due to high birth rates and the immigration of relatives, were facing problems of environmental degradation and a shortage of gardening land to meet the needs of the inhabitants.

Relocated marriages

A separate marriage survey was conducted in the relocation areas to shed further light on the problems which had been a central concern of the Porgera Women's Association since it was founded in mid 1989. The main complaint was that Porgeran men had been using compensation money to 'buy' new wives, most of whom were 'outsiders', and then deserting their Porgeran wives and children (see Chapter 2).[18] The sample for this survey was the first 100 relocated married men—approximately 25 per cent of the relocated men with extant marriages. Informants were asked

1. How many wives did this man have before relocation (which roughly equates to the time when the large compensation payments were made)? and
2. How many wives did this man marry after relocation?

Notes were made as to the place of origin of each wife, deaths, divorces and wives who left their husbands.

Increase in polygyny

Meggitt reported a 30 per cent polygyny rate for Porgera in 1957, based on a sample of 41 men, while Kyakas and Wiessner (1992:153) have more recently estimated a 20–25 per cent polygyny rate for Enga Province as a whole. Glenn Banks reported a figure of 8 per cent for Porgera in his own 1993 survey (see Chapter 3), but this figure cannot be related to the others as it relates to households rather than marriages.

The results of my own survey (Table 4.8) indicate a dramatic increase in polygyny from 19 per cent before relocation to 43 per cent by mid 1993. Between 1989 and 1993, a further 7 per cent of men in the sample had at some time been married to more than one wife, but were now in monogamous marriages because they had divorced one or more of the previous wives, or because one or more of the wives had left the marriage (*meri i ranawe*). This meant that, at some time between 1989 and 1993, 50 per cent of the men in the sample had been practising polygamy!

The 100 men in the sample had a total of 135 wives prior to relocation, and acquired 75 new wives between 1989 and mid 1993, making a total of 210 wives. This meant that the average number of wives had increased from 1.35 to 2.1 over that period. It is probable that this polygyny rate would decrease again, as there was an increase in the failure rate of the marriages contracted after relocation. Of the 135 marriages contracted prior to relocation, 15 (11 per cent) had already failed, with 13 wives divorced and two who ran away. Of the 75 marriages contracted after relocation, 15 (20 per cent) had already failed, with five wives divorced and ten who ran away. Nine of the post-relocation wives who left their husbands were non-Porgerans.

One practical reason for 'traditional' polygyny was the high male death rate due to warfare. The economic basis of polygyny was the need to cultivate more sweet potatoes to increase the number of pigs in the household herd. More wives meant that more sweet potato could be cultivated to feed more pigs, and pigs were the essential means for men to increase their personal wealth and prestige. But even in the past, the failure rate of polygynous marriages was high because of conflicts which stemmed from the opposing interests of men and women.

> For a man, marrying more than one wife was one of the roads to success...For a woman, having a co-wife meant sharing her husband with another woman, sharing the family's garden land and sharing the family's pigs to be given away in exchange between her relatives and those of her co-wife. The road to success for men thus divided the

Table 4.8   Types of marriage before and after relocation (per cent)

Type of marriage	Before	After
Monogamy	76	41
Polygyny	19	43
Serial monogamy	5	8
Polygyny to monogamy [a]	0	7
Now single	0	1

Note: [a] These were men who had previously had more than one wife at the one time, but who now only had one wife.

Source: Marriage survey data.

possessions and territory of women. Only wealthy leaders, skilled in handling social and personal relations were able to manage lasting polygynous marriages (Kyakas and Wiessner 1992:154).

The modern forces of money and education have distorted the practice of polygyny in ways which have had a further adverse impact on women and the family. Cash provides the means to literally buy wives. Men now marry for sexual purposes rather than the more economic purposes of the past. In Porgera, men could formerly only acquire additional wives if the first wife agreed or if she failed to have children. On the other hand, there was now very strong evidence that men were using the village courts (an introduced institution) to rewrite custom in their favour. This was made possible because women had no traditional voice in the public arena.

Today, throughout the highlands, cash is being used for brideprice payments, either directly or indirectly (when it is used to buy tradit-ional wealth). When cash only is used for marriage, Porgeran women classify that as an inferior marriage and say contemptuously: *'em i-baim long moni tasol'* ('he bought them with money only'). As women gained increasing freedom to marry the man of their choice, one may well ask why they agreed to marry a man who already had a wife or wives. The women may either have truly desired the man or merely wanted a rich husband with the idea that they would oust the previous wife or wives. The Western colloquialism 'gold digger' has been particularly apt in Porgera.

Women, although often victims, are not without power. A strong first wife can influence a husband to leave his second wife. For example, one woman I knew left her husband after he took a second wife. She took the children and moved in with relatives until (she said) he came to his senses. The new wife was felt to be no threat as she was 'lazy and only after money'. In this case, the first wife won. However, the more common result in Porgera has been the abandonment of the first wife (and her children) and/or increased domestic violence. Porg-eran women also said that, when a husband wanted to take a new wife and get rid of the old one, he would beat her so that she would leave and return to her relatives. According to custom, if the wife leaves, the husband does not have to refund the brideprice.

Although Porgeran women were very vocal in their condemnation of polygyny, in principle they were not totally opposed to it (in spite of their professed Christian values) if the husband followed custom and looked after all his wives and children. However, I only met two women in polygynous marriages in Porgera who indicated they were happy with their situation. Both these women were first wives who maintained their prestige and were in charge of the subsequent wives. I do not know what the co-wives thought of the situation.

The relocation house added further stress to the polygynous family. Often, there was a dispute as to which wife should occupy the relocation house. If more than one wife occupied the house, this frequently led to disputes between co-wives. This unhappy situation was common. In 1989, I tried unsuccessfully to convince a badly beaten woman to come with me to the hospital. She refused, as she said that, if she left her new relocation house, her husband would move in his new wife. She still had the house in 1993, but her husband was living elsewhere with his other wives.

Many women in Porgera (indeed throughout the highlands) have been suffering the effects of an increase in, and distortion of, the practice of polygyny. I support their viewpoint that this practice has no place in modern Papua New Guinea. Polygyny is as socially repugnant as other local 'customs' such as cannibalism, infanticide, domestic violence and tribal fighting for example. It is in violation of Christian beliefs, the National Constitution and the United Nations Declaration of Human Rights. Cynics will rightly point out that legislation has not diminished tribal fighting or domestic violence, and that the Christian churches have had little effect on polygyny, especially in the highlands.[19] Laws of this country are made by men, many of whom do, or would like to, practice polygyny themselves— especially the members from the five Highland provinces. Although it is not possible to legislate morality, nevertheless the problem still needs to be dealt with.

Increase in marriage to outsiders

Table 4.9 shows the extent of the increase in marriages to 'outsiders'. This table compares the place of origin of the wives whom the 100 surveyed men had married before the start of the relocation programme in 1989, with the place of origin of the wives whom they married after it had started. The results show that 64.5 per cent of the wives acquired after relocation (that is after receiving large compensation payments) were non-Porgerans, and 64 per cent of the wives were from non-Ipili speaking areas. The greatest increase was for wives from the Tari District of the Southern Highlands. As previously mentioned, there had been a high failure rate for the recent marriages to outsiders.

Table 4.9   Wives' place of origin before and after relocation (per cent)

Place of origin	Before	After	All wives
Porgera	79 (58.5)	19 (25.3)	98 (46.7)
Paiela	25 (18.5)	8 (10.7)	33 (15.7)
Laiagam	14 (10.4)	13 (17.3)	27 (12.9)
Tari	8 (5.9)	22 (29.4)	30 (14.3)
Wabag	4 (3.0)	2 (2.7)	6 (2.8)
Kandep	3 (2.2)	7 (9.3)	10 (4.8)
Chimbu	2 (1.5)	0 (0.0)	2 (0.9)
Hagen	0 (0.0)	3 (4.0)	3 (4.1)
Kopiago	0 (0.0)	1 (1.3)	1 (0.5)
Total	135 (100.0)	75 (100.0)	210 (100.0)

Source: Marriage survey data.

While most Ipili marry other Ipili, it was also traditionally common for Ipili men or women to marry outsiders—especially their Huli or Engan neighbours. This was to increase their population for defence purposes, to help with customary obligations, and to increase the potential for survival in a harsh environment. With the sudden influx of cash, the Ipili became more attractive as marriage partners, while their customary practice became dysfunctional. Because Porgera was now an attractive place to outsiders, family members of the non-Porgeran spouse would take advantage of the marriage ties and move in. This led to chain migration which compounded the outsider problem. Taken to the extreme, this could cause the Ipili culture to be extinguished through marriage.

Impact of marital breakdown

When marriages broke down, the two most common consequences were either divorce or abandoned wives and children. Other consequences were murder, suicide, or the wife abandoning husband and children.

During the period of this study, divorce in customary marriages was normally conducted through the village courts. Women claimed that the village courts were making it too easy for men to divorce. There was no mediation. This situation usually occurred when a man wished to take a new wife. The most serious allegation had to do with the repayment of brideprice. Village courts were making orders for women to repay the brideprice to their husbands in the event of divorce (I saw several such court orders). Failure to repay meant jail for the woman. This was certainly not custom. Women did not pay their brideprices in the first instance.[20] This was an example of men using the village court system to rewrite custom.

While men were finding it fairly easy to obtain a divorce in the village court, women were not. As women had no say in the courts, when a husband took a subsequent wife, they were forced to stay in polygynous marriages against their will and their religious beliefs. There had been cases of women being forced to stay in violent marriages. In one marriage, the wife either committed suicide or was murdered, which led to a tribal fight. She had repeatedly gone to the village court to try to end this marriage. There are methods of appeal under the Village Courts Act against decisions which do not follow custom, or where the aggrieved party was not permitted to present his or her case. Many women were still ignorant of the grounds for appeal. Even if appeals were lodged, the appeal system did not seem to work.

A second consequence of marriage breakdown was abandoned wives and children. The marriage survey, unfortunately, did not obtain figures on the number of wives who were still married by custom, but who were no longer being looked after by their husbands. This problem had been a concern of the Porgera Women's Association. The PJV's Welfare Officer confirmed that he spent most of his time dealing with complaints from women who stated that they had been abandoned by their husbands. These complaints were not only from Porgeran women, but also from the wives of PJV employees who did not see their husbands on their rostered days off work or receive money from their paychecks.

Notes

1   The terms of reference were based on the suggestions made by Dave Moorhouse, then on Placer's Porgera staff, in consultation with other individuals with extensive local knowledge—Polly Wiessner, Frank Faulkner, Phil Gibbs, Kurubu Ipara and Graham Hogg.
2   The mutually acceptable decision to relocate the residents of Alipis had been reached by the time that Robinson's final report was submitted.
3   The LNC is not to be confused with the Porgera Landowner's Association which, though formed in 1986, was suffering from credibility problems (see Chapter 2).
4   Frank Faulkner was the Senior Liaison Officer employed by what was then the Department of Minerals and Energy (later Mining and Petroleum).

5 The K1,000 disruption allowance was determined at a rate which would furnish a house using furniture made at Wanepop Vocational Centre in the Lagaip District of Enga. Only two houses were furnished before Wanepop was burned down.

6 This is not to be confused with clause 18.1 of the agreement between the National Government and the Porgeran Landowners which states: 'The Porgera Joint Venture is to be directed to make all necessary arrangements to ensure supply of electricity to individual houses—(a) in existing relocation cluster settlements with 12 months of the execution of this Agreement, [and] (b) in all similar future settlements necessitated by the issues of any mining tenements at the time of the construction of those settlements.' It is my understanding that the National Government did not in fact direct the PJV to do this, but it did become an issue, especially in Mungalep, Suyan and Kairik.

7 Garden contracts were issued by the PJV. Relocating families were encouraged to make gardens to replace the ones on land required for mine development. Payment for garden contracts was in three instalments; after garden cleared and fenced, when garden was prepared for planting, and when the planting was completed. In anticipation of a Relocation Agreement, 17 garden contracts had already been let by February 1988.

8 One problem noted during the first visit to the new houses was the lack of an outside water tap. Women complained it was too hard to wash clothes and all their small children inside the house. The outside tap became *the* feminist issue in the relocation programme. After 120 houses had been built, the outside tap was finally incorporated into the house design for all subsequent relocation houses, though it took several months before the original 120 houses had outside taps installed.

9 A number of specific maintenance problems were noted during the relocation survey and discussed with PJV's Community Affairs staff so that they could take remedial action.

10 In 1993, the PJV was favouring two methods of dealing with water supply problems. Where there was an available clean source, a gravity feed system with a free-flowing outlet would be installed. This method was in the process of being piloted at Kulapi at the time of this research. Where this first option was not feasible, the alternative was the installation of rainwater tanks connected to public buildings with good catchment areas, such as churches, schools or community centres. Tanks had already been installed in many areas of Porgera, as well as other areas outside of Porgera covered by the PJV's community relations programme.

11 Most Alipis residents relocated to Yarik.

12 The women of Kulapi, without exception, still listed the lack of good gardening land as their biggest concern in 1993. Those of the Pulumaini clan were especially aggrieved by their perception that the Tieni clan had gained an unreasonable advantage by moving to

Alipis to be near the company, and then being moved back to Yarik and given relocation houses near their existing food gardens.

13 This is what they told me, though it is hard to believe that they were not yet full after four years of use. This remains a mystery that I did not investigate!

14 This expedient, which was only feasible on hilly sites, could be regarded as a serious health hazard in high density living areas, because the effluent simply drained down the hillside.

15 Staff in the PJV's Community Affairs and Environment departments had long been aware of the problem, and had started programmes to produce seedlings for distribution and for youth reforestation projects in the SML. It was reasonable to assume that many people would become increasingly dependent on purchasing firewood for some or most of their needs.

16 Many residents of Alipis village had free electricity provided by the company before the relocation programme started.

17 Elcom staff did provide some education during connection, but this appears to have been patchy, and the leaflets that were distributed were in English.

18 Many Porgeran men received large amounts of money from the Mount Kare gold rush, as well as compensation money from the PJV. However, it was generally felt that gold rush money was spent on loose women, while compensation money was used to buy new wives. This fits with the notion that Kare money was not 'real' money (Davis Film & Video 1990).

19 A significant number of Porgeran pastors and other church leaders had entered into polygynous marriages since 1988.

20 According to Chris Ballard (pers. comm.), this trend was also evident in the Tari area, where men were divorcing their wives and obtaining a refund on the brideprice to finance a new wife.

5

Gardens and *wantoks*

Glenn Banks

This chapter is designed to illuminate the significance of the
subsistence sector in the local economy during the development of the
Porgera mine. I begin by detailing the physical environment at
Porgera which acts as the ultimate constraint on the productivity of
the subsistence system. The Porgeran gardening system prior to the
start of mine construction is then described, and the effect of the mine
development on the gardening system is investigated, firstly in
general terms and then focussing on two areas within the Special
Mining Lease (SML) where the agricultural system is under stress.

The basic demographic and economic information on the
'outsiders' (*epo atene*—'come stay') from the surveys carried out in late
1992 and mid 1993 as part of the Economic Modelling Project within
the Porgera Social Monitoring Programme is then presented. The *epo
atene* make up a significant proportion of the population, and play a
key role in the dynamics of the local economy. Finally, I draw together
the material on the subsistence sector and the *epo atene*, placing both of
them in the context of the total Porgeran economy at that point in
time.

The results of a number of separate investigations are described in
this chapter, drawing on primary and secondary sources. A review of
the literature on local gardening systems forms a basis from which the

effects of the mine can be discussed. Most of the substantive work was commissioned by the Porgera Joint Venture (PJV) prior to mine development, though some information also exists in patrol reports and in other studies by anthropologists and agriculturalists.

A central part of our own investigations was a survey which questioned people as to the food they had eaten in the previous 24 hours. For convenience, it is referred to as the 'diet survey', although I stress that it was not a full dietary or nutritional survey. The aim was to investigate the contribution of the subsistence component of the economy or, put another way, the extent to which the population was still dependent on food from their gardens. In total, 350 interviews were completed by the team, each lasting between 10 and 15 minutes.[1] Three areas within the SML (Apalaka, Yarik, Kulapi) and five outside the SML (Mungalep, Anawe, Paiam, Porgera Station, Tipinini) were visited. This represents a cross-section of the communities within the Porgera Valley. The survey was carried out from Wednesday to Saturday in a week in June which was a government (but not a PJV) pay week.

My previous comments on the accuracy of data from such surveys (see Chapter 3) apply to this one as well, although the very immediate and non-sensitive nature of the questions being asked should provide information that is more reliable than the average. There were no independent means by which to confirm the information given, though casual observation of cases of tinned fish and large bags of rice being carried by people in all parts of the valley confirmed their popularity. No information was collected on the amount of each food type consumed—the survey asked only whether or not the respondent had eaten various types of food in the previous 24 hours. Ultimately, this must limit the conclusions which can be drawn from the data, but the survey still provides a useful indication of consumption patterns across certain groups.

During the first week of fieldwork at Porgera we encountered community concern within the relocation areas over the pressure on gardening land. This concern was acknowledged as genuine by PJV Community Affairs staff, and the impact of future dumping in the Anjolek was seen as worsening this problem. As a result, the second week of fieldwork was directed towards a study of the availability and suitability of gardening land within the SML. Kulapi and Apalaka were the two areas investigated in detail. Twenty-two households in Apalaka and 18 in Kulapi were surveyed as to the extent of their garden holdings. The households chosen were simply those whose heads happened to be around on the three days we visited each settlement. The investigations involved interviewing the head of household as to the make-up of the household, the numbers of its pigs, access to land in other parts of the valley, and the number of gardens held, and then visiting the gardens with the interviewee. Wherever possible, all the gardens belonging to these households were visited, though some respondents did not want to visit their more distant gardens. At each garden we visited, the size, shape and intensity of cultivation were measured. Air photo analysis was used to compare the extent of gardens in 1971 (for Apalaka) and 1986 with the situation in December 1991, and contour maps provided a means of assessing the average slope angle for the various gardening areas.

The subsistence sector in the economy

The subsistence sector at Porgera has been described in a number of studies. However, these papers and reports all pre-date the mine, and no available information documents the changes in the subsistence system since the start of mine construction in 1989. From the earliest European contact, Porgera's subsistence agriculture has been viewed as less productive than that practised in other parts of the highlands. The early patrols from Wabag to Porgera in the late 1940s described the gardens of Tipinini and Porgera as being poor compared to the rest of Enga. Patrol reports noted the 'blue shale' rocks from which the 'poor' soils derive, and also the lack of surplus food available for exchange with the patrols. In the first ethnographic study of the Ipili, Meggitt (1957) also noted the blue shale soils of the Upper Porgera, with better, blacker soils downstream—though neither type was regarded as particularly fertile.

In spite of its low productivity, subsistence agriculture was still the most important element in the Porgeran economy prior to the start of the mine, its output being valued at an estimated K3 million in 1987 (Pacific Agribusiness 1987[1]:41, 45). In 1993, it remained a key element of the economy, even in those communities most affected by the mine and the consequent influx of cash.

The physical environment

The physical environment exercises a basic constraint on Porgeran agriculture. Soil fertility, slope angles, altitude and climate all act to inhibit the productivity of the gardening system. Recent changes, such as the massive in-migration and the loss of gardening land to the mine operation, have exaggerated the effect of these environmental factors.

Generally speaking, soil fertility is lower at Porgera than in valleys to the east, although soils exhibit extreme variability in fertility within small areas. The greatest fertility occurs on the flatter ridges and in pockets on steeper slopes (Pacific Agribusiness 1987[1]:29). Soils in the area are derived from sedimentary and colluvial material, and lack the depths of volcanic ash which appear in profiles to the east. Goldsmith and Mules (1990), in their geomorphic mapping of the Porgera area, distinguished between the colluvial bench land terrain (derived from the steep limestone terrain behind), which covers much of the lower portions of the valley, and the mudstone ridge and V-valley terrain of the Kaiya River area. These differences are significant for the Apalaka and Kulapi examples discussed below. For the moment though, this distinction highlights general variations in soil types, with the colluvial material tending to have relatively deep, peaty/clayey soils, and poor drainage. This compares with the generally shallower, better-drained soils which developed from the mudstone shales (Mules 1993).

The Porgeran climate is characterised as lower montane perhumid (McAlpine and Keig 1983, cited in NSR 1988). The meteorological data recorded at the Alipis mine site since 1974 shows average annual rainfall to be 3,678 mm per year. Data for 1991, from three other stations within a 10 km radius, reveal the marked influence of local topography and orographic effects on rainfall magnitude and intensity (PJV 1993:6). Although there is little seasonality in rainfall, the monthly totals can vary significantly, with the highest and lowest monthly totals recorded being 909 mm and 84 mm respectively. There are relatively few rainless periods of more than four days and droughts are rare. The absence of a distinctive drier season limits the occurrence of frosts relative to other parts of the highlands.[2] Linked to the high rainfall is regular extensive cloud cover, particularly in the higher altitudes. The mean daily temperature range for the Alipis mine site is 11–22° celsius, with little variation through the year. There is an average of 3.9 hours of sunshine per day, also with little annual variation. Wind speeds in the Porgera Valley are generally low.

The Porgera Valley has an altitudinal range from around 1,800 m (at the Kaiya River) to 3,500 m. According to Hughes and Sullivan (1988:5) the lower temperatures at higher altitudes limit the number of food crops that can be grown, as well as their yields. They compared the altitudinal limits of sweet potato gardens elsewhere in the highlands (productive to 2,700 m, with an absolute limit of 2850 m) with their observation that the upper limit of gardening averaged 2,400 m at Porgera. On this basis, they proposed that there was

> ...a strip of forested land about 60 km² in area and up to 3 km wide around the rim of the valley which may be capable of being cultivated, depending on factors such as soil fertility, but which is at present not utilised for that purpose. This area represents about 25 per cent of the potentially cultivable land in the valley.

This observation was used as the basis for statements in the Porgera Environmental Plan (NSR 1988) to the effect that expansion of agriculture above the existing altitudinal limits up to 2,700 m was one way to ease the increasing stress that would be placed on the agricultural system.

While the altitude/temperature relationship generally holds true, the relationship in any given location is also significantly affected by factors such as topography, aspect, rainfall and cloudiness. More specifically, at Porgera it is likely that the greater cloudiness and rainfall, compared to most other parts of the highlands, will significantly reduce the altitudinal limits of crops (and their yields) below the maximum levels recorded elsewhere. Significant expansions of productive gardens above 2,400 m may well not be feasible. During fieldwork in November 1992, it was noted that the highest house and garden on the Waile Creek road was at 2,650 m. However, this is not conclusive evidence that widespread expansion of gardens to this altitude is generally possible, since the garden there was very recent, and it is not clear how productive such gardens are in the Porgeran context.

The topography of the upper Porgera area necessitates that gardens are often constructed on slopes that would be considered steep elsewhere in the highlands. Allen (1982:98) and Scott and Pain (1982:137) both report findings from elsewhere in Enga where slopes over 35° are considered unsuitable for cultivation and are only used for hunting and pig foraging. The average slope of the gardens measured at Apalaka was 27°, and a quarter were 35° or over. Meggitt (1957:36) described Porgeran gardens as being on steep slopes, although his observation that 'few gardens are less than 40° to 50° from the horizontal, most are 50° to 60°, and a few are from 70° to 75°' is clearly an exaggeration. According to Bourke and Lea (1982:82), all the evidence shows that yields are greatest on slopes of 10° or less.

Slope angle acts as a constraint on the productivity of an agricultural system in several ways. Most obviously, the long-term productivity of the garden is reduced through the increased soil erosion which is likely to occur on slopes over 15° (Allen 1982:103–4). Gardening on steep slopes also probably requires greater energy inputs from gardeners than the equivalent garden on the flat.

The gardening system

As with the rest of Enga, the Porgeran subsistence agricultural system (as it existed before the development of the mine) is based on the sweet potato, which is universally grown in mounded gardens. A range of other crops—primarily pitpit, sugarcane, 'true' (indigenous) taro, corn, beans, cabbage, several species of greens and potatoes—are generally planted between, or on the periphery of, these sweet potato mounds.

Three main types of garden are generally distinguished (Pacific Agribusiness 1987[1]:26–7).

- First, there are the initial mixed gardens which are established after clearing of primary forest or secondary growth. A wide range of food and fibre plants are grown, though few if any sweet potato mounds are present.
- Mounded sweet potato gardens are generally established during the second cultivation of a mixed garden. The range of secondary crops is reduced as the area given over to sweet potato mounds increases (Pacific Agribusiness 1987[1]:28).
- The final type of garden is a house (or kitchen) garden surrounding the house, usually planted with vegetables (beans and cabbages are common) and sugarcane.

As in the rest of Enga (see Waddell 1972:42–49), two main types of sweet potato mounds are found at Porgera—composted (*mondo*) and uncomposted (*yukusi*). Composted mounds are formed by placing compost between existing mounds, allowing it to decompose, and then covering it with soil (Bourke and Lea 1982:80–1). Composted mounds at Porgera are up to 2 m in diameter and one metre high. Uncomposted mounds are found on steeper slopes, and are generally thought to be either an initial stage prior to the establishment of a *mondo* garden, or a simple rotational fallow with one or two successive plantings followed by lengthy fallows (Bourke and Lea 1982:81). These uncomposted mounds are smaller, often little more than 75 cm in diameter and

20 cm in height, and are 'usually associated with soils deriving from sedimentary bedrock' (Wohlt 1986:8).

Data collected by Wohlt (1986) showed the average Porgeran composted mound to be 1.46 m in diameter, significantly less than the average for Enga of 2.7 m, resulting in a smaller area per mound (1.7 m^2 compared to 5.7 m^2). Mounds were also lower in height in Porgera (61 cm compared to 75 cm), were more tightly grouped (2.29 m average spacing between mounds compared to 3.39 m for Enga), resulting in a higher mound density per hectare (1,901 compared to 866). They tended to have fewer vines planted per mound (28.1 compared to 48.7), but had higher planting densities per square metre of mound (16.8 compared to 8.5), and consequently a higher planting density of vines per hectare (53,443 compared to 42,291). Wohlt comments that

> [t]he Porgera figures make sense if the low proportion of garden in mounds implies poor soils or thin topsoils…and the high numbers of vines per square metre on the mound is an attempt to maximise the use of the soil thus concentrated.

Pandanus (*Pandanus jiulianetti*), the nuts of which are highly prized as food, are common within these sweet potato gardens, and are managed by a form of silviculture (Pacific Agribusiness 1987[1]:26). Plantings of *yar* trees (*Casuarina oligodon*) for timber generally occur within or on the fringe of the gardens, and these trees also have nitrogen fixing properties (Bourke and Lea 1982:80).

After three or four years with composted sweet potato mounds, the land is left to fallow.[3] Tall sword grass (*Miscanthus floriudus*), shrubs and trees dominate the fallow regrowth (Hughes and Sullivan 1988:9). The length of fallow is dependent on soil fertility and population pressure. Historically, Meggitt (1957) described the fallows as 'inter-generational', while the Social and Economic Impact Study (SEIS) describes fallows as being 'generally within the five to ten year range' at Porgera (Pacific Agribusiness 1987:29). A systematic survey of PNG agricultural systems has recently estimated the Porgera fallows to last longer than 15 years (Allen *et al.* 1995).

As in other parts of Enga, pigs are an integral part of the agricultural system (Bourke and Lea 1982:85). Wohlt (1986) shows that Porgera had the lowest ratio of pigs per person (0.61:1) in Enga Province. The gardens in use in 1993 were fenced to exclude pigs, but it is likely that pigs till and manure old gardens, as they do in the rest of Enga. They generally forage in forests and around houses during the day and are fed on inferior garden produce.

The garden surveys carried out by Jackson (1987) covered 43 households in the Porgera area and provided detailed information on the gardening system. Table 5.1 shows the approximate crop intensities which Jackson derived from the survey. He noted that the figures are inclusive, in the sense that all the crops were found together. Various other minor crops were also found, including pitpit, corn, pumpkin, greens and some crops, such as 'grass skirt' and 'rope' plants, which are normally 'bush' plants but are occasionally cultivated. There were variations in the figures for different communities—Suyan, for example, was found to have 60 per cent more crops per cultivated hectare than the average, compensating perhaps for that community's lower garden area per household. The ratio between sweet potato and taro also varied considerably, from 9:1 and 8:1 for Anawe and Alipis respectively down to 2:1 for Mungalep, and Jackson thought that there might be a link between recent in-migration and the predominance of sweet potato.

Various estimates have been made of the amount of gardening land available per household. The Porgeran agricultural system has generally been described as a low intensity system prior to the development of the mine, with a refined population density[4] of about 22 persons per square kilometre (Lea and Gray 1984, cited in Hughes and Sullivan 1988:4). This indicates that population pressure on land was low, and the agricultural system was sustainable. Meggitt (1957) noted that Porgeran gardens were larger than those in other parts of Enga, averaging between 0.3 and 0.4 hectares in area. Bourke and Lea (1982) report per capita (rather than per household) garden areas for Enga as a whole ranging from 0.05 hectares in the Upper Lai Valley up to 0.17 hectares in the Wapenamanda area. Allen (1982) found that three communities in Enga had between 0.24 and 0.31 hectares of cultivated land per person, while a generally accepted average for the highlands is 0.1 hectares of garden per person (Robin Hide, pers. comm.).

Jackson's (1987) survey found significant variations in garden area per household within the Porgera Valley (see Table 5.2). Jackson hypothesised that variations in household size (for which he had no data) may have been significant in explaining the variations in the garden area per household, or alternatively

the Alipis residents may have been using far more land than is normal in the Porgera valley—since this is not for cash crops, other reasons, including anticipated compensation, would need to be looked into.

Table 5.1   Crop and tree densities in the Porgera area, 1987

Crop	Unit	No. per hectare	No. per garden
Sweet potato	Mounds	2,100	1,150
Taro	Plants	350	190
Sugarcane	Clumps	140	75
Banana	Clumps	30	16
Pandanus	Plants	125	65
Tanget	Plants	350	190
Yar (Casuarina)	Plants	110	60

Source: Jackson, R.T., 1987. *Social Survey: Porgera*, Department of Geography, James Cook University for Placer Pacific Pty Ltd, Townsville: Table G-2.

Table 5.2   Porgera garden survey data, 1987

Community	Households surveyed	Mean gardens per household (metres)	Mean distance from household (hectares)	Mean size of garden	Garden area per household (mean) (range)
Mungalep	10	4.8	575	0.29	1.39 0.63–3.34
Anawe	10	3.8	613	0.64	2.43 0.45–5.31
Alipis	10	5.2	2,342	0.64	3.33 1.17–6.14
Suyan	10	2.8	244	0.19	0.53 0.29–1.18
Paiam	3	4.3	n.a.	0.14	0.60 0.30–0.86

Source: Jackson, R.T., 1987. *Social Survey: Porgera*, Department of Geography, James Cook University for Placer Pacific Pty Ltd, Townsville: Table G-.

The SEIS included surveys of 11 gardens amongst SML landowning clans. The average total area of an average of four gardens per household (with an average of six members) was 0.86 hectares, lower than the averages found by Jackson. It was estimated that a five-year fallow period would mean that each household required 4.86 hectares of garden land, while a ten-year fallow required 8.86 hectares per household.

Food shortages have occurred in the past at Porgera. The valley was visited in 1981 as part of an investigation into widespread food shortages in Papua New Guinea, carried out for the Director of National Emergency Services and Civil Defence (Wohlt *et al.* 1981). The study team noted that short-term (two to three month) food shortages were relatively common in Porgera, but longer-term shortages, when many Porgerans would have moved to stay with kin in the Wage Valley or the Tari area, were rare. The best explanation the team could find for this particular shortage was excessive rain in previous months, which gave rise to vigorous sweet potato vine growth but poor tuber development. The upper Porgera area was less affected than Kairik and Tipinini in 1981, partly as a result of cash income from alluvial mining being used to supplement garden foods. Yields from gardens being harvested were substantially down on the norm, and tubers were generally less than half the normal weight of 500 grams.

The impact of the mine

The SEIS noted that the Porgeran subsistence system is adaptable and dynamic (Pacific Agribusiness 1987). This is reflected in the way in which the system has adapted to the massive social, environmental and economic changes which have occurred since the start of mine production. The most significant changes which have impacted on the gardening system are the loss of land for the mining operation, the large influx of non-Porgerans, and the substantial amounts of cash which have been paid out by the PJV.

It was recognised, in studies conducted before the development of the mine, that the loss of gardening land within and around the SML could create major problems for some people (see Jackson 1987; Pacific Agribusiness 1987; Hughes and Sullivan 1988; NSR 1988:57). This was expected to be countered by the increasing cash-earning opportunities that would be available to the groups most affected. The Environmental Plan (NSR 1988) contended that the three most affected clans (presumably Tieni, Pulumaini and Angalaini) had

> ...already changed their economic base from pure subsistence to cash. The effects have been relative material wealth, modern leisure activities, a diet dominated by trade store foods and a relatively higher nutritional status, compared to outlying villages in Porgera and elsewhere in Enga. These economic trends have reduced reliance on subsistence agricultural resources.

At the wider valley scale, the impact of the project on gardening land was expected to be minor, as the mine would need only 2 per cent of the 230 km² of potentially cultivable land in the Porgera Valley. A number of 'safeguards' were expected to combine to ameliorate any adverse effects on gardening land over the life of the mine. These included the extension of land under cultivation to currently unused areas up to 2,700 m; reduction of fallows at lower elevations; introduction of new cultivars, composting systems and crops; and monetary compensation for gardens lost. Increased cash incomes associated with the mine were seen as reducing the dependence on gardens for food. In the longer term, with the closure of the mine, it was acknowledged that there might be a 'subsistence resource crisis', as employment and other sources of funds were lost.

Three more recent surveys have, as part of wider aims, assessed changes in the number of food gardens used by households in various parts of Porgera. The household survey carried out at the end of 1992 (see Chapter 3) asked respondents about the number (but not the area) of food gardens they had under cultivation. Bonnell carried out a similar exercise in a survey of 96 of the relocation homes (see Chapter 4). The diet survey carried out as part of the present study again asked a similar question. The results of these surveys are shown in Table 5.3, with the emphasis on the communities within the SML and at Tipinini, the area least affected by the mine development. This table shows averages for the entire valley of 3.1, 2.1 and 2.3 gardens per household respectively for the three surveys. The differences can be explained partly by the geographic spread of each of the surveys, and partly by the target group (relocation households versus more general groups). Several trends are evident in the data—Apalaka and Yarik appear to have more gardens than most other parts of the valley, while Kulapi has significantly fewer. These communities will be discussed in more detail below.

One very significant trend is the number of households in Porgera without gardens. This came out particularly in Bonnell's study of the relocated households, with 15 per cent of households having no food gardens. The diet survey figures showed that, among the SML communities, Kulapi had the most serious problem, with 26 per cent of households reporting no gardens, while Apalaka and Yarik had figures of 0 and 9 per cent respectively. Other parts of the valley, particularly those which had recently experienced large increases in the number of non-Porgerans living in the community, had significantly higher proportions of garden-less households. Of those interviewed at Porgera Station, for example, 53 per cent had no gardens in the valley, though it needs to be pointed out that most of those interviewed there were not Porgerans.

Table 5.4, based on occupation fees paid during 1993, shows the extent of the impact of mine development on the availability of gardening land by subclan group within the SML. The figures showing the proportion of the clan land untouched by the mining operation are the inverse of the proportion which had been cleared, damaged or lost to mine development. The Table shows that certain subclan groups (particularly the Tieni Waingolo, Yangua and Uape, the Pulumaini Ambo, the Angalaini Mapindaka, and the Tuanda Yapala) had lost large amounts of land in absolute as well as percentage terms. The Pulumaini losses may have been relatively greater, since these involved their lower-altitude gardening lands, and the result was that they had been forced to move into areas of primary forest, above the altitudinal limits of their previous gardens.

Access to land at Porgera for an individual is derived from cognatic kinship links—that is, through rights to land acquired from either parent. The implication of this is that individuals who lost land within the SML may well have had rights to land elsewhere—either in Porgera or further afield. Table 5.4 does not show the extent of subclan landholdings, or access to land, outside the SML boundary. On the

Table 5.3   Household size and garden numbers in recent surveys

Survey and community	Sample size	Mean household size	Gardens per household
1. Household survey 1992			
Apalaka/Yarik	32	7.1	3.8
Tipinini	35	5.7	2.7
Rest of Porgera	55	7.3	3.2
Total	**122**	**6.8**	**3.1**
2. Relocation survey 1993			
Apalaka	15	8.0	2.3
Yarik	21	7.0	4.0
Kulapi	24	8.5	1.2
Rest of Porgera	36	8.5	1.7
Total	**96**	**8.1**	**2.1**
3. Diet survey 1993			
Apalaka	12	10.8	4.3
Yarik	55	8.7	3.2
Kulapi	19	9.0	1.2
Tipinini	49	7.6	1.8
Rest of Porgera	243	7.7	2.1
Total	**378**	**8.0**	**2.3**

Sources: Banks, G., 1993. *Porgera Social Monitoring Programme: economic modelling project—First Report*, Unisearch PNG Pty Ltd for Porgera Joint Venture, Port Moresby; Banks, G., 1994a. *Porgera Economic Modelling Project—Second Report: gardens and wantoks*, Porgera Social Monitoring Programme Report 3, Unisearch PNG Pty Ltd for Porgera Joint Venture Port Moresby;. Bonnell, S., 1994. *Dilemmas of Development: social change in Porgera, 1989–1993*, Porgera Social Monitoring Programme Report 2, Subada Consulting Pty Ltd for Porgera Joint Venture, Thornlands (Qld).

other hand, there is no guarantee that individuals who had lost land were automatically able to exercise rights to other pieces of their subclan's land outside this boundary. Three questions which thus arise in the context of loss of garden land are

- the extent of subclan land ownership outside the SML boundary for those subclans listed in Table 5.4
- the extent to which individuals had retained and maintained rights to other land outside the SML; and
- the nature of the current mechanisms and authorities for handling disputes over land, in a context where land was being lost to the mine and the population was increasing.

The continuing economic significance of the subsistence sector, in spite of the large amounts of compensation which had been paid out

Table 5.4   Effect of mine development on land by subclan within the SML, 1993

Clan/subclan	Area owned in SML (hectares)	Area untouched by mining operation	
		(hectares)	(per cent)
Tiene/Waingolo	299.0	61.9	20.7
Tiene/Yangua	186.0	37.0	19.9
Tiene/Uape	269.0	145.5	54.1
Tiene/Lagima	89.0	78.4	88.1
Tiene/Kaimalo	32.0	11.0	34.4
Tiene/Akira	21.0	21.0	100.0
Pulumaini/Paramba	56.0	38.0	67.9
Pulumaini/Ambo	257.0	157.3	61.2
Pulumaini/Epeyea	21.0	-	-
Pulumaini/Yunga	22.0	22.0	100.0
Anga	2.0	2.0	100.0
Mamai/Andapo	9.0	9.0	100.0
Mamai/Kenja	54.0	28.0	51.9
Waiwa	54.0	32.9	60.9
Angalaini/Piko	40.0	35.1	87.8
Angalaini/Mapindaka (Yunguna)	103.0	60.3	58.5
Angalaini/Woyopen (Taunga)	67.0	67.0	100.0
Tuanda/Yapala	332.0	223.1	67.2
Tuanda/Ulupa	309.0	289.9	93.8
Pakean/Ringime	6.0	6.0	100.0
Total	2,228.0	1,319.0	59.2

Source: PJV records.

by PJV, emerged as a significant finding of the first phase of my study (see Chapter 3). The income and expenditure survey carried out in 1992 highlighted the inequalities in cash income in Porgera, with the top 10 per cent of the sample earning 54.8 per cent of the income, and the bottom 50 per cent earning just 2.6 per cent of the income. Of the sample of 220 interviewed, 40 individuals (18 per cent) reported no monetary income in the previous fortnight, and a further 25 (11 per cent) reported less than K10. When asked how they survived, those with little or no income were evenly split between those who relied on *wantoks*, and those who lived off food from their own gardens.

The 1993 diet survey revealed some significant patterns in the consumption of different food types, particularly the difference between subsistence garden food and store-bought food. Table 5.5 shows the proportion of respondents in different parts of the valley who had eaten tinned fish, rice, sweet potato (from their own garden), and greens (from their own garden). A probable interpretation of this data is as follows: people within the SML were eating relatively high proportions of store-bought food, but a significant proportion were also still consuming food from their own gardens. People living in communities outside the SML which had experienced large inflows of *wantoks* and others (that is Anawe/Paiam and Porgera Station) had a higher proportion of store-bought food and, for Porgera Station at least, lower levels of food grown in their own gardens. The communities outside the SML which had been less impacted by immigration (Mungalep and Tipinini) showed very low proportions of store-bought food, and high levels of food from their own gardens—everyone in Tipinini, for example, had eaten sweet potato (*kaukau*) in the previous 24 hours, and only two (out of 49) had eaten tinned fish.

Of the 380 people in the total sample, 329 people (87 per cent) had eaten *kaukau* in the previous 24 hours, and 226 (70 per cent) had obtained it from their own gardens; 193 (51 per cent) had eaten no store-bought food, and 57 (15 per cent) of them had eaten only *kaukau*. Only 28 people (7 per cent) had eaten solely store-bought food. These figures underline the fact that the bulk of the population in Porgera were still dependent on the subsistence sector for meeting at least part of their basic food requirements.

There is some evidence to support the assumption made in most of the studies done prior to mine development, that the loss of gardening land would be balanced by more cash and a shift to store-bought goods. If Tipinini is taken as a 'control', then it is clear that there was a

Table 5.5   Percentage of community members consuming food types in the previous 24 hours

Community	Sample (N)	Tinned fish (%)	Rice (%)	Sweet potato (%)	Greens (%)
Apalaka/Yarik	67	43	48	78	42
Kulapi	19	68	74	21	42
Mungalep	53	13	17	89	70
Anawe/Paiam	84	44	51	75	50
Porgera Station	96	56	59	47	33
Tipinini	49	4	2	100	69
Other	12	33	58	50	33
Total	380	38	43	70	49

Source: Porgera diet survey, 1993.

greater amount of store-bought food being consumed in 1993. However, even in the relocation areas most directly affected by mine development, the bulk of the population had eaten food from their own gardens in the previous 24 hours. There is obviously no linear relationship between the amount of cash going into a community and the switch to store-bought food.

There were differences in the foods eaten by male and females. The sample was made up of 263 males and 117 females. Fewer women had eaten tinned fish (31 per cent) or rice (38 per cent) in the previous 24 hours than men (42 per cent and 45 per cent respectively). The foods eaten also varied by the age of the respondents, with the proportion of people reporting *kaukau* from their own garden rising from 57 per cent for the 16–19 age group, to 82 per cent for the 40–49 age group, and 73 per cent for those 50 years and over. Taro consumption was even more influenced by age—from less than 10 per cent of those aged under 30 years, to 36 per cent of those aged 50 years and over.

It is also reasonable to expect to find variations in food consumption through the fortnightly pay period. As noted earlier, the survey was carried out during a government pay week—between a week and ten days after the more significant PJV pay Wednesday. One would have expected higher proportions of tinned fish, rice and other store-bought food to be eaten just after PJV pay days. In SML areas, regular payments such as royalties and occupation fees may well have influenced food consumption for short periods in the same way. Temporal patterns of trade store sales (see Chapter 3) certainly reflected recent PJV-related inputs, and these patterns of expenditure were probably closely related to food consumption patterns.[5]

In the SEIS, it was estimated that subsistence agriculture was worth K1 per person per day, or a total of K3 million per year in the Porgera Valley as a whole. The 1993 diet survey showed that this figure had probably increased in absolute terms. While there was now greater consumption of trade store-sourced foods, there was also a significant increase in the size of the population being fed, and most people were still reliant on the subsistence sector for many of their food requirements. If we assume that, for the valley as a whole, dependence on garden foods had dropped by 25 per cent, and prices for store-bought food had doubled over the intervening period, it is likely that the average figure per person per day for the value of subsistence food production (or the cost of replacing it with purchased food) was now approximately K1.50. With a population of 12,000 in the valley, this amounted to K6.57 million per annum—slightly less than the K7.3 million of direct PJV cash payments to Porgerans in 1993 (see Chapter 3).

From the data already presented, it is clear that the subsistence sector remained very important to the bulk of the population in Porgera. At the same time, the loss of land, the greater amounts of cash in circulation, and the influx of outsiders had affected the agricultural system in different ways in different parts of the valley. Two of the areas which appeared to be under the greatest stress were Kulapi and Apalaka, and these were chosen for more detailed investigation because they were the areas where most concern was expressed by residents and PJV staff. The aim of this exercise was to establish, in a preliminary way, the extent to which the subsistence gardening sector was under pressure in these two areas.

Apalaka case study

Apalaka is a relocation housing area situated at the end of the road which services the three relocation areas on the southern bank of the Kaiya Valley (see Map 1.1). The Apalaka relocation area was established in 1989, and there were 62 relocation houses in the area in 1993 (with an average of eight persons in each house), as well as a considerable number of bush material homes. Part of the relocation package included K1,400 to assist with the preparation of new food gardens for each household.

The Apalaka area comprises moderate to steep mudstone ridges and slopes, which are generally stable and well-drained. There are small areas of boulder clay colluviums, and local relief can be very steep. Soils are generally thin and largely residual, derived from the mudstone. Small areas have a greater depth of residual soils or a veneer of colluvium (Mules 1993). From my own brief observations in the field and from anecdotal evidence, it would seem that rainfall is lower at Apalaka than at Alipis. Apalaka, being slightly lower than Alipis and situated on a north-facing slope, should also have slightly warmer temperatures. Contour maps of the Apalaka area indicate that slopes average around 16.5°, though there is great variability, and the houses tend to be grouped on the flattest land, leaving the steeper slopes for gardens. The gardening areas range in altitude from 2,000 m on the banks of the Kaiya River to around 2,450 m on the slopes of Waruwari ridge, but most of the gardens are in the range between 2,100 m and 2,200 m. Air photographs show that the area around Apalaka has been used for gardening for many years. A set taken in 1971 shows that around 60 per cent of the area which was under cultivation in 1993 had already been cleared of primary forest for more than twenty years.

The Tuanda clan has primary rights to the land around Apalaka, including most of the land to the west of Yambu Creek, while the Waiwa clan owns the remaining 54 hectares immediately adjacent to the west bank of the creek. The Tuanda clan also has access to gardening land in the upper reaches of the Kaiya, although the boundaries of this access are not clear. Five out of 22 households interviewed for the garden survey said they had access to land in other areas—two in Laiagam, two at Alipis, and one at Yuyan. It is likely that some of the social changes brought about by the mine (permanent houses, fixed water supplies) had reduced the mobility of households within the SML, in the sense that people might no longer be prepared to walk considerable distances to gardens, and relocated landowners might be less likely to live in 'multilocal' households (see Burton 1991:10). These trends would have reduced the likelihood of these households maintaining gardens outside the SML.

Twenty-two households were covered by the garden survey in Apalaka, 13 of which were resident in relocation houses. A total of 31 gardens were surveyed in Apalaka, and these included the complete garden areas of 11 households (see Table 5.6). For these 11 households there was an average of 1.4 gardens per household, averaging 7,173m² in area, giving an average of just over 1 hectare of garden per household. Assuming a constant average garden size, and extrapolating to the gardens which were not surveyed, the average area per household for all 22 Apalaka households in the survey sample would be 2.1 hectares. With a total population of 183 in those households, this gives a mean garden area per person of 2,524 m²—higher than most of the comparable Engan figures discussed earlier. A total of 92 pigs were distributed between 19 of these households, giving an average of 4.84 per household, or a pig-to-person ratio of less than 0.5:1.

The average slope of the 29 gardens inspected in the Apalaka survey was 27°, with a range between 12° and 60°. A quarter of the sample gardens were on slopes of 35° or steeper. As previously mentioned, such slopes are generally regarded as having low productivity, high rates of topsoil depletion, and short effective lives. Fallow periods, to be effective, must be long. Residents were aware of this problem, and expressed concern at the frequent slips and slumps which occurred in the steeper gardens. The steep gardens were notable for their small uncomposted mounds (*yukusi*). Large composted mounds, up to 2 m in diameter and 1 m high, were predominant on the less steep slopes. We were told that, although most of the gardens had been cleared for many years, most had also been replanted after the relocation programme had been completed four years previously. The relatively few newly-planted gardens which we saw were being cut out of short scrub and sword-grass fallow. It seemed likely, in light of the SEIS findings, that the yields in the current gardens would fall rapidly in the next couple of years, particularly from the uncomposted mounds.

Table 5.6   Agricultural resources of Apalaka households, 1993

Variable	Total households in survey sample	Households with total garden area surveyed
Households	22	11
Mean size per garden	8,061 m²	7,173 m²
Mean gardens per household	2.63	1.4
Mean household garden area	20,959 m²	10,043 m²
Household garden area range	720–75,000 m²	720–32,250 m²
Mean household size	8.32	7.9
Mean pigs per household	4.84	2.8
Mean slope angle	27° (29 slopes)	30° (14 slopes)

Source: Porgera garden survey.

Nearly all of the moderate slopes in Apalaka territory were currently covered by gardens (see Map 5.1). A series of air photographs of this area (1971, 1986, 1991) were examined to assess the extent of change over the last 20 years.

- The area between Yambu Creek, the Kaiya River and Anjolek Creek had been under cultivation for many years. Even in 1971, the forest had been cleared to around 2350 m in places.
- Between 1971 and 1986, some areas had changed from gardens to regrowth, and some from regrowth to gardens, but it is not possible to say whether the extent or intensity of cultivation in the area had increased or decreased.
- Finally, the area covered by gardens had increased from 1986 to 1991, and with one exception, these gardens were all within areas which had been cultivated at some time in the past. The exception was that new gardens were being created from primary forest at higher altitudes. There were only a few very small areas which appeared to have reverted from gardens to regrowth over this period. In total, it appeared that there were now more gardens than at any one time in the past.

From the 1991 series, it is possible to make an estimate of the area being cultivated in 1993, although there are major problems with such calculations in areas of steep terrain. Furthermore, it is virtually impossible to distinguish current gardens from gardens which had been abandoned for one to five years. As a result, the figures which follow probably have a large margin of error built into them. Given these limitations, the photographs indicate a total area of around 100 hectares of land available in the territory bounded by Yambu Creek, the Kaiya River, the Anjolek Creek, and the ridge crest which runs almost directly from east to west (Map 5.1). Over 25 per cent of this area was still forested, but much of this was on the walls of steep gullies unsuitable for gardening. Another 4 hectares was taken up by roads and houses, especially the main settlement of Apalaka. This left around 70 hectares in gardens and fallow regrowth. It appears from the photographs as if a greater proportion was now under garden rather than fallow, and despite the reservations noted above, my field observations tended to support this conclusion.

If we follow the SEIS in assuming a figure of 4.86 hectares of garden per household with a five-year fallow period (Pacific Agribusiness 1987), and ignore the greater average household size

Map 5.1   Apalaka garden area, 1993

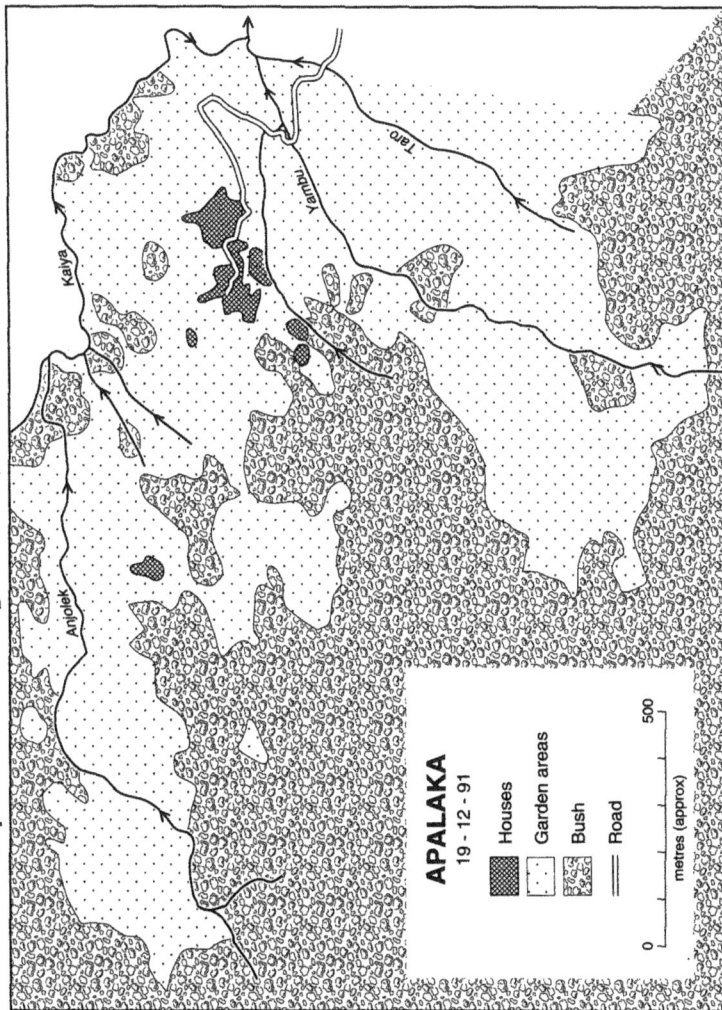

APALAKA
19 - 12 - 91

Houses
Garden areas
Bush
Road

0   500
metres (approx)

Banks, G., 1994a. *Porgera Social Monitoring Programme: economic modelling project—first report*, Unisearch PNG Pty Ltd for Porgera Joint Venture, Port Moresby.

found in the garden survey, the 62 relocation households at Apalaka would require 280 hectares of land to support the pre-mine agricultural system. Even allowing for a 25 per cent reduction in the dependence on gardens since 1987, the requirement would still be around 200 hectares, which implies that the Apalaka households must have had other gardens outside the immediate area defined from the air photographs. The implication of all of this is that the existing agricultural system at Apalaka would not be sustainable in the long term, even with greatly reduced fallow periods, if these people had no access to garden land elsewhere. Furthermore, there were numerous gardens and fallow areas (around 15 hectares in all) in the Kaiya 'compensation envelope' which were due to be affected by sediment from the dumping of mine waste in Anjolek Creek over the following 18 months (Parker 1992), and it was possible that additional areas of cultivable land would be lost, either by greater bed aggradation than anticipated, or by the triggering of new landslips or the reactivation of old landslips by the transport of sediment downstream. At the same time, access to Tuanda gardening areas to the west of the Anjolek would become more difficult, unless some positive steps were taken to maintain it.

Kulapi case study

The Kulapi relocation area is adjacent to, and south of, the Anawe plant site (Map 1.1). The gardens associated with the settlement range in altitude from 2,275 m to 2,500 m at the SML boundary, but most of the gardens are at an altitude of around 2,400 m. The gardening area comprises a mix of undulating mudstone ridges and moderate slopes on a boulder clay colluvium resulting from a partially stabilised landslide. Slopes are not as steep as those of Apalaka. The area is cut by three streams, and has several swampy parts. The soils are peaty/clayey, with gravel and large limestone and sandstone boulders, and drainage is generally very poor. Although Kulapi is close to the Alipis meteorological station, anecdotal evidence suggests that rainfall may be slightly higher, and the area is certainly in cloud more often than Alipis and Apalaka. Temperatures may be expected to be a degree or two cooler than Apalaka, given the higher altitude and fewer hours of sunshine. All these factors reduce the rates of growth of agricultural crops (see Chapter 4).

The present settlement of Kulapi dates from 1988, and was the first of the relocation areas to be established. As previously noted, the Pulumaini clan has lost large portions of its land to mine development, most notably the area which now comprises the Anawe plant site. The Pulumaini had few options for relocation, simply because the portion of their land which was not occupied by mine installations extends uphill from that site. Air photographs from 1986 show dense forest cover over most of the area which now contains Kulapi gardens. Three clearings of less than a hectare are shown on these photographs, the highest of which was at approximately 2,500 m. The upper limit of cultivation was around 2,350 m. As noted above, this is now the lower limit of the garden area. Most of the new gardens were cut from primary forest, and still contained large tree trunks in 1993.

In the Kulapi garden survey, 17 households were interviewed, and in 13 cases, visits were made to all of the household's food gardens. These 13 households had an average of 1.5 gardens each, with an average garden size of 2,890 m², giving a total area per household of roughly half a hectare (see Table 5.7). Extrapolating again to the gardens which we did not visit, we obtain a very similar figure for the average garden area of all 17 households in sample. Average household size in Kulapi was 11.3, which gives a mean garden area per person of just 470.5 m². Although the survey data indicate a much lower pig-person ratio than at Apalaka, this finding does not tally with our general observations in the Kulapi community, which appeared to have a larger pig population than any other Porgeran community we visited.

The average slope angle shown on contour maps of the Kulapi area is around 11°. For the 22 gardens inspected in the Kulapi survey, the

Table 5.7   Agricultural resources of Kulapi households, 1993

Variable	Total households in survey sample	Households with total garden area surveyed
Households	17	13
Mean size per garden	2,797 m²	2,890 m²
Mean gardens per household	1.88	1.54
Mean household garden area	5,314 m²	4,450.4 m²
Household garden area range	425–8,549 m²	425–23,608 m²
Mean household size	11.29	11.6
Mean pigs per household	2.7	2.4
Mean slope angle	17° (22 slopes)	16° (20 slopes)

Source: Porgera garden survey.

average slope was 17°, with a range between 0° and 35°. Mounds varied from quite large (1.5 m diameter) composted *mondo* down to small uncomposted *yukusi* on small areas of steep local relief. The gardens at Kulapi were markedly wetter than at Apalaka, with very poor drainage. Bonnell (Chapter 4) notes that, when they were first cleared, the soils had a high water table, and there was excessive leaf mould with a high nitrogen content. Agricultural experts who visited the area in early 1989 felt that time would cure the drainage and nitrogen problems, though improved agricultural practices would be the only remedy for the poor soil fertility. In fact, four years later, the drainage problems remained. The poor environment for agriculture at Kulapi is confirmed by the fact that relocation gardens took 15 months to start producing *kaukau*, compared to an average of nine months in other relocation areas. The diet survey highlights the gardening problems faced by the Kulapi people. They appear to have been far more dependent on store-bought food than the people at Apalaka and Yarik, and a much lower proportion reported eating *kaukau* from their own gardens in the previous 24 hours (see Table 5.5).

In absolute terms, there was still enough Pulumaini land for additional gardens at Kulapi, above the existing limits of cultivation. In practical terms, however, it was clear that the soils and climate severely restricted yields at the existing altitude, and further expansion up slope would not be desirable. Below the existing altitudinal limit of cultivation, there were only limited areas of forest and fallow remaining. From the 1991 air photographs, it appears that there are roughly 50 hectares of land below that limit, of which 5 hectares had been used for settlements and roads. Small blocks of forest made up another 5 hectares, largely unsuitable for cultivation. A large proportion of the remaining 40 hectares was currently under cultivation, with few areas of fallow (see Map 5.2). The long-term implications for the subsistence component of the economy at Kulapi were obvious and serious.

The role of the *epo atene* in the economy

The issue of 'outsiders'—the *epo atene* ('come stay') people—is interconnected with many of the other social and economic changes that have occurred at Porgera. 'Outsiders' place increasing stress on the subsistence sector, they are central to the redistribution of cash out of Porgera, and they are usually involved in social problems such as law and order (see Chapter 2). Burton (1991:4) comments that

Map 5.2   Kulapi garden areas, 1993

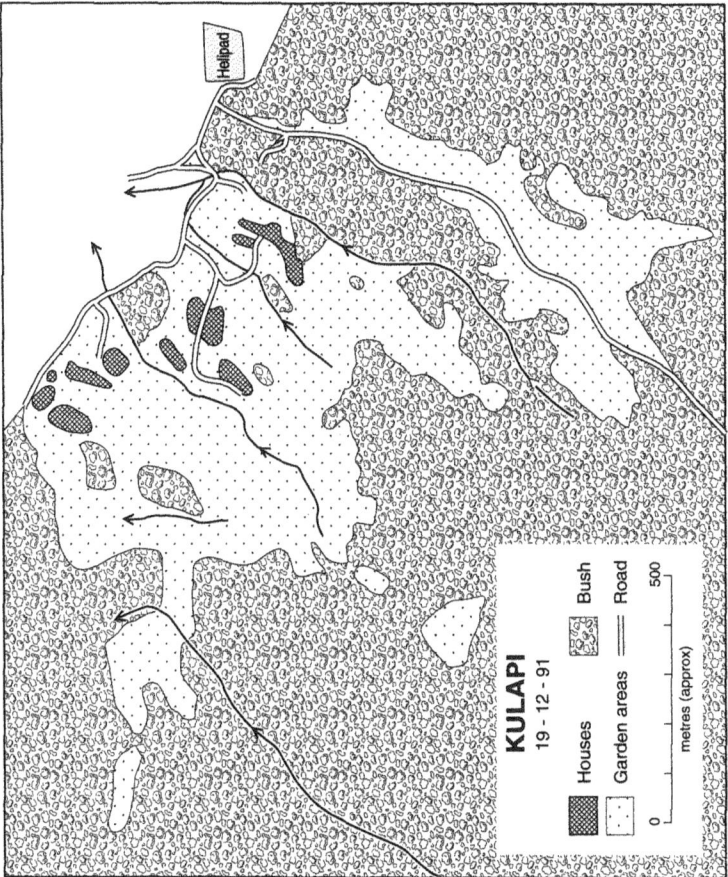

Banks, G., 1994a. *Porgera Social Monitoring Programme: economic modelling project—first report*, Unisearch PNG Pty Ltd for Porgera Joint Venture, Port Moresby.

more specifically from the company's point of view, the build up of *epo atene* (non-Porgeran) migrants around the mine area has been perceived as substantial and a threat to the harmony of company-landowner relations, and indeed to development generally.

The diet and income and expenditure surveys revealed some interesting facts about the role of the *epo atene* in the Porgeran economy. Three categories of people are discernible from the surveys—those born in Porgera ('Porgerans'), those born elsewhere but now living in Porgera ('*epo atene*'), and those born elsewhere who are just in Porgera for a short time, visiting relatives or selling goods at the market. These last I call the 'visitors'.[6]

In demographic terms, neither of the survey samples showed any clear distinction between the three groups, although there was a tendency for the Porgerans to be older than the *epo atene* or the visitors. Proportions of males and females varied slightly between each of the groups, but the greatest difference was between surveys, with the income and expenditure survey as a whole having 14 per cent females, and the full diet survey sample having 31 per cent females.

The most interesting result from the income and expenditure survey was the level of income received by each group in the previous two weeks (see Table 5.8). The *epo atene* had an income 50 per cent greater than that of the Porgerans, and they had notably higher earnings from PJV (K106 compared to K44 for Porgerans), while the visitors got more from wantoks (K22 compared to K13 for Porgerans and K10 for *epo atene*). The diet survey revealed slightly different patterns of activity, with more Porgerans in PJV employment, and fewer working for other employers or running their own business. Porgerans, not surprisingly, had more gardens, while visitors had very few, and the *epo atene* fell midway between the two. Significantly, only about 25 per cent of the *epo atene* had no gardens at Porgera.

The diet survey showed a clear division between the Porgerans, who ate the least store-bought food and the most *kaukau* and taro from their own gardens, and the visitors, for whom the proportions were reversed (see Table 5.9). These patterns presumably reflected the amount of garden land and the amount of cash to which each group had access, but they also point to significantly different economic situations and lifestyles for the Porgerans and non-Porgerans in the valley.

The diet survey provides an indication of the variable lengths of time for which the *epo atene* had been living in Porgera (see Figure

5.1).[7] Most of those who had been in Porgera for less than six months did not have their own home in Porgera, and were staying with *wantoks*, friends or others, and most of these people had come to Porgera to sell food or goods at the markets. The same survey data suggest that 34 per cent of the *epo atene* were from Mulitaka and Laiagam, 28 per cent from the Southern Highlands, and 33 per cent from other parts of Enga. Similar proportions were found among the visitors—20 per cent from Mulitaka and Laiagam, 40 per cent from Tari, and 33 per cent from other parts of Enga.

The non-Porgerans were distributed unevenly within the valley. While they accounted for 40 per cent of the total diet survey sample,[8] the proportions in each local community varied from just 4 per cent in Tipinini up to 71 per cent of those surveyed at Porgera Station (Table 5.10). Apalaka and Yarik both had low percentages, perhaps reflecting the successful identification of Porgerans (and exclusion of non-Porgerans) during the relocation programme. However, these sample data need to be treated with some caution, because a subsequent census of the Kulapi community found a total population of 730, of whom only 180 (or 25 per cent) were 'outsiders' (B. Robins, pers. comm.).

A comment by Robert Glasse, regarding Huli social structure and dynamics, would seem equally applicable to the situation at Porgera.

> Huli have a number of concepts of affiliation and corporate group structure which they use strategically when access to resources is in dispute. In my view these concepts cannot be meaningfully assembled into a seamless, consistent theoretical construct. Instead Huli employ the notions of attachment and detachment according to their individual assessment of self-interest at any given moment (1992:248–9).

The *epo atene* at Porgera are pursuing the same course. As long as they are able to take up residence in Porgera, in accordance with the related (though not identical) Engan, Porgeran, and Huli principles of group membership, and as long as Porgera is seen as an economically attractive venue, when compared to other parts of the highlands, then these people will continue to pursue the strategy of settling in Porgera.

As the mining company is well aware, the 'outsider' issue is complex and not amenable to a simple solution. Individual Porgerans must to a large degree accept responsibility for the influx of migrants within the valley. Not only have individuals allowed *epo atene* to reside in their areas, but many must have actively recruited people to the SML in the hope of gaining a greater compensation package (see

Table 5.8   Differences in economic status by residency type, 1993

	Porgerans	*Epo atene*	Visitors
Income and expenditure survey sample size	125	49	46
Mean fortnightly income (kina)	142.66	215.50	150.34
Diet survey sample size	224	116	30
Proportion with PJV employment (%)	13	7	-
Proportion with a business (%)	13	19	33
Average number of gardens	2.9	1.3	0.6

Source: Porgera survey data.

Table 5.9   Food eaten in the previous 24 hours by residency type, 1993 (per cent)

Food type	Porgerans	*Epo atene*	Visitors
Tinned fish	25	45	73
Rice	28	55	74
Kaukau (own garden)	83	63	35
Taro (own garden)	21	8	2

Source: Porgera diet survey.

Table 5.10   Percentage of non-Porgerans by community, 1993

Community	Non-Porgerans (%)
Anawe	65
Apalaka	17
Kulapi	68
Mungalep	15
Paiam	40
Porgera Station	71
Tipinini	4
Yarik	21
Mean	40

Source: Porgera diet survey.

Figure 5.1   Length of residence of non-Porgerans in Porgera, 1993
(n=140)

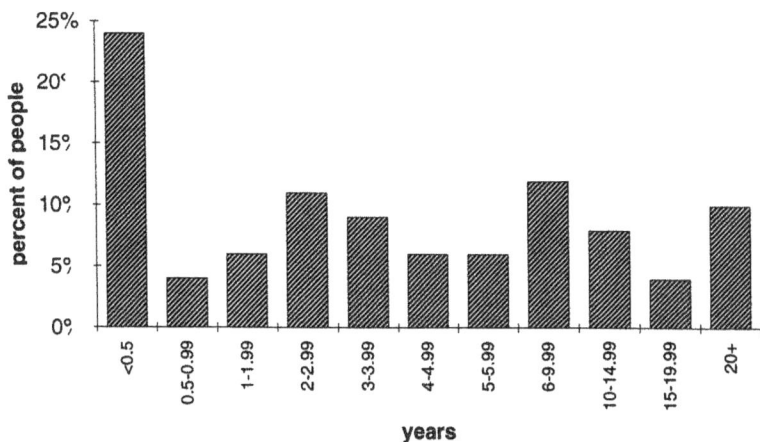

Source: Porgera diet survey

Burton 1991:40). A majority (three to one) of Porgerans, both inside and outside the SML, who commented on this issue, when we interviewed them at the end of 1992, expressed favourable opinions of their *epo atene*, who were seen to provide additional security to the households and communities with whom they resided. Porgerans were unwilling to use the law to overcome the lack of customary means for removal of unwanted kinsfolk, and their most common response to the question of why they could not get rid of the *epo atene* was one which cited the risk of security problems further down the Enga Highway.

Within the SML, the PJV had successfully worked with landowners to remove 'outsiders' from communities such as Kulapi. Outside the SML, there was no direct way that the company could do anything about the problem, though offers were made to provide landowners with advice on procedures for evicting unwanted *epo atene*. Company spending in other parts of Enga Province under the Tax Credit Scheme has partly been intended to reduce the motivation for people in these areas to leave home and travel to Porgera. However, until the level of government services and economic development in other parts of Enga and the Southern Highlands is improved, individuals will continue to see Porgera as the place for a new and better life, to which a cognatic descent system gives many of them access.

Conclusions

Porgera is an area where the physical environment has always limited the productivity of the subsistence agricultural system. In the past, this has been compensated for by the low population density, allowing a low intensity of use. Most of the studies carried out prior to mine development considered that these factors would mean a minimal impact of the mine on the agricultural system. The system could be intensified, and previously untouched areas, such as the zone between 2,400 m and 2,700 m, could be used to compensate for any loss of gardens associated with mine development. Greater amounts of cash were likely to bring a switch away from a dependence on garden foods to a diet based on store-bought foods. Severe problems were only thought likely to occur for small groups of people most affected by loss of land.

After three years of mine operation, several factors had combined to make some of these predictions obsolete. The massive in-migration of *epo atene* and other 'outsiders' had stressed the subsistence base of the Porgerans in areas within and around the SML. Greater use of higher altitude gardens (above 2,400 m) was limited by environmental constraints. Perhaps most significantly, the relatively inequitable distribution of compensation payments meant that the bulk of the population were still dependent on the subsistence sector for their basic food requirements. In absolute value, the contribution of the subsistence sector to the Porgeran economy had probably more than doubled between 1987 and 1993 as a result of local inflation and the greater population resident in the valley.

In the two areas studied in detail, Apalaka and Kulapi, the subsistence system appeared to be under increasing stress. At Apalaka, there was very little room for expansion of the area under cultivation, and additional pressure was about to be placed on the existing gardening land by the loss of up to 15 hectares associated with the failing waste dump in the Anjolek. The Pulumaini people at Kulapi faced a somewhat different problem, in that they were being compelled to construct gardens at high altitudes on poor soils, and the subsequent low yields were forcing them to depend on tradestore goods to a greater extent than other communities in the SML. Based on the evidence it does not seem reasonable to expect cultivation in Kulapi to extend up to 2,700 m, Although the cultivation zone had extended up to 2,700 m in some other parts of the valley (outside the SML), the poor soils and drainage, and the low sunshine hours, seem to have made this impracticable at Kulapi.

Notes

1   This survey was undertaken by Ben Imbun and five students from the University of Papua New Guinea.
2   Porgera escaped the effects of frosts which hit other parts of the highlands in 1981 (Wohlt *et al.* 1981).
3   Meggitt (1957) had previously described the system as reverting to fallow after the second crop.
4   Population per square kilometre of potentially useful land (i.e. land below 2800 m which is not too steep or too swampy to be gardened).
5   Compensation payments, one particular aspect of the cash economy, had another impact on the gardening system at Porgera. It was not uncommon practice for gardens to be planted, and houses built, by people in anticipation of compensation payments being made by the company when the area was needed for mine development. This was documented by Pacific Agribusiness (1987) and Jackson (1991), and was still occurring in 1993. However, such incidents did not represent the real role of gardens for the bulk of the Porgeran population, as reflected in the results of the diet survey.
6   The definitions in the two surveys varied. In the income and expenditure survey, respondents were asked whether they were born in Porgera, and whether they usually lived in Porgera. I defined the *epo atene* as those not born in Porgera, but now living there, and 'visitors' were those born outside Porgera who did not usually live there. The diet survey again asked if the respondent was born in Porgera, but also asked how long the respondent had been in Porgera, and whose house the respondent stayed in last night, rather than whether the respondent usually lived in Porgera. In this case, I defined the *epo atene* as those not born in Porgera, who had been at Porgera for over six months, or had stayed the night before in their own house, or in the house of a parent or husband.
7   It is worth noting that responses to this question could have been affected by people wanting to assert their perceived right to be in

Porgera by overstating their period of residence, or by older people, in particular, citing the first time they had visited Porgera, rather than the time when they had taken up residence.

8   Previous surveys found between 17 per cent (household survey, November 1992) and 43 per cent non-Porgerans (income and expenditure survey, December 1992). The variations probably reflect the difference between the targeted populations (see Chapter 3). A figure of around 40 per cent non-Porgeran residents in the valley is probably realistic, if somewhat conservative.

6

The next round of relocation

Glenn Banks

This chapter differs from the previous ones in that it is focused on a particular area, rather than an issue such as economic change. It establishes a social and economic baseline for the Kewai people on the north bank of the Kaiya River (see Map 1.1) within a Lease for Mining Purposes (LMP) which the Porgera Joint Venture (PJV) was seeking to acquire in 1993. These people were due to be affected by the spoil from the PJV's planned Anjolek Creek waste dump, and the company was therefore embarking on a compensation and relocation programme in accordance with an agreement negotiated with representatives of the affected community. The original intention of this study was to facilitate the monitoring of those social and economic changes which would occur in the community as a result of the company's proposed relocation programme.

Until the end of 1993, the Kewai people had been largely unaffected in the physical and material sense by the development of the Porgera mine. Although they had been able to both see and hear many of the changes occurring on the other side of the Kaiya River, they had not yet experienced the loss of land and huge amounts of cash compensation that had befallen the communities of the Special Mining Lease (SML). This is not to say that the Kewai were totally unaffected by the massive changes that had taken place in the previous five years. The people were very mobile, and a significant number spent most of their time out of the area, working for the PJV or living with *wantoks* within the SML. Many had lost access to the alluvial gold of the Kaiya River as a result of increased sedimentation, some had already received compensation payouts, and a few had picked up business contracts with the PJV. In addition, their expectations and aspirations, based on what they had already seen within the SML, were high. The baseline study which follows must be seen in this context—as a description of a community which was already changing, but which had yet to experience the magnitude of changes that had affected the SML communities.

One other point to note here is that although the brief was to establish a socioeconomic baseline for the people of the 'Kaiya River LMP', our study took in a wider area than that covered by the LMP. This occurred for a number of reasons. First, the mobility of the people meant that most had gardens and houses both inside and outside the LMP, and that many people who had an interest in the LMP did not reside within its boundaries. Conversely, there were some inside the LMP boundary who were not likely to lose gardens or require relocation as a result of the further development of mining operations. At the same time, some people resident outside the LMP boundary were liable to be affected by other people relocating to their neighbourhood, especially because the proposed relocation road would run outside the LMP boundary for most of its length. Finally, it was not always obvious on the ground where the LMP boundary actually ran. The area covered by our study therefore stretches from the Kaiya River almost to the ridge of Mount Tangawundi.[1]

A series of detailed interviews form the basis for this report. These were carried out over a three-week period in November and December 1993. Information was collected on the make-up of the household, the type of housing, household assets, involvement in the cash economy, food eaten in the previous 24 hours, and the number, size and location of gardens. Each interview lasted between one and four hours, depending largely on the size of the household and the number and location of gardens. In total, 45 households were interviewed (comprising 381 individuals), and 91 gardens surveyed. Each of the gardens was measured, crops were counted, and notes were made on the location, the setting, the slope and other relevant details. All parts of the LMP and surrounding areas were visited, although a problem was encountered at Nikianga, where some Seventh Day Adventist households were unwilling to be interviewed because of rumours about our role which were spread by the lay preacher.

The Department of Enga and PJV records of compensation payments made for the Kaiya LMP area during 1993 were collected and analysed. Fritz Robinson's detailed relocation study for the Kaiya LMP (Robinson 1993) proved very useful, as did the Kewai genealogies compiled by both Robinson and Kurubu Ipara (1993). The work carried out by Goldsmith (1993) and Mules (1993) provided most of the information on the geology and geomorphology of the area. Further discussions, formal and informal, were held with Fritz Robinson, Geoff Hiatt, Rob Goldsmith, Tona Yongape, Marala (PJV), Kurubu Ipara (Department of Enga) and Pawe Lembopa (Councillor), and fleshed out the information obtained from the surveys.

The Kaiya environment

The following description of the existing environment of the Kaiya LMP area varies markedly in terms of detail. The emphasis is on economic and, to a lesser extent, social measures from the household survey carried out in November and December 1993. Evidence on changes in the extent of garden coverage between 1971 and 1991 is taken from aerial photographs. Material on the physical environment (geology, geomorphology, soils and vegetation), demography, social services and political situation is drawn from existing reports and conversations with a range of individuals, and is open to correction and refinement by those who have (or had) a better understanding of the situation than myself. Where appropriate, I have made comparisons between the Kewai community and other parts of the Porgera Valley, as discussed in previous chapters of this volume, in order to provide a clearer picture of the social and economic situation of the Kewai people relative to other communities.

Physical environment

The physical environment of the north bank of the Kaiya River is similar to that of Apalaka on the south bank (see Chapter 5). The Kaiya River is 14.5 kilometres in length, running from an altitude of 3,200m below Mount Pangalin in the west down to the junction with the Pongema River in the east at an altitude of 1720m (Goldsmith 1993:9–10). The lower Kaiya, from the junction with Anjolek Creek to the Pongema, comprises a relatively steep V-shaped valley, with slopes between 10° and 50°, while the upper part of the valley is wider and flatter.

Goldsmith (1993:9) describes the geology of the valley as folded and faulted Chin Formation mudstone, with major structural elements trending northwest to southeast, although variations in the direction of the bedding are significant and have an impact on slope stability. The mudstone is generally of low strength, with high rates of erosion leading to the development of deep-seated slide blocks. The geomorphology of the area is dominated by a series of large dormant landslides, which make up the bulk of the flatter (and more populated) parts of the valley. Lepalama, for example, is situated on such a landslide (see Map 6.1). The headscarps of several of these landslides are visible high on the ridge. The soils on the dormant landslides are peaty to clayey, and are generally deep and poorly drained. On the steeper mudstone, the soils are residual clay and/or perched colluvial veneer, with generally good drainage (Mules 1993). The area is split by a number of small streams and creeks which drain into the Kaiya River. These generally have low sediment loads, although they are capable of moving relatively large amounts of sediment after heavy rain.

It has been pointed out (Chapter 5) that climatic data collected from meteorological stations in different parts of the Porgera Valley reveal the marked influence of local topography and orographic effects on rainfall magnitude and intensity (PJV 1993:6). The area under consideration here is mostly at a lower altitude (1,800–2,000m) than the Alipis mine site (2,250m), from which the most detailed records are available, and can therefore be expected to have higher average hours of sunshine, warmer daytime temperatures, and lower rainfall. These features were readily apparent during our work in the area.

In 1993, the northern side of the Kaiya Valley was mostly covered by primary forest, interspersed with garden areas. The density of gardens decreased with altitude, with large tracts of garden and short fallow separated by patches of forest close to the Kaiya River, but no gardens along the ridgeline which reaches up to 2,500m. This was in marked contrast to the southern side of the valley, where the relocation areas of Apalaka and Yarik had little forest remaining below 2,500m (see Chapter 5). A series of air photographs (from 1971, 1986, 1991 and 1993) show that gardens had certainly been encroaching on the forested land on the northern side of the valley for the previous 20 years, but the remaining forest cover was still in the order of 65 per cent of the total area.

Map 6.1 Location of houses in the Kaiya LMP, 1991 (after Goldsmith 1993)

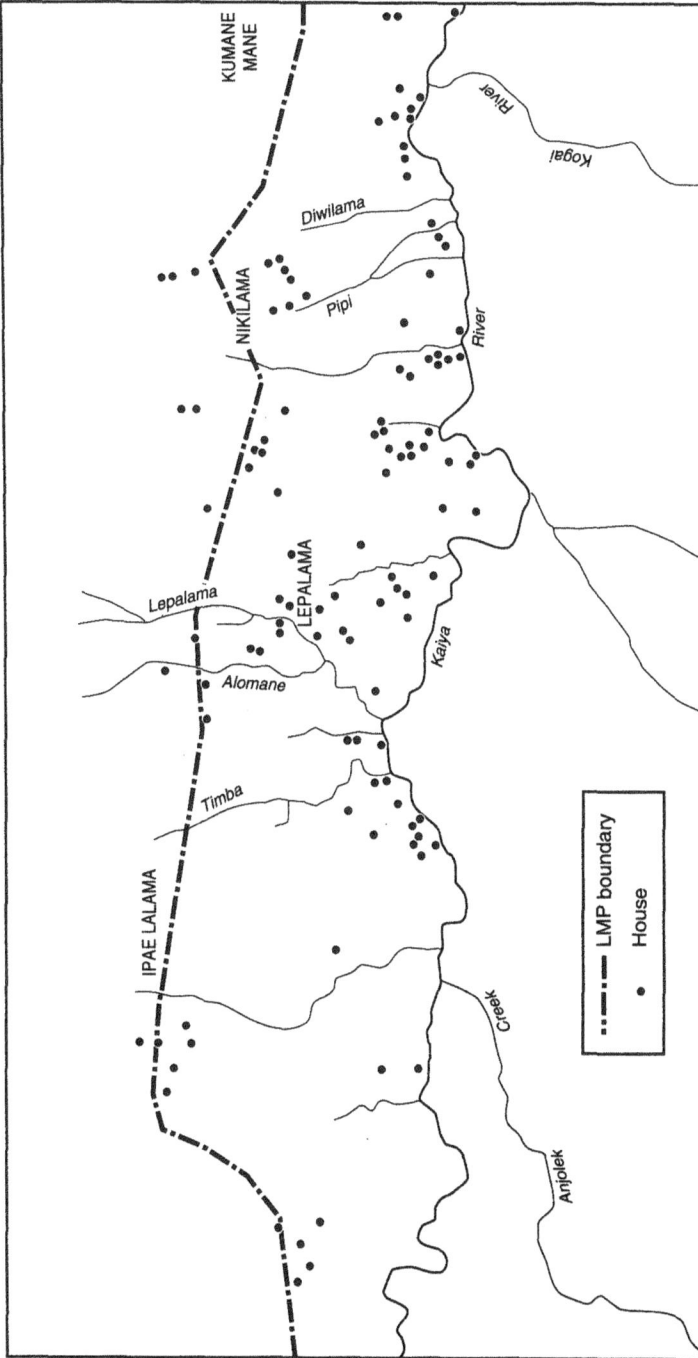

KUMANE
MANE

Kogai *River*

Diwilama

NIKILAMA

Pipi

River

LEPALAMA

Lepalama

Kaiya

Alomane

Timba

IPAE LALAMA

Creek

Anjolek

LMP boundary
House

Source: Banks, G., 1994b. *Kaiya River LMP Socio-Economic Baseline Study*, Porgera Social Monitoring Programme Report 4, Unisearch PNG Pty Ltd for Porgera Joint Venture, Port Moresby.

This 'lower montane' forest is similar to that found throughout the rest of Enga Province, the predominant species being beech (*Nothofagus*), with some oak (*Castanopsis acuminatissima*) and a mixture of other species (Pain *et al.* 1982:35–7). In economic terms, one of the most significant tree species is Karuka (*Pandanus jiulianetti*), which appears to be more widespread on the northern side than the southern side of the Kaiya.

The people

The Kewai clan have primary rights to the area covered by the LMP. The boundaries of the Kewai territory extend up to Mount Tangawundi, which forms the prominent ridgeline to the north of the Kaiya River, down to the Kaiya River itself on the southern side, along the Kaiya to the east to a point almost halfway between the Kogai junction and the bridge, and for an unknown distance upstream to the west, probably as far as Mount Pangalin and the ridge at the head of the valley. Significantly, this is the ridge which separates Porgera from Paiela.

As Burton (1991:9) points out, Porgeran 'clans' are simply lines of descent, and are named after lineage founders. Given the cognatic descent system of the Ipili, membership of the Kewai clan is not fixed or determined, and individuals are able to assert multiple clan affiliations. In the sort of situation which confronted the Kewai in 1993, this can lead to a large number of people trying to assert their links into the 'clan' so as to gain access to the anticipated benefits of relocation and compensation. Within the Kewai 'clan' there are several important 'lines' (or 'sub-clans' as they are generally known in Porgera), each of which can be divided into further distinguishable (though not mutually exclusive) groupings. Figure 6.1 represents the genealogy of the major Kewai lines, as far as I have been able to ascertain it.

Like other Porgerans, the Kewai have links with groups to the east (Enga), the south (Huli), and especially the west (Paiela). The Kaiya Valley was one of the routes into Paiela territory, there are links through marriage to the Paielan Komo clan (Peri 1994), and it was evident that a relatively large number of Paielan-born people had moved into the area during the previous five years. No detailed census of the area had been carried out during this period, so no accurate estimate of the local population could be made. Company staff working on the relocation programme had mapped 130 houses in

Figure 6.1   The main lines of the Kewai clan

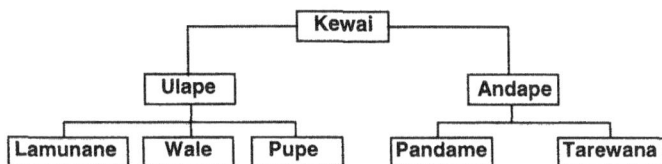

the area, most of which were not permanent residences. On the basis of our own fieldwork, the genealogical work of Ipara (1993), and Robinson's (1993) relocation study, we reckoned that the resident population was between 600 and 800, while a total population including absent persons could have been as high as 1,000.

For the 45 households in which we conducted our interviews

- household size varied from one to 30, averaging 8.47, and yielding a total of 381 residents
- there was a virtually identical number of males and females (190 to 191)
- 163 (or 42.8 per cent) were under 15 years of age
- 330 (or 86.6 per cent) were born in Porgera; and
- there were 64 other family members absent, who were not counted in the total.

The average household size was towards the higher end of the range found by previous surveys in other parts of Porgera, which went from 6.8 for a sample of 122 households (Chapter 3), to 11.3 for a survey of 17 households in Kulapi (Chapter 5). The fact that many of these households were likely to be relocated may account for this higher number; the average household size during the first SML relocation survey was 13 (Robinson 1991:4). The percentage of children under 15, and the percentage of Porgeran-born residents in the sample, were more clearly within the range of previous local surveys. The balanced sex ratio contrasts with the findings of the 1992 household survey (Chapter 3), where a higher ratio of males to females was found in all parts of Porgera. This may indicate a recent movement of families into the Kaiya area. Further evidence of a recent movement of people into the area is contained in the age profile of our survey, which shows a large proportion of 25–29 year-olds (see Figure 6.2). This is unusual in an area from which out-migration could have been expected, as this age group would be one of the most mobile and thus most likely to leave. Here again, it suggests the movement of young people into the area in anticipation of benefits from the relocation and compensation packages.

The population was scattered throughout the area, with three main settlements (Kumane Mane, Nikilama and Lepalama), and a tendency for groups of four or five houses to be clustered together at garden sites. Twenty six (58 per cent) of the households interviewed had more than one residence. The general pattern was for a family to live in one house for the greater part of the year, but to spend short spells at their other home or homes. In some cases, the secondary homes were garden houses. Map 6.1 shows the location of the houses (not all of which were primary places of residence) revealed in a December 1991 air photograph, and highlights the scattered nature of the population.

The population was also very mobile, with people 'commuting' to Yuyan, Apalaka and Yarik on a daily basis. Some residents had departed the area on a more permanent basis, because the Nikilama and Lepalama areas were isolated, even by comparison to Yuyan, and they evidently wanted to get closer to the road and all the benefits that this would bring, or was thought likely to bring. More recently,

---

Figure 6.2   Age profile from the Kewai household survey, 1993

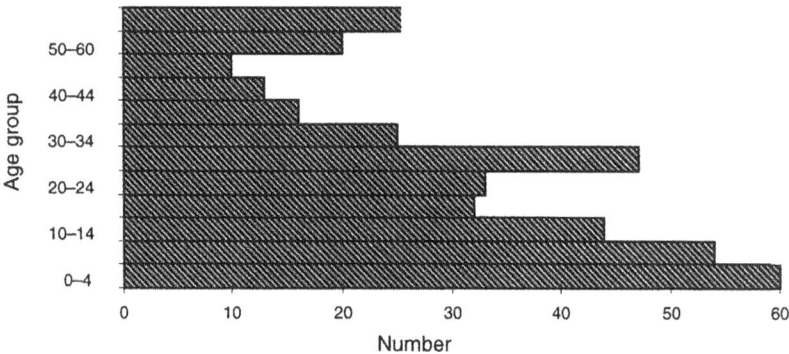

Source: Kaiya household survey, 1993.

---

individuals and family groups had utilised their links with Tuanda, Tieni and other clans to gain better access to the material benefits of mine development, and this had further consequences for the proposed relocation programme which are discussed later in this chapter.

Social infrastructure

This section is based on the responses to interview questions about housing, water supply, cooking, cleaning and toilet facilities, with the addition of some basic information about access to health and educational facilities.

Two broad types of housing could be distinguished

- the 'true' Porgeran house has a low, rectangular profile, with a timber frame, double thickness pandanus walls, a palisade of vertical or horizontal timber and a pandanus roof
- the 'imported' type has a high-pitched roof and square design, with kunai thatch being used as roofing material, and woven bamboo 'blind' being used for the walls.

In practice, the distinction had already broken down, because the area displayed a wide range of house designs and materials. Canvas and heavy nylon sheets ('sails') were found on roofs, there were several houses on stilts (a design imported from the Hewa people), and cardboard and timber were common wall materials. Of the 59 houses which we surveyed, only eight were 'true' Porgeran houses. One relocation house had already been built in the area, although the owner was not using it because he worked for the PJV and lived in Yarik.

Cooking was generally done inside the main house over an open fire. Only nine (20 per cent) of the households surveyed had a separate 'haus kuk'. The relocation house was the only one with a stove. Firewood was the source of fuel for all of those in the survey. Creeks and streams were the main source of water for all the houses except for the one relocation house, which had a rainwater tank. For this reason, most of the houses were located relatively close to the water supply, although the ridge-top settlements were some distance from the creeks. Forty-four gallon plastic drums were used as an additional store of water by some households. Most of the streams and creeks in the area were used by one or more households, but the Kaiya River had never been an important source of drinking water, and was certainly not used for this purpose in 1993. The Kaiya river was previously used for bathing and washing by some households, but these activities were now confined to the smaller creeks and streams.

All toilets were of the basic pit type (some not even covered) except for the relocation house, which had an improved pit, with a concrete floor and corrugated iron walls and roof.

The area apparently had an aid post at Nikilama for some time, but this had since been closed, and the nearest medical facility was the aid post at Yarik. Bonnell (Chapter 2) has highlighted the serious shortage of reliable information about the health status of Porgerans and the performance of the local health services throughout the Porgera area, and we were unable to obtain any better data for the Kaiya area. Like other Porgerans, the Kewai had certainly gained better access to educational facilities since 1991. The nearest community school was at Apalaka, and there was another one at Yuyan. However, staff resources in both schools were stretched, with five teachers for 225 pupils up to Grade 3 at Yuyan, and three teachers for 145 pupils up to Grade 1 at Apalaka. Eighty-one of the 384 people in our survey had schooling of some kind, though just 26 of the children were currently attending school.

Access to this particular part of the Porgera Valley was generally difficult. The area had no direct vehicular access, the closest being the road from Mungalep to Yuyan (see Map 1.1). People had previously gained access to other parts of Porgera along tracks to Yuyan or by crossing the Kaiya River. In mid 1993, the Porgera Development Authority erected a new footbridge over the river, between Lepalama and Yarik. At least eight helipads dotted the area, providing convenient access for PJV Lands and Community Relations staff.

Two churches were active in the area: the Seventh Day Adventist church had a lay-preacher, church and compound area at Nikilama (with a congregation estimated to be roughly 200 people), while the Apostolics had a church at Lepalama. There was a volleyball court at Nikilama which was in regular use. Alcohol was not a major problem for the community: we were told on several occasions that drinking was something that happened at Apalaka or Yarik, not on their side of the river, even though some Kewai did presumably cross the river to partake in this activity. In the survey of expenditure patterns discussed below, no-one reported any spending on alcohol in the previous two weeks, and this might have been due to the strength of the Adventist church.

Economic status

Given its proximity to the alluvial gold of the Kaiya River, this area has had longer and greater exposure to the cash economy than other parts of Porgera.[2] Until recently, the Kewai were heavily involved in alluvial mining, and even in 1993, this was still the largest source of income for the local residents. Although this was already a diminishing resource, the Kewai, along with others along the Kaiya and the Porgera, were due to be compensated for their loss of access to it. Nevertheless, the Kewai community is one in which average incomes had probably dropped since the start of construction in 1989, and this may have had some bearing on the level of expectations within the community.

I shall now discuss the economic status of the Kewai people in 1993 with reference to the results of our survey, looking specifically at amounts and sources of income and expenditure, material wealth and assets, and food eaten in the previous 24 hours. The survey revealed that the Kewai had a variety of sources of income, the most significant of which was alluvial mining. Table 6.1 compares the Kewai figures with those obtained in 1992 for other areas of the Porgera Valley (see Table 3.8). Table 6.1 highlights several other features of the Kewai situation. The figures for royalties and occupation fees were lower than elsewhere, while the proportion of households which had received PJV compensation was higher, although the value of this compensation to date had been relatively low. Almost 50 per cent of the households were involved in the sale of crops or produce. The proportion involved in a business (11 per cent) was lower than in all other parts of the Porgera Valley we surveyed in 1992, but the number and proportion (30 per cent) of households involved in alluvial

Table 6.1   Annual value and distribution of cash income for the Kewai community (1993) compared with other parts of Porgera (1992)

Income sources	1992 Porgera survey (N=122)			1993 Kewai survey (N=45)		
	Income (kina)	No. of recipients	Kina per recipient	Income (kina)	No. of recipients	Kina per recipient
Royalties	41,308	43	961	1,045	8	131
Occupation fees	8,454	33	256	140	1	140
PJV compensation	241,250	32	7,539	14,254	16	891
Cash cropping	6,054	41	148	4,610	22	210
Alluvial mining	18,150	14	1,296	27,577	14	1,970
No. in business	n.a.	30	n.a.	n.a.	5	n.a.

Source: Porgera household survey and Kaiya household survey.

mining, and the value of that activity to the community, were significantly greater than they were elsewhere in the valley.[3]

The data obtained from survey questions relating to income received in the past two weeks are shown in Figures 6.3 and 6.4. Sixteen people in the 45 households we surveyed were in paid employment. A total of K5,004 was received by these households at an average of K111.20 per household for the fortnight. The information was significantly skewed by one household, which had received a K2,000 compensation payment from PJV during the period in question. This was left in the data because it appears to be typical of the way that the local economy functions, with a sequence of 'windfalls' of various sizes and sources occurring to different households throughout the year. The data show that

- excluding the large compensation payment, alluvial mining and money from *wantoks* provided the greatest source of income to the community; PJV wages accounted for 11 per cent of the income received, though this figure is certainly an underestimate, as several household heads did not know how much money their adult children had brought home in wages from PJV

- the Kewai income figures were generally below those previously found in other parts of Porgera (with the exception of Tipinini) in our income and expenditure survey.[4] There were variations in the significance of the 'other' category for the Kewai (67 per cent against 5 per cent in the rest of Porgera), the lesser importance of wages from any source (15 per cent against 48 per cent), and the complete absence of any profits from businesses, which accounted for 28 per cent of income in the 1992 Porgera-wide survey (see Chapter 3)

- ten households (22 per cent) reported no income for the two week period.

Table 6.2 is based on the answers given to survey questions about the ownership of a range of material assets.[5] Compared to other parts of Porgera, the Kewai generally had fewer material goods than those inside or close to the SML, and similar amounts of assets to those in Tipinini. This is somewhat surprising, given the long history of alluvial mining, and may relate to a focus on consumption rather than investment in goods or businesses. Clark (1993) has postulated that

Figure 6.3   Number of Kewai households receiving income from various sources, 1993

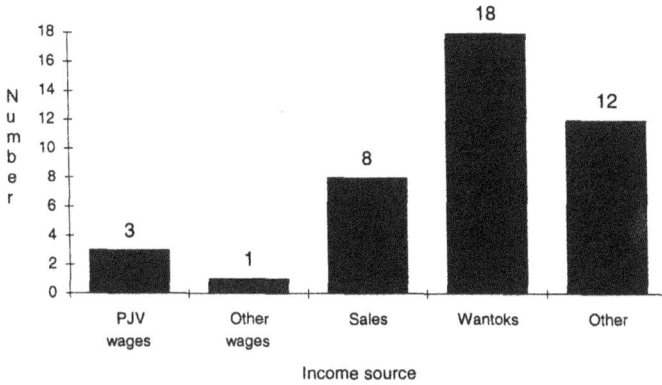

Source: Kaiya household survey.

Figure 6.4   Value of Kewai household income from various sources (total = K5,004)

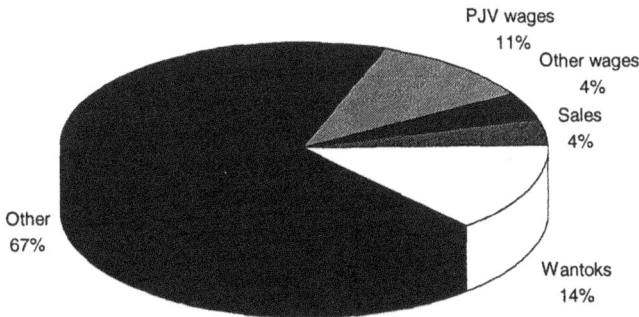

Source: Kaiya household survey.

there may have been cultural constraints against using the alluvial gold from Mount Kare for investment purposes, and the same argument may apply in this case.

This same constraint may also have influenced the patterns of investment revealed in Table 6.3. This table highlights both the low proportion of families with investments, and the low value of these investments, when compared to other parts of the Porgera Valley. The figures even understate the extent of this discrepancy, because one household accounted for the bulk of the total value (K12,000). The survey also revealed that the Kewai had contributed a total of K8,055 and 132 pigs to traditional exchange (brideprice and compensation payments) in the previous 12 months, which meant an average of K179 and 2.9 pigs across the 45 households. Twelve households (27 per cent of the sample) had contributed cash, while 17 households (40

Table 6.2   Material assets of Kewai households, 1993

Major assets	% of households	Minor assets	No. per household
Watch	20	Lamps	1.18
Radio	27	Axes	2.16
Tape recorder	16	Spades	2.09
Sewing machine	4	Shoes	0.64
Washing machine	0	Mattresses	2.22
Fridge	2	Pots	3.07
Stove	0	Bush knives	2.09
T.V.	0	Buckets	0.76
Video	2	44 gallon drums	0.76
Generator	2	Blankets	4.20
Car	0		

Source: Kaiya household survey.

Table 6.3   Investment patterns among the Kewai and other Porgeran communities

	Total value (kina)	Value per household	% households with investments
Kewai community (1993)	14,501	322.24	27.0
Other Porgeran (1992)	217,042	1,779.03	50.0

Source: Porgera household survey and Kaiya household survey.

per cent of the sample) had contributed pigs. In other parts of Porgera, we had found that 63 per cent of households surveyed contributed cash, and 61 per cent contributed pigs, to ceremonial exchanges, which meant an average of K2203.18 and 5.4 pigs per household (see Chapter 3). In summary, our measures of material wealth did not reflect the long history of alluvial mining in the Kaiya area, possibly because of cultural factors, or else because the mobility of local residents was associated with the movement of money out of the area.

The questions relating to expenditure in the last two weeks produced the results shown in Figures 6.5 and 6.6. Total expenditure amounted to K5,125.90, but here again, the figures for the value of different types of expenditure are skewed by the distribution to family members (included in the 'other' category) of the large compensation payment noted earlier. It may be noted that the amounts spent by a large proportion of households on store-bought food were significantly higher than those recorded in the 1992 Porgera household survey, where this category accounted for just 8 per cent of the value of expenditure (see Chapter 3).[6] On the other hand, savings and investments were significantly lower than those recorded in the earlier survey—4 per cent as against 32 per cent.

We do not have much information regarding Kewai people's involvement in business. We saw four trade stores during our surveys, but all were closed. Three PJV field contracts for the filling of gabion baskets had been awarded to the 'Kewai Clan', and several individuals had obtained other field contracts for the construction of relocation homes, liaison services and the like. Of the 45 households interviewed, five were involved in one or more businesses. Four of these had one trade store each, while the fifth family had four trade stores, three PMVs, and some unspecified PJV contracts. It is likely that individuals were involved in other businesses outside the area, but the only evidence of this was the five trade stores in Apalaka and Yarik owned by Kewai people which we came across in survey work in early 1994.

The responses to the question about food eaten in the previous 24 hours revealed some interesting patterns which clearly reflect the economic position of the Kewai people. Table 6.4 shows that, compared to other parts of Porgera, the Kewai were involved significantly in both the cash and subsistence economies. All reported eating *kaukau* (sweet potato), and 79 per cent reported eating greens, from their own gardens. These proportions were significantly greater than those found in other parts of the valley, with the exception of the

Figure 6.5

Figure 6.5   Expenditure patterns of Kewai households by number of persons, 1993

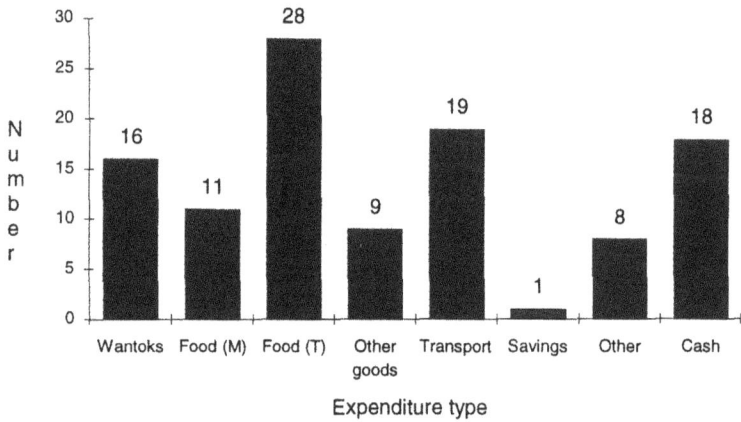

Notes: M = market; T = trade store.
Source: Kaiya household survey.

Figure 6.6   Expenditure patterns of Kewai households by value, 1993

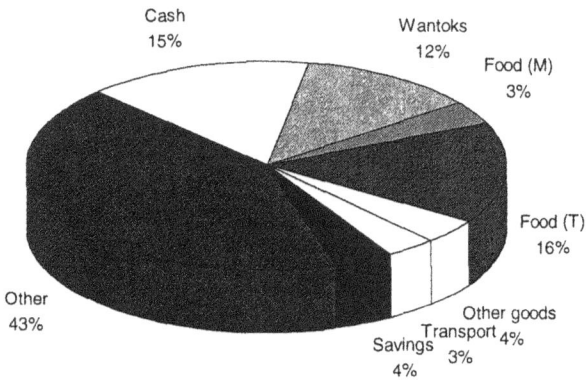

Notes: M = market; T = trade store.
Source: Kaiya household survey.

Tipinini and Mungalep communities (see Table 5.5), indicating that garden food retained a major role in the Kewai economy. It should also be noted that 67 per cent of Kewai households reported eating pandanus, and 33 per cent reported eating taro, from their own gardens in the previous 24 hours. At the same time, the figures recorded for rice and tinned fish (70 and 72 per cent respectively) were as high as those previously found in the most store-dependent parts of the SML. This shows that these communities have the cash to pay for such items, and may also reflect changes in dietary patterns that have occurred as a result of long exposure to the cash economy. It reinforces the view that the availability of cash has brought about a 'consumption' focus among the Kewai.

The gardening system

As in other parts of Porgera, the gardening system is based around mounded sweet potato, with a range of other crops also being cultivated (see Chapter 5). In our survey of the Kaiya area, we measured 91 current gardens, using a tape and an inclinometer, which represented 67 per cent of the total of 136 gardens belonging to the 45 Kaiya households in the survey. The gardens which were not surveyed were all at some distance from the houses, and often the interviewees were not prepared to spend the time required to take us to them. The average size of gardens surveyed was 2,024m², less than that which we found at Apalaka (8,061m²) but similar to that found at Kulapi (2,797 m²).

Table 6.5 compares the data obtained for those 26 Kewai households whose total garden area was surveyed with the corresponding data obtained in the Apalaka and Kulapi garden surveys (see Chapter 5). If the average garden size is used as a surrogate for the 45 Kewai gardens we did not measure, then the average garden area per household for the full sample comes to 6,118m². This is higher than the

Table 6.4	Percentage of Kewai and other Porgeran community members consuming food types in the previous 24 hours				
	Sample	Tinned fish	Rice	Sweet potato	Greens
	(N)	(%)	(%)	(%)	(%)
Kewai community (1993)	45	72	70	100	79
Other Porgeran (1992)	380	38	43	70	49

Source: Porgera diet survey and Kaiya household survey.

Table 6.5   Households with total garden area surveyed in Apalaka, Kulapi and Kaiya

Variable	Apalaka	Kulapi	Kewai
Households	11	13	26
Mean size per garden	7,173m²	2,890m²	1,958m²
Mean gardens per household	1.4	1.54	2.11
Mean household garden area	10,043m²	4,450.4m²	4,486.3m²
Household garden area range	720–32,250m²	425–23,608m²	0–14,225m²
Mean household size	7.9	11.6	8.47
Mean pigs per household	2.8	2.4	2.2
Mean slope angle slopes)	30° (14 slopes)	16° (20 slopes)	21° (64

Source: Apalaka, Kulapi and Kaiya garden surveys. '

figure for the 17 Kulapi households surveyed (5,314 m²), but well down on the figure for the 22 Apalaka households (20,959 m²).

One notable feature of the Kewai gardens was the size of the mounds, with a high proportion of new small mounds with one vine per mound. It was notable that, unlike the situation at Apalaka, these smaller mounds were found on slopes of all angles, not just steeper slopes. This may have been the result of a misunderstanding of the compensation agreement, whereby the gardeners were under the impression that every mound, regardless of size, would be eligible for the same amount of compensation. We also noted some unusual gardening techniques: large mounds (1.5m in diameter, 0.75m in height), with each of the ten or so vines planted on a small mound on top of the large mound, and mixed mounds, with a variety of crops (pitpit, taro, sugarcane) growing on the mounds in addition to sweet potato. Although there were a large number of new gardens, it was not clear whether these were the number that would normally be expected, or whether they reflected the number of new immigrants into the area, or represented an attempt by the existing residents to put in extra gardens in the expectation of compensation.[7] At the same time, the small average number of pigs per household was almost certainly related to the presence of the Seventh Day Adventist church at Nikilama, because 22 households, mainly in that area, claimed to have no pigs.

Although an estimation of garden area from air photographs is difficult for a number of reasons (see Chapter 5), it is apparent from the 1991 series that around 35 per cent of the area bounded by the Kaiya River and the ridgeline, between the Anjolek and the Kogai, was covered by current or recent gardens (see Map 6.2). This was approximately half of the proportion estimated for Apalaka. There were several new gardens which would not have shown up on the 1991 photographs, but primary forest still accounted for well over half of the total area. The gardening system thus appeared to be far less stressed than that of Apalaka or Kulapi. There was still ample bush and fallow land to support the current population under the present agricultural system. However, to judge by what had occurred at Apalaka and Yarik since the original relocation exercise, this situation was likely to change rapidly over the course of the following year. The main factors in this process would be the physical loss of land due to the spoil, the construction of roads and relocation houses, and the greater number of people that the area would have to support following the immigration which was expected to occur.

Political situation

The development of the Porgera gold mine over the previous six years had brought profound changes to most communities within the SML and along the highway from Tipinini to Alipis. Large cash payments for loss of land, the relocation programme, a large influx of non-Porgerans, and the creation of new employment and business opportunities had brought about a range of other social, economic and political changes. One of the most significant of these was the growth of Porgeran political organisation, as represented by the Landowners' Association, the Community Issues Committee (CIC), the Women's Association, and a variety of youth and church groups.

Yet the Kewai community had been substantially sidelined by this process, and had indeed lost the central position which the alluvial resources of the Kaiya River had previously bestowed on them. Before the creation of the Kaiya LMP Committee, the churches were the only significant 'political' organisations in the area, and Pawe Lembopa, as the local councillor and CIC member, was the only link to the larger Porgeran political scene. The creation of the LMP had now led to a further degree of political organisation amongst these people, and gave the community much greater direct access to senior PJV personnel. Like the SML landowners, their land would now be earning money for them.

Bonnell's comments on the social, economic and political role of women in Ipili culture (Chapter 2) are also relevant to the Kewai

Map 6.2 **Distribution of Kaiya gardens and forest (1991), with anticipated impact of the Anjolek dump**

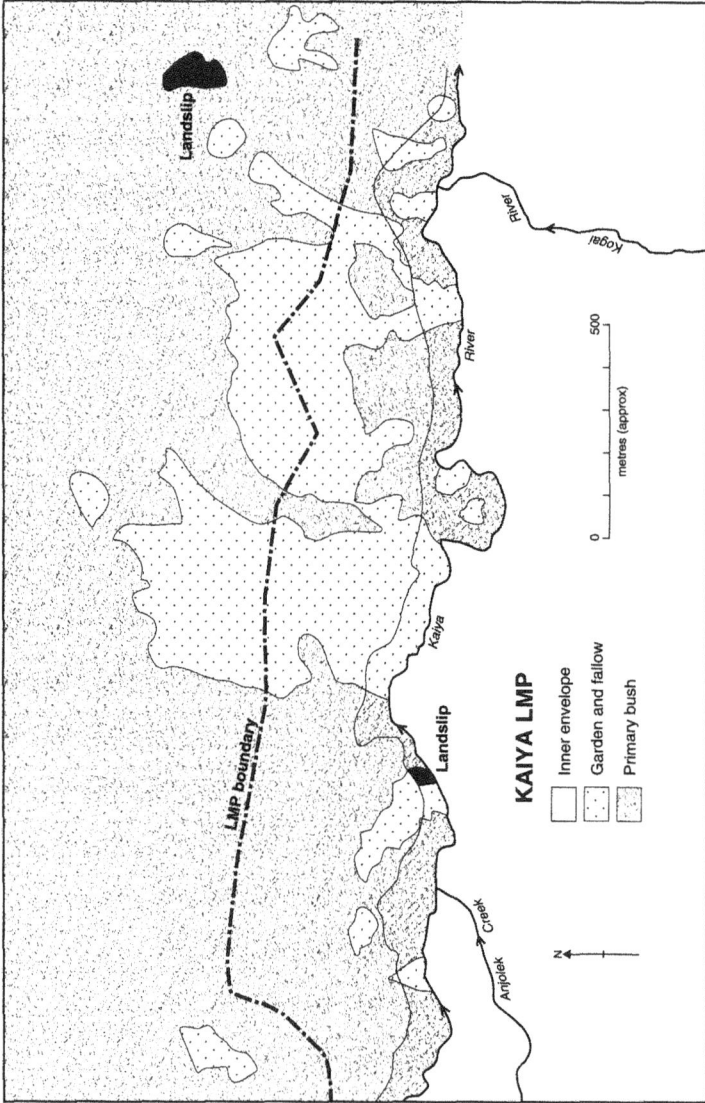

KAIYA LMP

Inner envelope

Garden and fallow

Primary bush

Source: Banks, G. 1994b. *Kaiya River LMP Socio-Economic Baseline Study,* Porgera Social Monitoring Programme Report 4, Unisearch PNG Pty Ltd for Porgera Joint Venture, Port Moresby.

situation. In 1993, local women's economic role was still largely confined to the subsistence sector, although there were a number of Kewai women employed by the PJV. With their social status and political influence still largely confined to the private sphere, women were unlikely to be in a position to influence important decisions and processes concerned with the impending programme of relocation and compensation.

Hopes, aspirations, expectations and fears

As part of the survey we asked the respondents to comment on their hopes and fears for the future. We prompted them with questions concerning the movement of outsiders into the area, the facilities which they would like to see, and their concerns about the compensation and relocation programme. The responses indicated that people were generally not opposed to the idea of losing some of their land to the spoil, or to the proposed compensation and relocation programme.

From the 45 households covered in the survey, the numbers giving specific responses to these questions were as follows.

- The most sought-after facilities were a school (15 respondents), an aid post (also 15), road construction and improvements (12), a permanent bridge (10), a shopping centre or large trade store (8), a government agricultural station (8), a new church (6), a locally owned PMV (4), and a recreation centre.
- Two respondents expressed concern about the loss of land to road construction, and one about the loss to the PJV generally.
- Seventeen respondents commented on the loss of income from alluvial mining due to the waste dump, while eight specifically wanted compensation for this. Seven thought that the increased sediment in the river was already affecting their gardens, and one mentioned the impact on hunting by the river bank. Three said that the company should not dump waste into the river, and four believed that it should carry out an environmental impact study before dumping any more. Three people simply stated that 'the river is polluted', and one pointed out that the people needed the river for laundry and bathing.
- Eleven respondents said that they did not want people relocating to their area, and 13 wanted compensation from

the PJV or the people themselves if this were to happen. Three people said they had no problem with this prospect.

- Nine respondents were concerned about the question of where they could be relocated, and 18 were worried about the level of compensation which they would receive for the loss of land (including gardens) or for relocation itself. Two people said that they would not move if the compensation was inadequate. Four people wanted the company to supply them with relocation houses, and not just to compensate them for moving, while three said that they wanted bigger relocation homes than those previously built in Apalaka. One person wanted business contracts with the PJV as part of the compensation package.
- Two respondents remarked that the Kewai had so far missed out on the benefits of mine development, and had been 'cut-off' and 'ignored' by the company, which had been dealing only with the SML landowners. Two others felt that there had been an unfair distribution of benefits to 'outsiders'.
- Five respondents had no comments, or were unsure what to say, in response to all of our queries.

These concerns were generally much the same as those brought up by community representatives in meetings with PJV staff, the minutes of which were made available to me. In many cases, their own questions reflected some impatience about the timing of road construction and the payment of compensation for the alluvial resource, as well as a desire to have some input into the scope and form of the relocation programme, including the route of the road.

The impact of the mine on the Kaiya

By the end of 1993, the Kewai had experienced little material impact from mine development, aside from the loss of access to the alluvial resource in the Kaiya River due to sedimentation associated with the development of the waste dumps in the Mungrenk and Anjolek creeks. Although the extent of the dumping had so far been limited, the river was already carrying an increased sediment load which was enough to deter all but the most determined alluvial miners. It was clear that this resource had provided an important source of cash for the Kewai for a number of years, and the loss of access to it had affected the incomes of the local people, as well as their attitudes towards the mine development as a whole. This loss was almost always the first point which our respondents raised in the interviews, and some seemed to be unaware of the fact that the level of compensation for it had already been agreed, and that payment would take place soon.

The area had also been affected by the immigration of *epo atene*, especially relatives from Paiela, who wanted to move closer to the mine in order to gain a share of the benefits distributed by the company, including the relocation and compensation package which had recently been put in place. To some extent, this movement reflected the misinformation that was circulating in the area: one person said that he had been told that the loss of any house, regardless of condition, size or type, would make him eligible for relocation. At the same time, the Kewai community's 'grandstand view' of the growth of mine facilities and the settlements at Apalaka, Yarik, Olonga and Timorope had raised local expectations to the point where they appeared (to PJV staff working in the area) to be much higher than they had been before the relocation programme in the SML during 1988 and 1989. People now wanted roads, schools, aid posts, trade stores and cash, and almost everyone expected to receive a relocation package. These unrealistic expectations would obviously have some impact on local perceptions of the compensation paid for the Anjolek waste dump, not only by those directly affected, but also by other members of the local community.

The Anjolek dump

The Anjolek erodible dump was a part of the overall waste rock disposal plan for the Porgera gold mine approved by the PNG Department of Environment and Conservation. By March 1994, the plan was to dump a total of 72 million tonnes (mt) of incompetent (easily eroded) waste material into the head of the Anjolek Creek over the following nine years. Another 25mt of colluvium was expected to enter the Kaiya river system from the construction of the Mungarenk 'displacement dump', which was intended to store competent material. In the first two years of dumping, over 40mt of incompetent material was expected to be delivered into the river system. Parker (1992) predicted that, given the proposed dumping schedule, the Anjolek runout zone would reach its maximum extent at the beginning of 1997, by which time the toe would have migrated some two kilometres into the upper Porgera. The toe was then expected to retreat to the Kaiya-Pongema confluence, remain there for several years, and then retreat rapidly up the Kaiya with the reduction in the rate of dumping. By the end of dumping (in 2002), after delivering 97mt of material to the system, the runout zone was predicted to have just 13.3mt of sediment stored in it (down from a maximum of 31mt), while all the other material should have been carried further downstream by fluvial action, as had already occurred with spoil from the Anawe dump.

Parker (1992) estimated that the mudflow would aggrade the bed of the Kaiya River, between the Anjolek and Pongema confluences, by up to 35m below Apalaka to about 15m at the junction with Taro Creek. This aggradation was expected to occur quite rapidly, with the toe of the slide reaching the confluence with Taro Creek by the beginning of 1995. The mudflow might also reactivate a number of large, currently dormant landslides. It was this combination of predicted physical effects which had resulted in the negotiation of the proposed compensation and relocation package for the Kaiya LMP.

An examination of the 1991 and 1993 air photographs reveals that around 60 per cent of Kewai gardens then fell within the LMP boundary, which had been established by reference to the maximum possible extent of the impact of the mudflow. A significant proportion of these (around 25 per cent) were also within the inner 'compensation envelope', which is the area that would definitely be lost to the spoil (see Map 6.3). The immediate impact of the dumping of the spoil would then be the loss of 15 per cent of the total Kewai garden area. While this figure itself is not very high, our own observations in the field indicated that the gardens nearest to the river were among the most productive.

The proposed compensation and relocation programme

The agreement which had been signed between the PJV and the clans affected by the proposed Anjolek dump (including the Kewai) was the outcome of nine months of negotiation between the various landowner agents and PJV representatives. The most significant components of this agreement were the relocation package and the compensation package.

The relocation component stated that

> In respect of affected landholders' families, the PJV will: (i) construct relocation houses to replace their vacated houses, such relocation houses to be of the same construction and built to the same standards

Map 6.3   **Predicted impact of the Anjolek spoil, with the proposed relocation road and housing areas** (after Parker 1992 and Goldsmith 1993)

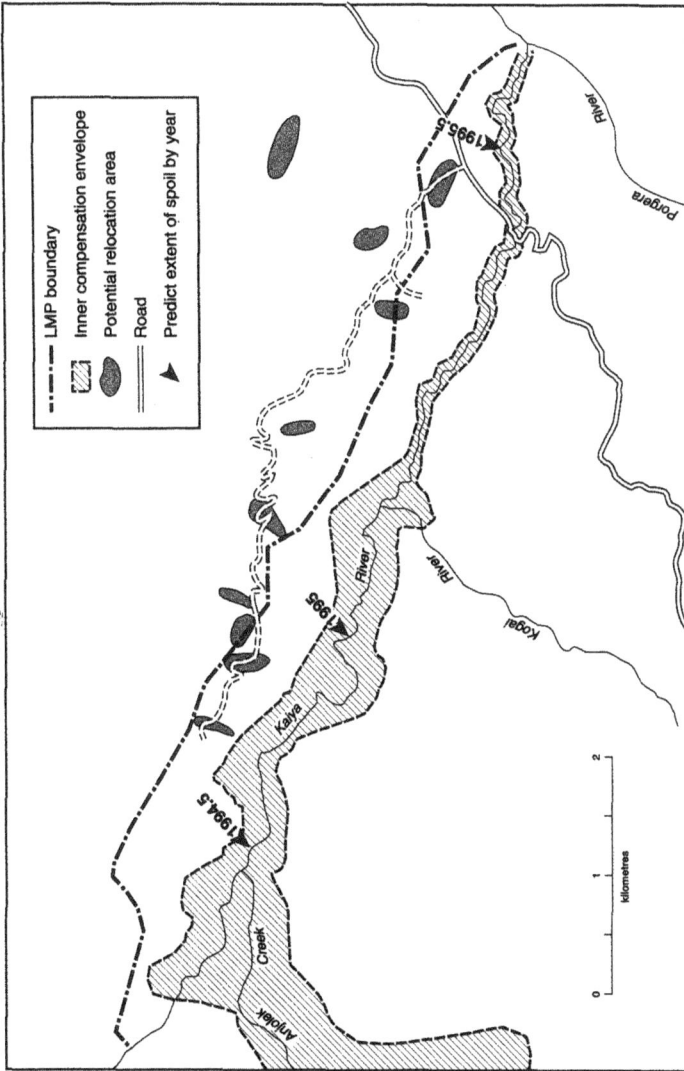

Legend:
- LMP boundary
- Inner compensation envelope
- Potential relocation area
- Road
- Predict extent of spoil by year

Source: Banks, G., 1994b. *Kaiya River LMP Socio-Economic Baseline Study*, Porgera Social Monitoring Programme Report 4, Unisearch PNG Pty Ltd for Porgera Joint Venture, Port Moresby.

as offered in respect of families relocated for the purposes of the PJV's activities under its Special Mining Lease No. 1 – Porgera, such houses to be wired to Elcom standards and complete with an external power box ready for connection; (ii) provide road access to the main cluster of relocation houses;

The key phrase in the above is 'affected landholders' families', defined in the agreement as

True Landholders (YUU ANDUANE) who had prior to 3rd August 1992 and still have a primary residence within the LMP area. These individuals will appear in the genealogies which are being prepared and will be agreed between the PJV and the relevant Landholders;

Long term relatives, particularly WANA, married into the clan and who have a primary residence prior to 3rd August 1992 in the above area; and

Long-term invited outsiders (EPO ATENE) of ten (10) years permanent residence in the above area.

Given the general mobility of the population, and especially the recent movements towards the roads and the SML communities, there were a significant number of Kewai people who would simply not be eligible for relocation under the terms of the agreement, because their main place of residence was now outside the LMP area. Likewise, the *epo atene* who had moved in over the last five years would not be eligible.

The relocation package also included the following undertakings by the PJV

- agreement to meet the reasonable costs of relocating each family of eligible landholders, with a payment of K1,000 to the head of each family for hardship and disturbance, and provision of rations to commence on the date on which the family no longer had access to traditional gardens, and to continue until the food gardens in the new locations were ready to harvest, or else for a maximum period of nine months
- sympathetic examination of the situation of any relocated landowners who were affected in a special or unusual manner
- construction of an aid post by the main cluster of relocation houses, with an extra relocation house for the orderly, subject to agreement by the government to staff this facility and supply appropriate drugs and medicines

- construction of two more relocation houses for the church pastors, although these would remain the property of the congregations rather than the pastors
- clearing of a sports area for a basketball court and volleyball court, and supply of initial sporting equipment for these
- construction and maintenance of two footbridges across the Kaiya River.

According to the agreement, relocation would occur 'as necessitated by the PJV's activities'. Relocation of 40 households in the Anjolek area, on the southern side of the Kaiya River, was already underway by early 1994. On the northern side, an assessment of the value of the forest and 'improvements' in the inner envelope had already been completed, and those households which were eligible for relocation had been identified. At that stage it appeared that 40 Kewai families were due for relocation around the middle of 1994, although the actual effects of the spoil might cause this number to increase. Recent arguments between the company and the community, and also within the community itself, had concentrated on the question of who should get a relocation house. Many of the community representatives appeared to be arguing less in terms of eligibility under the agreement than in terms of 'political correctness', which in this case meant a preference for people with some standing in the community.

The compensation package stipulated rates for various economic and non-economic trees, which were based on those paid under the SML compensation agreement. These rates were generally somewhat higher than those recommended by the Valuer-General, which had last been revised in November 1993 (DLPP 1993). For example, a mature pandanus (*karuka*) was valued at K8 in the Valuer-General's schedule,

Table 6.6   Rates of annual fees payable for the Kaiya LMP

Type of payment	Kina per hectare
Bush and nuisance compensation	12.30
Cleared land	9.22
Damaged land	18.45
Lost land	21.52
Non-Renewable Resources Fund	6.15
Occupation fee	5.00

Source: Kaiya LMP compensation agreement.

but K12 in the Kaiya LMP compensation agreement. Compensation payments of this type had already started within the LMP area, primarily in respect of the damage done by clearing helipads and by surveying and cutting the LMP boundary. By the end of 1993, a total of 32 claims had been paid, with a total value of K28,848.50. The distribution lists contained 216 names, but there was some duplication, as some individuals received a share of as many as nine of the claims. There were 146 different individuals named on the lists, and their receipts ranged from K3,172.60 down to K17.40, with an average of K197.59 per person.

Since the inner envelope contained around eighty hectares of Kewai land, and the minimum PJV compensation payment for a hectare of bush was K9,000, then the Kewai could expect a minimum of K720,000 cash compensation for the loss of these eighty hectares. Given that some of the inner envelope consisted of gardens, and the compensation rates for these were more than K14,000 per hectare, the total was certain to exceed K1 million. The compensation to be paid for the damage caused by building the relocation road to Lepalama would make a substantial addition to this total.

The compensation package also established the rates of the annual fees to be paid over the whole LMP area, under the various categories shown in Table 6.6. The fees for cleared, damaged and lost land were mutually inclusive, so that K27.67 would be paid for a hectare of damaged land and K49.19 for a hectare of lost land. The Non-Renewable Resources Fund was to consist of a series of trust funds established 'for the benefit of the landowners and other people of the Porgera area'. If we assume that the Kewai had primary rights to 387 hectares of land inside the LMP, then their total annual receipts under this element of the package would be worth at least K9,000, and might turn out to be worth twice that amount.

Separate compensation agreements had been negotiated for the loss of access to the alluvial resource and for the sedimentation of the river system. The agreement for the alluvials involved a single lump sum of K311,755 'to be invested or distributed as directed by the landowner representatives' of the clans who lived along the Kaiya, between the Anjolek and Pongema junctions. The agreement for the sedimentation was based on a rate of 1 toea per tonne of material dumped in the failing dumps, and in this case also, the distribution was to be determined by the landowner representatives. At the end of 1993, both of these 'heads of agreement' were awaiting government approval of the genealogical studies being carried out by the company to determine which groups would be eligible for these monies.

Overall, the compensation and relocation package offered significant benefits for the Kewai, including better access to and from the area, improved access to health facilities, significant amounts of cash compensation, and superior housing for many local families. However, it was already evident that such benefits had not guaranteed a long-term improvement in the quality of life (at least in Western terms) for the residents of the SML communities. Like them, the Kewai stood to lose a large proportion of their lower-altitude garden land, and the likely influx of people to the area would put further pressure on the remaining land.

It could also be argued that some Kewai people would not be adequately compensated for their losses under the terms of the compensation package. For example, the rates of payment for some economic crops, albeit higher than those recommended by the Valuer-General, could still be said to seriously underestimate their current value. We watched one morning as six large clusters of nuts were knocked from one pandanus tree, and were reliably informed that each of these clusters could fetch K4 in Apalaka, or up to K10 if they were roasted and transported to Wabag for sale. While the harvest of six nuts from one tree is unusual, and other studies generally give a figure of one or two nuts per tree per year (Rose 1982:164), it is hard to see how the Kewai would be adequately compensated for the permanent loss of pandanus trees by the one-off payment of K12 for a mature tree. Such problems may reflect the way that certain crops have acquired market values in addition to their value as subsistence resources, and it is not clear how they might be resolved. It would not be equitable to change the rate paid to the Kewai alone, while a substantial increase in the rate paid for pandanus under all compensation agreements would probably call into question the relative value of some other crops, which might in turn necessitate the renegotiation of all these agreements.

Conclusions

In 1993, the Kaiya LMP area contained a fairly small population living in a relatively isolated situation. They had formerly had access to alluvial gold in the Kaiya River and ample land suitable for gardens. Many of the Kewai have moved from the area (though not permanently) to gain better access to the road at Yuyan and, more recently, the benefits of mine development at Apalaka and Yarik. They had lost income in recent years as a result of the increasing sedimentation of the Kaiya. Our survey evidence suggests the existence of well-established cash consumption patterns, especially relating to the purchase of food, and yet the subsistence sector remained an integral part of the local economy.

The creation of the Anjolek failing waste dump was about to bring huge changes to the Kewai community. There were great expectations that the compensation and relocation package would bring substantial benefits to all, and some people were bound to be disillusioned at the eventual distribution of the benefits, while a minimum of 80 hectares of land would be lost, including 15 per cent of the current gardening area.

The evidence from other parts of the Porgera Valley, as discussed in previous chapters of this volume, shows that the benefits do not necessarily mean a positive long-term change for the communities which receive them. In particular, cash compensation had mostly been consumed or poorly invested, and there were relatively few individuals who were in a secure financial position or who had secured long-term benefits from such income. These problems were not a function of the compensation packages themselves, which were seen to be adequate by those who received them, and which appeared quite generous to an outsider like myself. But once payments had been made or benefits distributed, there was little follow-up action by company or (more significantly) government officers to assist and advise the recipients on such matters as the best way to invest their money or maintain their houses.

In the Kewai case, the limited flow of information from the mining company to the local community was reflected in the abundance of false rumours. Several people told us, for example, that they were expecting a relocation because they had been told that everyone would get a house, and there was widespread ignorance of the terms of the compensation agreement for the alluvial gold resource. These rumours were feeding the expectations of the local people, while senior company personnel placed too much reliance on local representatives to pass on the information derived from formal meetings between them. These lines of communication did not seem to be working too well, either in the Kaiya area or in the rest of the Porgera Valley.

Notes

1 The area of the new LMP which lay south of the Kaiya River (below Mungalep) was specifically excluded from our terms of reference.

2 Descendants of Joe Searson, the first of the long-term miners who arrived in 1948, still live at Kumane Mane.

3 Although we did not collect systematic data on this point, it appeared that much of the current alluvial mining was being carried out on irregular trips to Mount Kare, where the Kewai had some land rights, but we also saw some alluvial miners working (successfully) in the Kaiya area.

4 It is important to note that the income and expenditure survey carried out in late 1992 was directed at individuals, whereas the current survey was included as part of a household survey, so direct comparison is not possible.

5 These questions were of two types. In the case of larger or more expensive goods, a simple 'yes' or 'no' answer was recorded, while in the case of more common items, we asked how many of them each household had. In hindsight, it would probably have been better to ask the second type of question for all the goods.

6 No spending on alcohol was reported in the Kaiya survey, although this was now included as a separate category of expenditure.

7 There were two one-person households with no gardens at all.

7

Business as unusual

Glenn Banks

This chapter presents the results of four weeks fieldwork at Porgera during March 1994, arising in part from a recognition that my earlier account of the cash economy (Chapter 3) had not adequately addressed the role of 'business'. Since 1990, the value of Porgera Joint Venture (PJV) business contracts to local Porgeran businesses had been equivalent to the value of all cash payments made by the company in the form of compensation, wages and royalties. Given its size, political importance and recent history, the business sector in Porgera was a major 'issue' in the local community.

My earlier discussion of this issue left a number of important questions unresolved.

- Were the businesses owned by Porgerans, or did they lease them to, or act as front-men for, larger non-Porgeran business interests?
- Were the 'Porgeran' business owners native to the Porgera Valley or were they 'new' Porgerans?
- How were the businesses run, did they have light or heavy debt burdens, and what was being done with the profits?

The rationale for the present study was to

- provide an independent review for the company, the government and the local community of the results of five years of business development at Porgera associated with the construction and operation of the Porgera gold mine

- provide background material for the review of the Porgera Joint Venture's Business Development Plan; and
- provide a baseline against which the future growth and development of the business sector in Porgera could be monitored.

A variety of methods were employed in this study. A survey of all formal businesses in the valley was carried out in March 1994, locating them on a series of maps, interviewing the owners and establishing a database for future information. Our definition of a 'formal' business entailed the possession of a large asset such as a building, public motor vehicle (PMV) or plant of some kind, thus excluding market traders and sellers of second-hand clothes (see Chapter 2).

In some cases, the owners were not available, in which case the interviews were held with the manager or staff of the business. Information collected included: the type and ownership of the business; its history (including the origin of the initial capital); the value of stock, turnover, cash, credit, profits and investments; the extent and nature of debt; the accounting system used; business or management training levels; employees and wages; problems being faced; the owner's future plans; and the type of assistance required from the government and the mining company.

As with all surveys of this type, the quality of the information collected relies heavily on the honesty and knowledge of the owner concerned. For nearly all the smaller operations, the information relating to turnover, profit, credit and stock levels is the store owner's own estimate, and in some cases these appear unlikely. Usually, these are cases where the owner had little idea of the figures concerned, rather than a deliberate intention to mislead, and this serves to underline the informal way in which these 'formal' business operations were being run. In most cases, we were able to check that the figures for stock were reasonably accurate, simply by looking at the amount of stock on the shelves. Occasionally, lists of customers with outstanding credit were displayed or produced for us to check. The relative number of customers in different stores could be roughly confirmed simply by counting the number who entered during the 20–30 minutes that we were in the store carrying out the interview.

The information collected on each business varied along a continuum, from those where only the basic dimensions of the building and its location were recorded, through those where we were able to collect limited information about its ownership, to those where the entire questionnaire was completed. Some businesses were missed as a result of our reliance on the road system: for example, four small closed trade stores were present in the Kaiya LMP area in late 1993 (see Chapter 6). On the other hand, PMV business owners were virtually impossible to interview because they spent most of the day driving. However, most business operations with fixed assets were located very close to the road.

PJV records of all formal business contracts (excluding labour-only contracts) were analysed and discussed with a range of parties, including landowner representatives. Discussions about business at Porgera were held with a number of people, including PJV staff, Porgera Development Authority staff, business owners and managers, landowner representatives, and Enga Provincial Government staff. Several significant Porgeran businessmen[1] were interviewed in depth, to provide 'profiles' and to gain an insight into the factors behind their relative success. Finally, a return visit to Porgera on unrelated fieldwork in late 1994 allowed the opportunity to update and correct the data in an earlier draft.

Business at Porgera: some issues

In this section, I discuss some general issues which have influenced the development of business at Porgera. These include the philosophy behind business development, the basic constraints of both the Porgeran setting and the mine development, the limitations of Porgeran attitudes to business, and the issue of umbrella companies verses multiple business entities.

The philosophy of business development at resource projects

Local and provincial business development has been an integral part of resource developments in Papua New Guinea for some time. Initially, the mining development agreements placed emphasis on the local (i.e. Papua New Guinea) supply of goods, along with employment, training and localisation issues. Included in the original 1967 *Bougainville Copper Agreement* was a requirement (Clause 9(a)) that, 'so far as is reasonably and economically practical', the company should use supplies, plant, machinery and equipment manufactured or produced in the country. The renegotiated 1974 agreement contained a new clause (Clause 10A) which related to the conduct of the company's business advisory services. These were to be made available on 'as widespread a basis as is reasonably possible to all areas of the Bougainville District'. The second and final section of this clause stated that the company 'shall not be required to spend more on its said business advisory services in any year than the amount so spent by it in the year ending the 31st December 1974'.

The original 1976 Ok Tedi Agreement contained a large section on local business development. In summary, this stated that

- the company was to promote, support, encourage and lend assistance to establishment of local businesses in the area, particularly those enterprises supplying goods and services to the project or the town
- the company was not obliged to lend money to any enterprise
- maximum use was to be made of Papua New Guinean sub-contractors, where the price and quality of the service was comparable to those obtainable from elsewhere
- insofar as it was practical, the company was to give first preference to landowners
- at least one full time, experienced business development staff member was to be employed by the company
- a business development programme was to be prepared, making provision, where practical, for various specified contracting services, for training, and for various types of activities and assistance by the company; and
- the business development programme was to be reviewed annually, with a view to 'securing the maximum benefit to Papua New Guineans and local enterprises from the operations of the Company and the carrying out of the Project'.

A draft of the Standard Mining Development Agreement which was prepared in late 1985 adopted the Ok Tedi requirements in Clause 21, relating to local supplies and business development.

The Mining Development Contract for the Porgera mine development contained one clause (Clause 14) relating to local business development. This clause provided the formal context for the PJV business development programme

14.1 The Joint Venturers, in consultation and co-operation with the State and the Engan Provincial Government, will:
(a) Within nine (9) months of the effective date (12th May 1989), devise a business development programme which will encourage and assist

people from the Enga Province with preference to Porgerans, to establish businesses to supply materials, equipment and services to the Project, provided that the Joint Venturers shall not be obliged to grant or lend money or provide materials to any person or organisation,
(b) Conduct an annual review of progress being made on the implementation of the business development programme and make such variations to it as may be required by changing circumstances, and
(c) Employ full-time staff experienced in setting up and managing business enterprises
> i) To assist Papua New Guineans who wish to or have set up businesses to service the project;
> ii) To assist in the implementation of the business development programme and variations thereof;
> iii) To liaise with the appropriate officials from the State and the Enga Province; and
> iv) To provide advice and assistance in the development and implementation of long-term business enterprises which can continue after the Project is terminated.

Similarly worded clauses were included in the agreements between the national government and the Enga Provincial Government, and between the national government and the Porgera landowners.

Such negotiated guidelines and agreements are generally very broad, but in all cases they reflect a concern from the government that the projects provide a basis for local business development. A report by the International Monetary Fund (IMF) prepared for the Papua New Guinea government in 1993 pointed out that business development programs and favoured status for PNG suppliers amounted to 'implicit taxes' on the operator which effectively lowered the national government's own taxation revenue from the project. The IMF believed that such implicit taxes were better replaced by direct income taxes (Callick 1993:4). O'Faircheallaigh (1985:238) has offered a different perspective, noting that

> It can be argued that a number of LDCs [including PNG] have concentrated too heavily on a revenue-maximising strategy and that the limited 'direct' economic impact of mining is in part due to their consequent failure to exploit other economic opportunities generated by mineral development.

Business development has been included in the agreements, and as an integral part of the overall approach to new resource developments, largely in response to pressure from the local community and the relevant provincial government. These parties have been concerned to see that they are able to derive maximum economic benefits from the mine development, thus excluding others from obtaining a greater share.

Mining companies have had additional motivations for becoming involved in local business development. Clearly, there are economic advantages in having local businesses which are able to supply goods and services to the mining project at competitive rates. In addition, local business development contributes to the maintenance of a social environment conducive to the continuation of the resource project, and to mitigating its social impact. This is an important factor, because it highlights the social and political objectives which underpin business development programs at least as much as their economic objectives.

Basic business parameters at Porgera

There are a number of basic constraints to business development at Porgera—location, the pre-existing economy, the nature of the mine development, educational standards, the social environment, and land availability.

The location of Porgera, 130km west of Mount Hagen at the end of the Enga Highway, places severe economic constraints on business development. Transport costs alone effectively rule out the development of manufacturing industries which are able to compete nationally or even regionally. The proposed Porgera–Tari road would reduce this constraint to some extent, placing Porgera in a more central location in a regional sense, but the timetable for its construction was unclear in 1994 (and is still unclear today). Of course, Porgeran businesses are located close to the mine itself, and this has conferred advantages on those businesses which are able to offer goods and services to the mine. Theoretically, if not practically, Porgeran businesses should be well placed to compete with Engan and other Papua New Guinean companies for contracts from the company.

The physical environment at Porgera places constraints on business development in the area. Firstly, the high altitude, soils and climate of the area severely limit its potential for cash cropping (Pacific Agribusiness 1987[1]:31–6). There is also a serious lack of stable, relatively flat land, a problem underlined by the 1991 landslip at Porgera Station itself. On the positive side, the impressive scenery of the area could potentially be used as a basis for tourism, and there is some possibility for commercial vegetable production, particularly at the lower altitudes.

There was a limited amount of business activity in Porgera prior to the start of mine construction, but the small scale of the existing business sector has continued to act as a constraint on its further development. While a larger business sector might have conferred economies of scale on the whole area, the limited size of the sector has meant that few Porgerans are gaining the necessary skills in business management.

The nature of the mining operation itself places constraints on the types of businesses which are likely to be able to supply goods and services. The operation is a capital-intensive one, reliant on high-technology capital equipment and specialised inputs and maintenance services. Much of the capital equipment and many of the inputs have to be sourced from offshore, or through specialised national firms.[2] The most plausible area for local business is the supply of basic services—such as freighting, transport, supply of food, laundry services (Pacific Agribusiness 1987).

The 'fly-in fly-out' (FIFO) pattern of commuter mining for the non-local component of the project workforce has been a source of considerable concern in the local community. The belief has been that, with these workers and their families living in Porgera, there would be much greater scope for the development of local businesses. Money would 'stop' in Porgera rather than be spent in other parts of Papua New Guinea or offshore. A report by an economic consultant engaged by the Porgera Landowners' Association provides support for this argument, estimating that K12 million has been lost to Porgera each year as a result of the FIFO policy (Kiri Consultants 1993). The construction contracts alone for the additional houses required by a resident workforce would certainly have been a large boost for local contractors. However, I doubt whether the on-going economic advantages to Porgera would have been as large as predicted in that report.[3] In any case, the 'FIFO debate' was not going to be decided on strictly economic grounds. Quality of life, safety, and other social issues have been more important than economic factors in determining where the bulk of the workforce resides.

Educational levels among Porgerans are generally low, and this counts against a locally-owned business sector. Experience from around the world suggests that, even with higher education levels and a business background, around 80 per cent of small businesses will fail in their first year. In the analysis of our own survey results, it was notable that the six largest businesses in Porgera were owned by people who spoke English. But the general lack of education and business experience were not problems which could be quickly overcome. While the low educational levels of Porgerans generally have meant that joint ventures with outside firms and individuals can be an attractive proposition, they have also meant that many Porgerans are vulnerable to sharp operators, many of whom have come to Porgera with attractive sounding deals for local businessmen.

The current social environment at Porgera is not conducive to the development of a large business sector. Clearly, the low population base of the valley (an estimated 12,000 people) places a limit on the size and scope of those businesses which are economically viable. In addition, the high level of personal violence and inter-clan fighting are disincentives to investment in Porgera by both outsiders and Porgerans. The costs of security measures, from fences to security guards, are high, while the risk of damage to plant, violence against staff, and theft of stock all act as disincentives.

Land, or more precisely the lack of relatively stable freehold or leasehold, has also been a major constraint to the development of a business sector in Porgera. The lack of secure access to land has discouraged a number of large outside businesses from locating in Porgera. Locating on customarily owned land adds a further level of complexity to the operation of a business. While Porgerans themselves are more easily able to locate business operations on their own clan land, banks are generally reluctant to lend to businesses without freehold or leasehold title.

Umbrella companies versus multiple entities

Around all major resource projects, the developer faces the issue of whether to establish and support an umbrella landowner company or to utilise multiple entities which reflect tribal or clan differences. One business development consultant has offered several reasons for considering 'a single entity to be the best means of representing the local people's interest in [dealing] with a developer' (Egan 1994:4), including reduced inter-clan jealousy, a focus for the developer's attention, a pooling of financial resources, and a uniting influence. The umbrella stands as a symbol of the local community's involvement in development alongside the mining operation. An umbrella company can also serve as a role model for local business people, ideally illustrating how an effective business operates. It is also possible for an umbrella company to establish a series of small businesses to which it can provide advice and assistance until it is deemed appropriate to sell the business to the manager(s)—in essence acting as a 'business incubator'.

On the other hand, the umbrella company concept has several problems. It means putting all your eggs in one basket, and if it gets into trouble (as has happened at Bougainville, Ok Tedi, Misima and Porgera), this can count against the mining company. Good practical management, suited to Papua New Guinea's social and cultural environment, is required and again the record on this count is not great. A single umbrella company can in some circumstances be seen as a branch of the mining operation, particularly if the mining company offers management services. Finally, the dividends paid by a large company with a broad base of shareholders are not likely to satisfy everyone, and there will be local entrepreneurs who feel they would benefit more from having their own dealings with the mining company.

In summary, there are advantages and disadvantages to each approach, and in theory it should be possible to have a successful blend of both. Under this scenario, the umbrella company picks up the larger contracts, while individuals and business groups pick up smaller ones. This is the approach which has been adopted at Porgera, and although business development has not met everyone's expectations, I do not believe that exclusive reliance on either an umbrella company or individual entities would have provided a better result.

Bisnis is not business

There are important cultural factors which impinge on the development and performance of the business sector at Porgera. These factors revolve around the understanding and expectations of 'business'. In large part, they derive from the pre-existing social and economic system of the Ipili. The prior economic system was based on mounded sweet potato production, which in turn was used for the raising of pigs. The product was partly for subsistence and partly for exchange and distribution, both to kin and to non-kin. These exchanges and distributions ranged from contributions to relatively structured forms of exchange, such as brideprice or death compensation payments, to more personal obligations to distribute food and other resources to immediate kin.

Wealth for a man was created through the production of pigs for the accumulation of wives, which then increased his capacity to produce more pigs for distribution. Prestige and status was in large part linked to distribution, and the extent of the obligations to himself which a man could build up. In this sense, then, the aim was to maximise net outgoings (Gregory 1980:636). Although rhetorical, political and fighting skills were also some of the criteria by which a man was judged, this conflation of the production system and social status—the entanglement of the economic and social spheres—is most significant for this discussion. Distribution of pigs and other goods by a man can be viewed as a form of investment—it created obligations for the recipients to eventually 'return' the investment (Finney 1987:10). But, as Gregory (1980) notes, it was an interest-free form of investment, which kept both parties in a state of 'mutual reciprocal dependence', and the repayment period was flexible.

The economy was based around a limited range of goods, and importantly, the 'leakage' of production out of the system was not great. There was some trade between Ipili and other language groups, particularly the Enga to the east and the Huli to the south, but it is not likely that the extent of resources traded were significant when compared to those used for internal distribution and consumption, and in any case, every outside trade transaction returned some resource to Porgera. There were entrepreneurs in the trading system: Ballard documents Huli traders who acted as middlemen, and through a series of exchanges of different goods in different parts of the valley, eventually obtained up to eight times as much as what they had originally traded (Ballard 1994:141). But this was done with the intention of putting the traded resources obtained back into the exchange and distribution network within Huli territory.

Planning was an integral part of the pre-contact socioeconomic system—from the planning of gardens (an annual cycle) to pig rearing (at least four years), trips for trade and karuka harvesting (probably irregular events), and perhaps most significantly, the planning associated with the ongoing maintenance of networks of exchange, distribution, obligation and reciprocity—both inside and outside Porgera.

There are several obvious conflicts between the pre-contact system and the operation of a business in the cash economy. The conflation of personal and productive systems, and the pressure of obligations to kin, drain resources away from a business. Maintenance of the exchange networks, with their emphasis on the maximising of net outgoings, clearly clashes with the system of modern business which seeks to maximise net incomings, especially as a means to accumulate capital (Pomponio 1992:181).

In addition, businessmen continually find themselves obligated to assist kin in a range of projects (brideprice, school fees, a bag of rice, and so on) in such a way that the owner is relying on repayments under the relatively flexible traditional system, while the business incurs debts in the formal economy. And yet it is often these same kin who contributed in some manner to ensure that the business was able to start in the first place.

It is also far easier for individual Porgeran businessmen to leak resources out of the local economy in a way which attains little or no benefit in either the traditional or modern sphere. Although conspicuous consumption of a Landcruiser, for example, may carry some prestige value within the community, there are no real benefits to an individual's business, in modern or traditional terms, from spending on overseas travel.

Expectations of business by Porgerans are also important. In large part, businesses are seen as a means by which a person can accumulate resources for use in the traditional sphere—such as wives and obligated kin and non-kin (see Finney 1987). Cash, assets and capital accumulation *per se* are not generally seen as ends in themselves, but rather as a tool which can be employed to acquire status within the community, either through distribution or conspicuous consumption, and to further the political aspirations of the businessman.

Individual Porgerans are constrained by, and are able to control, these factors to varying degrees in the running of their businesses. For Porgerans, they are part of the business environment—it is simply not possible to ignore them. The most successful businessmen are those who are able to successfully manage the extent to which these obligations and expectations impinge on the running of their business—a point which Finney (1987:63–4) has made about successful Gorokan businessmen.

The practical implication of all these issues is that, although many Porgerans have received large amounts of cash compensation from the mine development since 1989, this has not been transformed into a sustainable and viable business sector in Porgera. The reason lies in the pressures exerted by kin to distribute and contribute to exchange, and by the fact that leakage out of the system is far more likely with cash than it is with pigs. In light of my previous estimates of the use of compensation payments (Chapter 3), the remainder of this chapter will focus on the estimated 20–25 per cent which has been invested in local business, and will assess how effective this investment has been.

Business development 1984–1994

In this section I trace the development of business in Porgera over a period of ten years. The chronology is patchy, and as such is presented in three parts. In the first, a brief potted history is provided, drawing primarily on records at hand, particularly the Social and Economic Impact Study (SEIS) and notes taken by myself during several visits to Porgera. The second part traces the development of the umbrella Porgeran landowner company, Ipili Porgera Investments Pty Ltd (IPI). The rise and fall and rise of IPI provides an interesting illustration of many of the problems of businesses at Porgera, and particularly those associated with the mine development. The third part presents the result of a survey of all businesses in Porgera in March 1994, which revealed a number of trends symptomatic of the local business sector. Finally, I review the success of the 1990 PJV Business Development Plan and, with the benefit of hindsight, discuss its strengths and weaknesses.

Business at Porgera: a brief history

The following account is drawn largely from four reviews and surveys carried out in 1984, 1987, 1990–91 and 1992–94, respectively, and anecdotal information collected from PJV staff and local businessmen.

The first systematic review of the Porgera business sector is contained in Talyaga's (1984) socioeconomic impact study. He noted that the 1980 census showed 97 households in Porgera District operating trade stores. In 1984, there were 15 trade stores in Alipis alone, though only four of these were operating, and all were 'half empty'. Twelve of these were owned and operated by local families, and the other three by 'other ethnic groups'. All of these trade stores had been built with cash accumulated by the individual owners, most of which had come from the sale of gold. The 1980 census also found that 19 households in Porgera District operated PMV businesses.[4] Again, these were owned and operated by individuals or families, although Talyaga (1984:82) notes that they had been purchased on a clan basis during the 1970s. They often operated at a loss due to 'unfamiliarity with economics of transport and lack of knowledge [of commerce]'. Apart from trade stores and PMVs, a sawmill at Alipis (owned by an outsider and commercially of little value) was the only other business activity recorded. Talyaga (1984) concluded the economic section of his report by stating that people were participating in the cash economy, often being guided by traditional values. There was plenty of cash around but 'people lack the knowledge to utilise it properly' (Talyaga 1984:83).

The SEIS (Pacific Agribusiness 1987) reported the results of a survey by the PJV Business Development section, which counted 143 trade stores, 93 of which were operating. On the other hand, it found that only seven vehicles were now owned by Porgerans. A number of business groups and companies were active in Porgera by this time. Several of these had sold 'shares' to Porgerans, though share certificates were rarely issued. These included

- Ipili Timbers, which operated two mobile sawmills, employing 18 local people. It was owned by a man from Mount Hagen who had married into the Tieni clan. It was an important source of timber for the PJV during mine construction. However, its inability to secure access to a timber resource at reasonable rates was a problem; at one point, leases were issued to two different groups for the same resource. The business ceased operating in 1992.
- Porgera Brothers and Exploration Pty Ltd was a gold-buying operation set up by a Tari man, who had married into the Alapklain clan, in conjunction with a national Member of Parliament. Porgera Enterprises Pty Ltd was set up by the same two men, and had entered into a joint venture with a Singapore-based group to sluice for gold. Equipment (valued at K30,000) had arrived at Porgera, but the company had no mining lease, nor even permission from the local landowners, and the enterprise had folded. The remains of the equipment were still present on the road below Mungalep in 1994.
- Aiyene Mine Explorations Pty Ltd was formed by members of the Waiwa, Tieni and Tuanda clans to act as an umbrella company for the Special Mining Lease (SML) landowners. Its purpose was primarily to win contracts associated with the mine development. Problems were experienced when it was discovered that control of the company effectively rested with outside interests.
- Ipili Amena was a company formed by the Anga and Kewai clans of Yuyan to operate trade stores, mining and transport

services. Porgera Joint Venture (not to be confused with the mining company) was formed as an offshoot of Ipili Amena after an internal argument. In a joint venture with Basu Coffee, a large steel bulk store was built at Porgera Station, but an argument over the ownership of the land on which it was located meant that it was unable to operate.

- Porgera Yutane Business Group was a Mungalep-based private company, the chairman of which was also the chairman of IPI. This group had interests in gold buying, transport and a trade store, and had plans for a bus service, contracts with the PJV or IPI, a picture theatre, and the construction of houses for rent. This business later became part of Kutato Family Trading.
- Mandi Golden Business Group was established to carry out mining, operate a trade store, and establish a piggery.
- Alipis Development Corporation was an unregistered company, established by five Tieni people. At the time, they were operating a successful trade store (for which they had taken out a K1,500 loan) and running a Dyna truck. They had plans to expand into coffee and vegetable buying, the operation of a bakery, and the purchase of a 16-seater bus to travel between Porgera and Laiagam.

A subsequent trade store survey carried out by the PJV Business Development section in 1990–91 found a total of 72 operating stores in the Porgera Valley at that time, excluding the larger wholesale or retail businesses. Figure 7.1 shows the geographical spread of weekly turnover and stock levels measured in this survey. In the accompanying brief report, the author noted constraints on the accuracy of the data that were collected, similar to those I have previously noted for my own survey data. But it is clear that Porgera Station and Suyan were the major centres of retail activity at that time, while the ratio of stock levels to turnover appeared to be high throughout the valley.

Inventory of existing businesses in Porgera

During the fieldwork conducted in March 1994, I undertook a survey of all the existing business operations in the area. This involved driving along the roads, from Tipinini westwards, noting the details of all commercial structures and, in those cases where the owner was present and willing to be interviewed, asking a series of questions relating to the business. The entire Porgera Valley was covered over a

Figure 7.1   PJV trade store survey findings, 1990–91

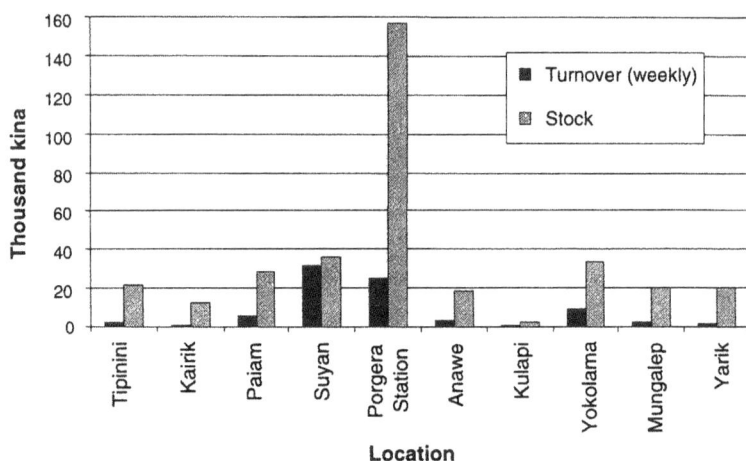

Source: Porgera business survey.

two-week period. For the purposes of analysis, the valley was divided into 11 smaller areas (see Map 7.1). The information on each business was entered into a spreadsheet, its location was noted on a map, and in many cases a photograph was taken to facilitate the construction of a database on formal business activity in the valley.

In total, 382 business premises were noted during the survey. In a number of cases, more than one type of business was recorded for each premises, the most popular combination being that of the trade store and 'kai bar' (fast food outlet), of which there were 11 examples, mostly around Porgera Station. One hundred and nineteen business owners were interviewed, and details of ownership were found for 234 businesses. It is worth reiterating the types of business which, for one reason or another, were not included in the survey. These were

- market and roadside sellers
- PMV and labour-contracting businesses
- businesses at some distance from a road; and
- a number of ephemeral businesses which may have been mapped but whose owners were not interviewed because they were not open at the time of the survey.

Map 7.1   Areas distinguished in Porgera business survey

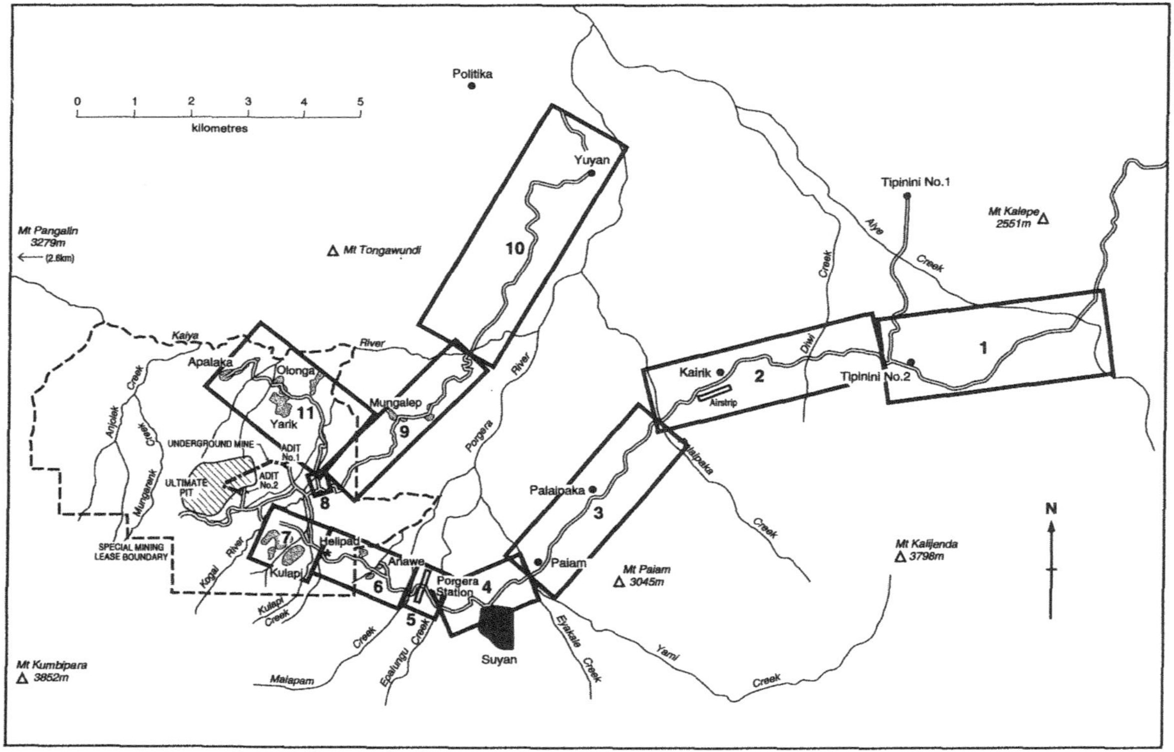

Source: Porgera business survey.

In addition, there were six trade stores whose owners were present but declined to be interviewed. Two large wholesale/retail businesses (the IPI Supa Stoa and Paiam Kumbipara Enterprises) were not included in this particular survey, but relevant data were collected later in separate interviews, and are included in the discussion which follows the presentation of the survey figures.

The following analysis is divided into three parts. In the first, significant findings from the aggregate figures are discussed. In the second, the businesses are divided geographically, because there are interesting and important differences in the figures for each area. Finally, the sample is divided into several different categories of business enterprise, which is another useful way in which to analyse the current business sector in Porgera.

The following figures emerge from the aggregate data.

- There were 284 trade stores (120 of which were open); 36 local bakeries; 28 fuel stations; 8 tyre repair shops; 5 chicken projects; 3 gold buyers; and 2 sawmills.

- A total initial investment of K372,000, or an average of K3,680 per business, was recorded for a total of 101 businesses.

- General savings were the most common source of seed capital, accounting for 38 per cent of businesses. This was followed by wages and alluvial gold earnings (22 per cent each), PJV compensation (16 per cent), sale of cash crops (10 per cent), *wantoks* (6 per cent), and a bank loan (5 per cent). Although general savings were the most common source of capital for both Porgerans and non-Porgerans, Porgerans were more likely to have used PJV compensation and alluvial gold earnings, while non-Porgerans relied more on wages.

- Cash holdings of K57,000 (an average of K550 per business) was recorded for a total of 103 businesses. Bank balances of K312,000 (an average of K9,450 per business) was recorded for the 33 businesses which had a separate passbook.

- The stock levels of 211 businesses were recorded, but 91 of these were businesses which were closed and we were informed that they had no stock. For those which were open, the total stock was valued at K167,000, or an average of K1,390 per business.

- For the 116 businesses which gave credit, the total credit outstanding was K144,000, or an average of K1,240 per business. Only 15 businesses (or 11 per cent of those interviewed) gave no credit.

- Eight businesses had debts totalling K55,200 (an average of K6,900 each), while 103 businesses had no debts.
- There was a total weekly turnover of K73,000 for 115 businesses interviewed, or an average of K635 per business. There were an estimated 4,000 customers daily, while the businesses had 61 paid staff and 117 unpaid staff.
- Sixty-four of the businesses had electricity, of which 35 used small generators. Porgeran owners accounted for 66 per cent of those with electricity. Forty-four businesses had vehicles, and 45 had freezers.
- Sixteen out of 119 owners interviewed had some business training, while 89 wanted to attend courses on how to run a business. Nine of the businesses had current tax compliance certificates.

The geographical pattern of business activity shows some striking differences between areas. The turnover, stock and credit levels by area are shown in Figure 7.2. The figures for Paiam Kumbipara and the IPI Supa Stoa have been added to those found in the main survey, and underline the fact that the commercial heart of Porgera is the Station area. Indeed, it seems to have become even more dominant than it was in 1990–91, though this situation was likely to change with the development of the Paiam township.

There was also a significant difference between the areas along the main road leading up to the SML (from Tipinini through to Anawe) and those within or through the SML (Kulapi to Yuyan and Apalaka). This point is highlighted in Table 7.1, which divides the survey data between these two geographical areas. Clearly, the first of these areas has a more professional business sector, with more trained managers, more paid employees, higher weekly turnover and, most strikingly, a far higher level of business bank savings. This appears to equate with a significantly lower percentage of Porgeran business owners, implying that 'outsiders' with business experience are taking a significant share of the Porgeran business sector. It is notable that Yokolama, the one location within the SML which has a low percentage of Porgeran owners (46 per cent), is also the location within the SML which has the highest turnover and highest credit levels. It is likely that turnover would have been increasing for short

Figure 7.2   Business turnover by area, 1994

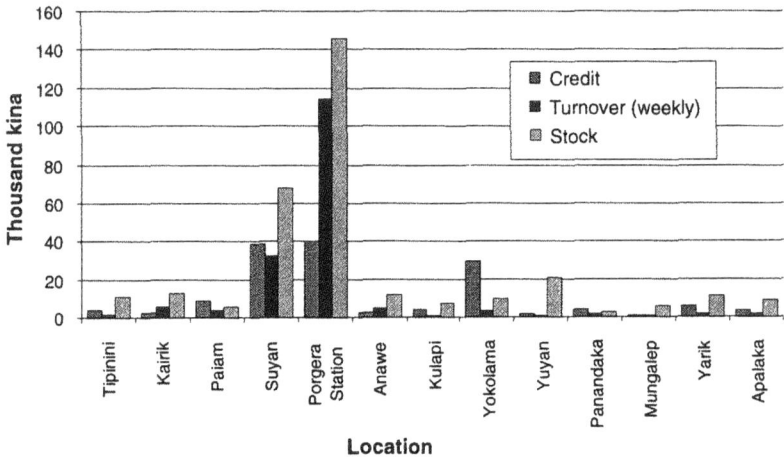

Source: Porgera business survey.

Table 7.1   Summary of differences in business activity by area, 1994

	Up to the SML	In or through the SML
Number of businesses	209	173
Number interviewed	69	50
Percentage Porgeran owned	60	88
Initial capital investment	K256,004 (average 4,196)	K115,859 (average 2,896)
Weekly turnover	K62,500 (average 961)	K10,710 (average 214)
Cash holdings	K43,332 (average 774)	K13,417 (average 285)
Money in bank	K307,598 (average 11,830)	K4,000 (average 571)
Customers	2,849 (average 43)	1,006 (average 22)
Trained managers	15	1
Paid employees	58	3
Unpaid employees	80	37

Source: Porgera business survey.

periods within the SML, as royalties and compensation were paid out, though many SML residents tended to shop in Porgera Station anyway.

We make a number of observations about the more specific spatial pattern of business activity.

- Tipinini had 26 businesses, with less than 1 per cent of the total turnover in the valley, but over a third of the cash holdings, thanks to one temporarily cash-rich business.
- Kairik had 40 businesses with 8 per cent of the total valley turnover.
- Paiam had 30 businesses, but only 44 per cent of the 18 for which ownership could be determined belonged to Porgerans. Weekly turnover was K4,040, or 6 per cent of the total for the valley. Five of the owners had management training, the highest of any area.
- Suyan had 47 businesses, and the highest weekly turnover in the valley (44 per cent of the total), as well as the highest number of customers. Half of the 20 businesses for which ownership could be determined were owned by non-Porgerans. But it should be noted that the Ela Motors outlet is included in these figures, and this accounted for the bulk of Suyan's weekly turnover.
- Porgera Station had 40 businesses, with the highest initial investment, the highest credit levels, largest bank balances, and highest stock levels. Weekly turnover was second only to Suyan, and accounted for 19 per cent of the total valley turnover.[5] Over half the total debt recorded in the survey, half of the kai bars, the greatest number of stores with electricity, and 45 per cent of the paid staff, were located in Porgera Station. Sixty per cent of the businesses were Porgeran owned, where ownership could be identified.
- Anawe had 26 businesses, with 86 per cent being Porgeran owned. These stores accounted for 7 per cent of the weekly turnover of the Porgera Valley.
- Kulapi also had 26, and all of the 21 for which ownership could be determined were Porgeran owned. Turnover was low, accounting for just 2 per cent of the survey total.

- Yokolama had 17 businesses in a very small area below the Yoko One camp. Only 46 per cent of the 13 businesses for which ownership could be determined were owned by Porgerans. Weekly turnover from the survey was 4 per cent of the survey total. Levels of credit were particularly high in Yokolama.
- Yuyan had 26 businesses, spread along a 5-kilometre stretch of road from the bridge over the Kaiya River to just short of Politika. Ninety-five per cent of the 21 for which ownership could be determined were Porgeran owned. Weekly turnover accounted for just 1 per cent of the survey total. Stock levels were very high, reflecting the historical importance of Yuyan as a trading centre which has declined with the growth of the Porgera mine. None of the businesses had positive bank balances.
- Panandaka had 18 businesses, which accounted for 3 per cent of the total weekly turnover. The value of stock was the lowest of any area, none of the businesses had positive bank balances, and 86 per cent of the 14 for which ownership could be determined were Porgeran owned.
- Mungalep had 32 businesses, including some on the stretch of road leading down to the Kaiya River. Ninety-five per cent of the 21 for which we were able to determine ownership were Porgeran owned, and turnover accounted for just 1 per cent of the valley total, although we were told that several more stores were generally open than was the case on the day of our visit. Credit levels were the lowest found for any area. Again, none of the owners interviewed had any money in a business bank account.[6]
- Yarik (including Timorope) had 29 businesses. Eighty-one per cent of the 27 where ownership could be established were Porgeran owned. Turnover accounted for 2 per cent of the valley total, and none of the owners interviewed had any money in a business bank account. Fewer customers were reported in Yarik than in any other area.
- Apalaka had 25 businesses, with a weekly turnover of just 2 per cent of the survey total. Of the 20 businesses for which I was able to establish ownership, 95 per cent were Porgeran owned.

A number of relatively distinct types of business operations could be discerned from the survey results, and I will divide the sample into four main categories. Clearly, not all businesses fit exactly into one or other of these categories, but they are useful as tools to discuss some of the main issues raised.

The first category, which contains at least a third of the survey sample, is made up of small-scale unsuccessful experiments in business, which are normally trade stores with corrugated iron rooves, corrugated iron walls, and wooden or dirt floors, measuring about 4 by 3 metres. One typical example was a store opened in 1989, after the owner received a K1,500 compensation payout in connection with the upgrading of the highway to Porgera. He purchased K300 worth of stock from the IPI Supa Stoa, but after this was sold it was not replaced. Income and profit from the store was used for personal consumption. The store closed in mid 1990 and had not been reopened by 1994.

The second category consisted of small-scale ephemeral businesses. These were either 'failed experiments' in the making, or part-time stores with more social than economic value. One such store was established in 1992 with a K3,000 compensation payment which the owner received from the PJV. The roof and walls were of corrugated iron, and the dirt floor measured 6 by 5 metres. The store had K1,200 worth of stock and K100 of credit outstanding. Stock was purchased from Mount Hagen on an irregular basis. Turnover was of the order of K20 per day, with around 20 customers spending an average of K1 each. The owner stated that the store was his 'garden', and emphasised that it was not run on a strict business footing.

The third category consisted of medium-sized retail businesses, run on a more formal basis. The owner of one such business had come from Wabag and was leasing a 180 square metre building, with corrugated iron roof and walls and a concrete floor, from a local Porgeran for K1,600 a week. The business had electricity, a freezer, and a hot food servery. The owner began operating in late 1993 with K600 worth of stock. At the time of our survey, the business had K8,000 worth of stock, cash of K200, and credit outstanding of K700, despite the deposit scheme which the owner was trying to enforce. Seven staff were then being employed.

The fourth category comprised the largest and most serious business operations. One such wholesale and retail business occupied a building measuring over 250 square metres in area, with corrugated iron walls and roof, and a concrete slab floor. It was established in 1988 with K4,000, largely from money earned on the Mount Kare goldfield. The business had a pool table and dartboard, generator, a vehicle, a freezer and a hot food servery. The business had about K10,000 in cash, credit outstanding of K1,500 and stock valued at K8,000. Turnover was around K300 per day, with about 100 customers spending an average of K3 each. The business employed four paid staff and two unpaid family members, with a wage bill of around K100 per week. It was owned by a Porgeran with no formal management training.

From the survey data, I estimate that the approximate breakdown of the 382 businesses would be: 67 per cent in the first category (failed experiments); 18 per cent in the second (ephemeral businesses); 12 per cent in the third (medium-sized retail); and 3 per cent in the fourth (wholesale and retail).

The Ipili Porgera Investments story

IPI was incorporated as a company on 25 August 1983, at the initiative of several prominent landowners and the management of PJV. Commercial operations began in 1984, with a security contract from the mining company and a movie theatre in Alipis. Shares were promoted among the local landowners, and by 1985, around 5,000 shares, valued at K1 each, had been issued and paid for. A limit of 500 shares for any one individual was written into the Memorandum of Association. At this stage, the PJV provided direct management, while four Porgerans sat on the board as trustee directors.

The rise of and fall of IPI is shown in Figure 7.3. The graph shows a rapid but controlled rate of growth from 1984 to 1989. Shareholding, assets and turnover increased, and the company diversified into new areas, such as wholesale, retail, hospitality and construction, primarily by means of joint ventures. Joint venture partners were generally well-established companies with proven track records, such as Sullivans, Pangia and Poons. During this time, the PJV controlled IPI's strategic policy and ran the business on a day to day basis. Dividends were paid over this period (see Table 7.2), the net worth of the company increased rapidly, shareholders were happy, and the company appeared well-placed to pick up a large number of the contracts associated with the construction and operation of the mine. The SEIS noted that, as of 14 April 1987, there were 2,687 shareholders, of whom 2,014 were males and 673 female (Pacific Agribusiness 1987).

April 1989 was a turning point for the company for a number of significant reasons. Firstly, the PJV stood aside from the management of IPI, though it retained an advisory role to the board. This decision was made primarily because of the perceived conflict of interest between being the principal source of contracts and being the manager of the largest local contractor. IPI's independent accountant and adviser, who had been with the company since 1983, became the general manager. In 1990, he instituted a new policy direction and style of management, with three stated objectives

* to increase the wealth of the shareholders
* to be self-sufficient in management in order for IPI to establish and control its own businesses; and
* to provide employment for Porgerans and technical and management training for local businessmen.

One of the manifestations of this policy was the disassembling of the existing joint ventures. Another was a revaluation of the company's assets which allowed for a substantial loan to be obtained from the Papua New Guinea Banking Corporation (PNGBC).

This major shift in management policy coincided with the letting of the major construction contracts for mine development and associated infrastructure, such as Suyan township and Kairik airstrip. IPI picked up many of these contracts, but deficiencies in its management structure, cost control, and supervision of sub-contractors meant that

Figure 7.3   IPI asset and liability levels, and shareholders funds, 1984–93

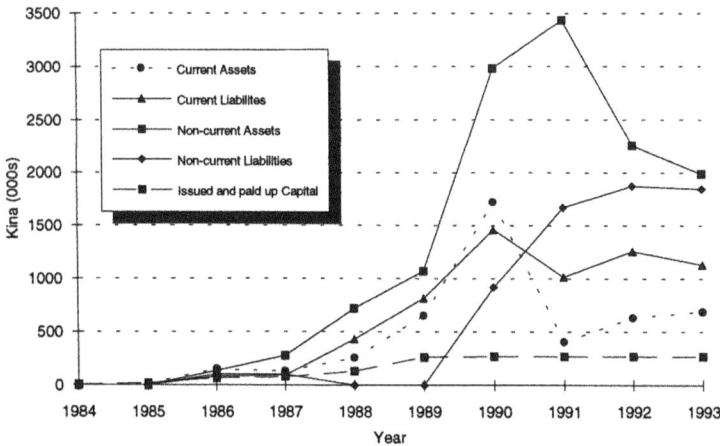

Source: IPI records.

the company accumulated trading losses of around K1,500,000 during 1991 and 1992. The newly formed Ipili Porgera Construction was the major source of these losses. The extent of the problem was not clear at the time, due partly to the rapid increase in the size of the business, and partly to the fact that the company operated without a full set of accounts during that two-year period. The full extent of the problem only became obvious in early 1993, when an audit of the books was carried out, and a set of 1991 accounts was prepared. To make matters worse, the landslip at Porgera Station caused a substantial writing down of the value of IPI's equity, effectively stripping K1 million from the balance sheet. A further K250,000 had already been expended on drawings and initial works for a commercial centre at the station, and this was added to the losses.

These three factors—the push for 'self-sufficiency in management', the rapid expansion in the size of the business, and the landslip at Porgera Station—placed IPI in a situation where it was unable to continue trading without the support of the bank, its principal creditor. In a tripartite agreement between the board of IPI, the PNGBC and Placer Niugini, signed in December 1993, a plan was devised whereby a wholly-owned subsidiary of the PJV, known as Yelgun, would be appointed as manager in an effort to reconstruct the company.

By mid 1994, IPI was reduced to a core of profitable businesses: the Supa Stoa, the Mountain Lodge hotel, a newly established fuel station, a collection of rental properties, a security service, and a 30 per cent share in IPI-Poons joint venture which held the PJV's catering contract. The medium-term plan was to try and reduce the debt burden inherited from IPI Construction, whose interest payments were barely covered by the current trading profit. There was some hope (though no great expectation) of debt relief granted by the national or

Table 7.2   IPI shareholding and dividends paid, 1986–90

Year	Issued and paid up shares	Dividend paid (kina)
1986	17,740	34,042
1987	75,691	-
1988	76,858	66,928
1989	130,685	31,484
1990	268,000	-

Note: In 1989, shareholders were given a bonus 2-for-1 share offer, hence the increase in the volume of shares in 1990.
Source: IPI records.

provincial governments, or by the PNGBC, which was partly based on the argument that IPI was the only landowner company in PNG which had not previously received government assistance.

By November 1994, the situation had improved markedly. An interest rate reduction was granted by the PNGBC on the outstanding debt, and all arms of the company were trading well. The collapse of the Umi bridge near Lae had badly affected supply (and thus trade) for a month but, despite this setback, it was anticipated that the company would achieve a profit of K300,000 for 1994—the first year-end profit since 1988. Working capital was now a positive factor in the balance sheet, and this had allowed for expansion into new, generally small enterprises, such as body hire, asset recovery, and glove cleaning.

To understand the significance of this story, it is necessary to consider what IPI meant to the local community, and also what it meant to the PJV. The financial failings of IPI were brought up at a Community Issues Committee (CIC) meeting between Porgera landowner representatives and PJV Community Relations and Business Development staff in early 1993. The minutes of the meeting record that the landowner representatives were 'shamed' by the failure of IPI. They saw the role of IPI as that of picking up the big 'spin-off' contracts from the mine development, while other Porgerans got the small contracts. One leading representative said that the landowners saw IPI as an umbrella or mountain under which they could all shelter as Mount Waruwari was gradually removed by the process of mining. It is clear that IPI was seen as a symbol of the contribution of the mine to development in Porgera, which reflected as much on the Porgerans as it did on the PJV. Several landowner representatives were calling for IPI to be wound up and its assets divided up amongst the Porgeran people, yet there appeared to be a certain element of self-interest in this proposal, from those representatives who might hope to gain the distribution of assets. The general feeling, as reflected by comments at the CIC meetings, appeared to be that local people wanted IPI to succeed, and they appreciated the PJV's continued willingness to assist with the management of the company.

The PJV became involved again in the management of IPI for two related reasons: first because of its importance to the Porgerans, and the political pressure which the community thus exerted, and second because the failure of IPI would reflect badly on the PJV at the local, provincial and national level. There was also an element of social insurance involved, since there was a risk that the failure of IPI could be used as a weapon by groups within the community which were generally opposed to the mining company. The PJV's resident mine manager, who was also the managing director of Yelgun, said that IPI was a 'flagship'—a visible sign of the PJV's involvement in the community and its contribution to the development of Porgera. On the other hand, he did not envisage a long-term role for Yelgun in the management of IPI, and if the directors lost their battle to keep the company alive, the short-term political fall-out might have to be accepted as part of the least expensive long-term option.

Porgera Joint Venture's business development efforts

I have already pointed out that the PJV has an obligation to provide business development services in Porgera. A business development plan was first developed in 1987 to provide guidance for the direction of the company's business development efforts. This was updated in 1990, after the signing of the Mining Development Contract, and was approved by the Department of Trade and Industry. This plan was due for a further update and revision in 1994. I shall briefly discuss the 1990 plan before reviewing the directions and efforts of the Business Development office in 1994.

The 1990 Business Development Plan (PJV 1990a) included a discussion of the constraints on business development in Porgera and Enga, similar to that presented earlier in this chapter, and a review of both business development programs in general and the activities of the PJV Business Development section in particular. In the section dealing with the implementation of the plan, the objectives of the PJV Business Development section were described as follows

> [t]o assist the peoples of Papua New Guinea, but particularly the peoples of Enga Province, to improve their economic infrastructure, particularly close to the mine, to a point where they can have a meaningful and profitable input to the mine. The economic development will be of a nature that will facilitate a smooth transition for the social changes accelerated by the mine development. The infrastructure should be large enough to create an internal life of its own and not be 100% dependant on the mine market. The infrastructure will be based on commercial enterprise, not on Government or Mining company subsidies.

One point which needs to be stressed here is that the PJV was concerned to support and assist commercial, sustainable businesses; it was not interested in handouts. In line with this policy, and in contrast with some other resource developers in PNG, the PJV gave neither loan guarantees nor seed capital. There was also an implicit emphasis on assisting Porgerans to succeed in business in Western terms; there were no romantic ideas of adjusting Western business practices to fit the Porgeran environment. Such an 'alternative' plan, if it could be devised, might succeed in the short term, but almost certainly would not lead to a long-term, sustainable business sector at Porgera. This is not to say that the PJV's business development assistance failed to reflect the difficulties of the Porgeran business environment; only that this was secondary to the main concern to establish commercially viable businesses. The strategy adopted to achieve this objective above was to develop a commercial business centre at Porgera Station through which Porgerans and other Engans could be involved in a wide range of commercial activities. The schedule to the Business Development Plan listed 110 opportunities for future business development in a 'function list', detailing the timing and experience required to carry out each function. Of these 110 functions, 12 implied the presence of non-Engan interests as joint venture partners. Approximately one-third of them had been established by 1994. The biggest impediment for most of the rest had been the lack of land for commercial development.

In 1994, the PJV Business Development section had a professional staff of eight—two expatriate managers, three accountants, and three business development officers (two in Porgera and one in Wabag).[7] In the Porgera office, much of their effort was directed at the maintenance of existing contracts, primarily assisting the contractors with administrative and accounting functions. The demand for such assistance had grown since the Internal Revenue Commission required that all PJV contractors have a current Tax Compliance Certificate. The Business Development section also had an important reporting function, compiling quarterly reports for the Department of Trade and Industry Goods and Services Committee (DTIGSC) on the PJV's compliance with the various development agreements, as well as attending its quarterly meetings.[8] Another focus was the discovery and negotiation of new contract opportunities arising from the current mining operation. There were a number of projects in the pipeline (both mine-related and non-mine related), including
- the recovery and resale of low-cost mine assets
- various services connected to the development of Paiam

township, including a bank, a pharmacy, a commercial centre, a PJV Community Affairs office building, a motor dealer, and tyre sales; and

- the revitalisation of a viable local sawmill, following the closure of the two which were covered by our own survey.

There was also an initiative to establish 'offshore' investment programs for individual Porgerans, which could be considered as a more sustainable use of compensation funds, even if it meant that capital was lost to the local Porgeran economy in the short term. For it could reasonably be argued that it was more productive and sustainable to have the returns from these investments enter the local economy over time than to have the capital injected immediately into a business which was likely to fail.

The bigger picture

It is clear that the Porgeran business community had a very limited range of activities and options in 1994. This was a characteristic shared with most other rural areas of Papua New Guinea, the main difference being that Porgera had far more money to spend. On the other hand, Porgera is a difficult business environment, even for a well managed business. Apart from the location constraints and the lack of secure land titles, the local economy has also suffered from an uneven level of PJV inputs, most especially in respect of monthly variations in the amount of compensation payments (see Chapter 3). The volatile social environment has increased security costs for businesses, both the cost of insurance and the wages of security guards, while the banks have grown nervous about lending money for businesses in Porgera.

For Porgerans, the social and cultural obligations which follow from possession of a successful business reduce their ability to continue to reinvest funds into the business. In the case of IPI, the demands made by directors on the company (for vehicles and other perks) may not have been the main cause of the company's financial problems, but do serve to illustrate the way in which personal and business interests seem to invariably become confused. Interestingly, only one of the successful Porgeran businessmen we spoke to felt that he had this problem under control. The others all noted this as the biggest problem which their businesses faced, and were well aware of the potential impact of the intrusion of personal matters into the business sphere (see Finney 1987:63–4).

There are ways for businessmen to reduce the pressure to distribute their business earnings. Biersack (1980) has observed that conspicuous wealth and consumption make a person more vulnerable to the requests and expectations of kin, although the sharing of this wealth and consumption is also the means by which prestige has been obtained in the past. Several Porgeran trade store owners had found that they were better off renting out their shops to non-Porgerans and simply collecting the rent, because this was a less visible form of accumulation. A number of Porgerans were investing in other parts of the Highlands, in Port Moresby and even overseas, partly as a means of keeping a distance between their wealth and their kin obligations, partly to reduce the visibility of their capital accumulation, and thus to limit the pressure to distribute these resources, and partly because of the greater investment opportunities which existed outside Porgera.

The other major finding of our own survey was the almost total lack of business training among Porgerans. Although business experience can be a substitute for formal training, it is unlikely to be useful if the businesses continually fail. Training in all the most basic aspects of business management was in high demand in the community, and would undoubtedly have improved the performance of many of the businesses surveyed. On the negative side, the training of businessmen and women would lead to the closure of many of the stores, because the reason why the area has been able to support so many stores is that most have been run unprofitably. The PJV Business Development section involved the Small Business Development Corporation in running business training courses in Porgera. These were initially well attended, but the level of attendance subsequently declined as a result of various problems in the organisation of the courses. Our own survey results suggested that there was still a demand for training courses among local business owners, and a new training programme had been developed in November 1994, which covered basic business and book-keeping skills.

Mining company contracts

The supply of goods and services to the PJV has been arranged through contracts which are issued in accordance with Clause 14 of the Mining Development Contract. The essential features of this clause are repeated in each of the quarterly review reports submitted to the DTIGSC.

[P]reference [will] be given to:
1. Porgerans;
2. Engans;

3. Other Papua New Guineans;
4. International companies,

provided:
1. there is no impact on schedule;
2. the specifications are adhered to; and
3. the cost is competitive.

Contracts at Porgera have been a source of contention, at both the local and provincial levels, largely because of misconceptions about what a 'contract' is. In addition, the PJV has been unnecessarily defensive in its presentation of the contract figures, which therefore merit closer examination. In this section, I shall also consider the types of contract which have been issued, and their real value to the Porgeran business community.

The numbers

The construction and operation of the Porgera mine have been handled by separate entities—Placer Dome Construction and the PJV respectively. As a result, despite the substantial temporal overlap between these two phases of development, contracts have also been divided between these two categories. The third (June–September) quarterly review report to the DTIGSC for 1993 (PJV 1994) provided details on the final figures for the construction phase, because construction officially ended with the completion of Stage IVa in October 1993.

- A total of 322 construction contracts were awarded between 14 February 1989 and the end of October 1993, with a total value of K184,344,863.
- Porgeran contractors (including joint ventures) received 80 contracts (or 25 per cent of the total number) with an actual value of K29.16 million (or 16 per cent of the total value).
- Other Engan contractors (including joint ventures) received 88 contracts (or 27 per cent of the total number) with an actual value of K34.17 million (or 18 per cent of the total value).

The report went on to state that such figures 'demonstrate clearly that the terms of the SML agreement...have been met during the four stages of construction at Porgera'.

The fourth (October–December) quarterly review report for 1993 provided comparable data on the contracts awarded under the heading of 'operations'.

- A total of 721 operations contracts were awarded between 1983 and the end of December 1993, with a total value of K99.8 million.
- Porgeran contractors (including joint ventures) received 353 contracts (or 49 per cent of the total number) with an actual value of K24.4 million (or 24.4 per cent of the total value) of these contracts.
- Other Engan contractors (including joint ventures) received 198 contracts (or 27.4 per cent of the total number) with an actual value of K28.9 million (or 29 per cent of the total value) of these contracts.

The report also noted that recent increases in the value of contracts awarded to Ipili-speakers 'indicates the maintenance of the preference clause'.

Closer examination of the Porgeran contract figures shows why they have been contentious. Of the 80 Porgeran construction contracts

- 31 went to youth or women's groups for 'environmental rehabilitation' (tree planting)—these were all relatively small, labour-only contracts
- 18 were for plant hire, and two were for road maintenance equipment
- 17 were for construction projects, including the PJV Environment and Assay buildings, Paiam school, relocation housing, Suyan township housing, and the like
- 12 were for freight, garbage disposal, and catering services.

Twenty-eight of the contracts, including all the construction contracts, went to IPI, either separately or in association with joint venture partners. Only 14 of the Porgeran contracts were worth more than K500,000 (six for plant hire, three for catering, and five for construction), and ten of these went to IPI.

Rather than examine the full total of 353 operations contracts awarded to Porgerans, it is more manageable to discuss the 57 contracts which were still current in 1994. These contracts were generally representative of the range of operations contracts awarded, except for the fact that they excluded the 'field contracts', which I shall discuss separately. Of these 57 contracts

- 19 were for bus hire
- 14 were for plant hire
- seven were freight contracts
- three were for hire of labour

- three were for security services
- two were for catering services
- two were for garbage collection; and
- there was one contract each for incinerator operation, SML fence construction, market construction, sewage truck, cleaning, vegetable supply, and animal capture and disposal.[9]

These contracts had a total value of just over K18 million, which represented about three-quarters of the value of all the operations contracts awarded to Porgerans to date. But an important qualification needs to be made about the value of these contracts. In all but three cases, they were paid on a 'rates' basis, which meant that the value of the contracts as represented in the quarterly reports was an estimate of what the contractor could usually be expected to earn over the life of the contract. In practice, few Porgeran bus, freight and plant contractors were actually able to realise these amounts for a number of reasons, including an inability to provide reliable service, occasional lack of work, and maintenance problems. The bus hire situation illustrates this perfectly. There were 21 PJV bus hire contracts in 1994, although it was acknowledged by the company that there was only work for 15 buses. The greater number of contracts was required so that, on any one day, at least 15 buses would turn up for work. This was because there had been problems with buses failing to turn up, especially during holiday periods when the owners were apparently liable to use them for personal business.

As a result, there was a substantial difference between the expected value of the contracts and the actual amount paid to date. The fourth quarterly report, for example, showed that, while the total value of the contracts awarded to Porgerans was K24.4 million, the amount actually paid to Porgeran contractors to date was only K15 million. The actual value of contracts paid was only being adjusted at the end of those contracts.

A further point raised by the landowners was that the full value of any contract awarded to a joint venture between a Porgeran and a non-Porgeran entity was being counted as the value of a 'Porgeran' contract. For example, the full value of the IPI-Poons catering contract was included in the Porgeran category, despite the fact that IPI only held a 30 per cent interest in the joint venture. Of course, the proportion of the total value of the contract which actually remained in Porgera might well have been greater than the equity share of the Porgeran partner in the joint venture, once the value of local wages and other local purchases was taken into account, but the PJV was preparing to acknowledge the point at issue by amending its method of calculating Porgeran contract values.

Given the local cultural constraints on business development and the high-technology inputs required by the mining company, the contract figures reflect well enough on the PJV's efforts. With a few exceptions, Porgerans were given all the contracts which they were qualified to carry out. Porgeran representatives have sometimes argued that Porgerans should be given contracts even if they are not qualified to carry them out, as they will pick up the necessary skills as they go along or else subcontract the work to someone else, but this is simply not feasible when one considers the often highly skilled nature of the mining operation and the tight schedules which require that contracts be completed quickly.

What is a contract?

The 'contract' has been seen by many Porgerans as the key to success in business, but the reality of the Porgeran business environment in 1994 was that a PJV contract had more status value than economic value. There were remarkably few Porgeran contractors who were actually making money from the project. Furthermore, most of the value of many Porgeran contracts was accounted for by goods (for example fuel and plant) purchased from outside Porgera, and there were some contracts to which the Porgeran contractor was contributing very little indeed. I shall now consider a number of specific contract types in order to assess both their projected and actual profitability, and the proportion of the value of 'Porgeran' contracts which actually accrued to Porgerans. Four specific types of contracts are discussed: freight, bus hire, field contracts, and operational contracts. In each case, a typical contract (rather than any actual contract) is considered in light of the figures discussed with me by the contractors themselves and by PJV staff.

A bus contract was typically listed as being worth K60,000 over two years, though this figure underestimates the amount that could be earned, because it represents the average of what was actually being realised by the contractors. Bus contractors were paid at a rate of K30 per hour. Assuming a five-hour day and a six-day week, this would have meant a gross income of K900 per week or K45,000 per year. The bus contracts were put together in such a way that a Porgeran could use his contract as a means of obtaining a bank loan to buy a new PMV, worth around K34,000, and pay off the loan over the two-year life of the contract. Repayments on such loans were about K1,600 a month in 1994. In theory, then, after two years, the bus contractor should own the bus and have made a significant profit which can be reinvested in the business. In practice, none of the bus owners were making profits of this order, and after two years, most of the buses were not in a suitable condition to continue operating on a PJV contract. The main problem was the lack of spending on repairs and maintenance, which in turn led to the owners being unable to provide a consistent and reliable service.

If we look at the budget breakdown (Table 7.3) in terms of final destination of the money being spent, we can safely say that all of the loan repayments and at least 75 per cent of the running costs (fuel, tyres and repairs and maintenance) accrued to non-Porgeran businesses, leaving a maximum of 42 per cent of the contract value to accrue in Porgera. Furthermore, most of the bus drivers were non-Porgerans recruited by the Porgeran contractor, thus reducing the proportion even further. And since the number of bus contracts exceeded the volume of available work, for reasons already mentioned, there would only be an average of 3-4 hours of work for each bus on those days when all the buses showed up for work—barely enough to meet the financial commitments of the owners.[10]

Although I could not construct a budget for a typical freight contract the following information does allow some comments to be made. In 1994, the PJV was paying K165 per tonne for freight from Lae to Porgera. For a typical 24-tonne load, this was equivalent to K3,970 per trip. A semi-trailer should be able to average four loads a month, while a twin-steer truck could complete five, and some of the new trucks were managing more. Average annual income should therefore

Table 7.3   Typical two-year bus contract budget, 1994

Item	Kina
Loan repayments for bus purchase	38,000
Driver's wages	7,000
Fuel	10,000
Tyres and tubes	4,200
Repairs and maintenance	12,000
Profit	20,000
Total	89,200

Source: PJV Business Development records.

have been K190,000 for a semi-trailer and K238,000 for a twin-steer. The PJV provided some assistance with fuel and tyres, and sometimes also had backloads needing transport down to Lae. The contractors could also secure backloads from other sources, and some of the larger, non-Porgeran companies were certainly doing so. The PJV considered that its freight rates had a K10 per tonne 'Porgeran factor' built in to cover the additional expenses involved in working in the Porgeran environment. The company's own estimate was that there should have been a profit of K1,000 per trip for the operators. And yet, like the bus owners, all the Porgeran freight contractors were in trouble, and this could once again be put down to a lack of maintenance and a lack of management. Freight contracts do require greater organisation than bus contracts, and even one missed trip could cost the operator a great deal. Several Porgerans had previously shown that it was possible to make profits from freight contracts, but only one or two had used the profits to consolidate their businesses, and at least one previously successful freight contractor had subsequently folded due to a lack of attention to the maintenance of the business.

The incinerator contract held by a Porgeran business group highlights many of the problems of what I call 'operational contracts' in the Porgeran business environment, and also the means by which these can be overcome. The PJV had constructed the high-temperature incinerator to dispose of the combustible waste generated by the mine. The contract to operate the incinerator was originally awarded to the business group in May 1993. In December 1993, a garnishee order was taken out on the contract earnings by a creditor of one of the two principals. Apparently, the money was owed for personal expenses which were unrelated to the business group. With assistance from the PJV, the group was able to continue operating, and the money was repaid. The principal involved agreed to step aside, and the contract was transferred to the other principal's own business group. In March 1994, Kulapi villagers living in the vicinity of the incinerator complained that this person was feeding his pigs on garden waste which should have been burnt in the incinerator. This claim was vehemently denied by the person involved, who believed that others in Kulapi were jealous of his success.

These two incidents highlight the way in which personal matters come to impinge on all types of businesses in Porgera. Unless the business owner is able to deal with such problems, the contract will be lost, and the business will fail. In the case of this particular contract, the support of the PJV was essential for survival. The business group was paid a guaranteed set rate each week, and employed eight staff, including the principal. Three of these staff were Porgerans, while the rest were from other parts of Enga. The projected cashflows showed that wages accounted for about 60 per cent of the value of the contract, other running costs accounted for about 25 per cent, and the remainder was potentially profit. When interviewed in late March 1994, the principal was finding the contract rather tight financially, but felt that he would be able to reduce costs to give a better return. The ongoing nature of the incinerator contract was typical of several of the operational contracts awarded to Porgerans: the sewage truck and the rubbish contract were two other examples. They allowed a steady source of income which could potentially be used as a source of long-term investment inside or outside Porgera.

Most of the operations contracts issued by 1994 were 'field contracts'. The PJV's contract listing indicated that these were a relatively recent phenomenon, because it showed that more than 180 field contracts had been issued to Porgerans since February 1993, but it seems that they had simply not been captured by the contract reporting system before that time. Field contracts are generally short-term, labour-only contracts which are relatively low value and thus not even regarded as 'business' by some Porgerans. They have been let for revegetation, scrub clearing, relocation garden clearing, relocation house construction and the like. Most have been let to individuals, youth groups or women's groups. Although they were generally valued at less than K2,000, the field contracts had the advantage that virtually all of this value accrued to Porgerans. In this respect, ten K2,000 field contracts are worth as much as a K100,000 contract from which only 20 per cent of the value stays in Porgera. On the other hand, the potential for investment of funds derived from the field contracts has rarely been realised, and this point has commonly been overlooked because the field contract has not had the status of the higher value, capital intensive contracts.

Notes

1 Businesswomen, while not totally absent, were very rare.
2 In the first half of 1994, 47 per cent of the value of PJV Warehouse purchase orders went to national suppliers.
3 The consultant made unrealistic assumptions, such as treating Porgera as a 'closed' economy, and then constructed a model of this economy which contained faulty equations, with input figures which misrepresented the relevant factors.
4 Gibbs (cited in Pacific Agribusiness 1987) had counted 25 'passenger vehicles' owned by the Ipili in 1979.
5 If the IPI Supa Stoa and Paiam Kumbipara operations were included in the figures, the predominance of Porgera Station as the economic heart of the valley would be further underlined. The current IPI Supa Stoa weekly turnover (one-third retail and two-thirds wholesale), for example, was equal to that of all other business combined.
6 By November 1994, business in Mungalep had virtually ceased to exist as a result of a large-scale tribal fight which had destroyed a number of the trade stores surveyed in March. The largest businessman in Mungalep was one of the central protagonists.
7 The Wabag office was intent on revitalising the Enga Vegetable Marketing Depot as a source of supply for the PJV caterers at Porgera, as well as other regional markets, and on providing assistance to reopen the local pyrethrum factory.
8 The government had two business development officers of its own based in Porgera, but their capacity to operate independently of the PJV's Business Development section was limited by their lack of a vehicle.
9 I would query some of these figures. The market construction contract, for example, was awarded to the 'Hiwanda landowners', who are thought to reside in the Southern Highlands Province, while two of the plant hire contracts were no longer current, and there appeared to be duplicate records for security, garbage collection and catering. Removal of these anomalies reduced the number of Porgeran contracts to 51.
10 By November 1994, the devaluation of the PNG kina had changed the financial parameters substantially. A new PMV now cost K57,000, and the cost of fuel, tyres and repairs had also gone up. The PJV had increased its contract rate from K30 to K33 per hour. The profitability of bus contracts also seemed to have improved, because half of the contractors had made enough money to buy new buses since April that year. IPI owned three of the bus contracts, and were managing several others for local Porgeran owners.

Porgera—whence and whither?

Aletta Biersack

Ipili speakers span two valleys—the Porgera Valley, home of the eastern Ipili, and the Paiela Valley, home of the western Ipili (Biersack 1995a). Porgerans and Paielans share a language, a culture, and a common, but also divergent, history. In the past, and still today, marriage, travel, and trade linked Porgera with Paiela to the west, the Tari basin to the south, and Enga-speaking areas to the east of Porgera. Their position today, however, is not merely a regional one. Colonial and post-colonial history, and in particular the gold mining for which Porgerans are justly famous, have exposed them to global markets, multinational corporations, and the state of Papua New Guinea, with its own laws, provincial government system, and international partnerships. The categories that are ubiquitous in this volume—the Special Mining Lease (SML), the SML clans and sub-clans (here called lines), and the SML landowners—signify novel entities and statuses. The SML is itself a fiat of the state of Papua New Guinea. The SML's boundaries were established to facilitate the investments of the Porgera Joint Venture (PJV), an amalgamation of several multinational corporations in partnership with the state of Papua New Guinea. Understanding the tensions and dynamics of gold mining depends upon understanding how the SML lines, and those designated as the SML 'landowners' (*yu anduane*), interact with neighbours at the valley, regional, and provincial levels (cf. Jorgensen 1996; Sagir 1997). Since the SML has arisen from the needs of the PJV and the powers of the State of Papua New Guinea, global capital and the state are fully implicated in any analysis of that interaction.

Today, there is a general 'breakdown of law and order', the refrain of Bonnell's insightful and rich report (Bonnell 1994). Tribal fighting is recurrent and disruptive. Is this escalation in conflict an inevitable trauma of development, a by-product of capitalist penetration and processes of 'modernisation'? Or is it better understood as the complex outcome of the interaction of local and national (or global) orders of determination? Here I shall argue that the task of accounting for this escalation, as well as explaining why the situation is not more explosive than it actually is, requires that we conceptualise Porgera as the subject of plural, cross-cutting, sometimes mutually reinforcing, but also sometimes contradictory orders of determination. The conflict of today should be understood in terms of the way that new, mining-related concepts of entitlement and endowment interact with traditional mores and, more specifically, the way that the SML zone, an artefact of global capital and state jurisdiction, interacts with antecedent social networks, themselves rooted in traditional social organisation. My argument, in a nutshell, is that the interaction is complex. On the one hand, the privileges of a few are bolstered through the codifications of mining, but on the other hand, the openness and inclusiveness of Ipili society is informally preserved. The greater the exclusiveness, the greater the conflict; yet the sharing of wealth and other resources levels economic disparities, promotes harmonious relations, and upholds traditional values and morality.

My discussion begins with the 'whence?' of the title, with a summary of the salient features of the traditional system. It proceeds to the title's 'whither?', exploring the fractures and tensions of the mining era as a by-product of multiple orders of determination operating in conjunction. Using my own research in the Porgera–Paiela region,[1] as well as the abundant information supplied by the reports of the Porgera Social Monitoring Programme, I shall then suggest how the recent codifications which stem from mining interact with anterior arrangements, and how, in effect, the seemingly innocuous institutions of kinship and marriage are politicised and deployed in 'altered contexts' (Gewertz and Errington 1991) to enable SML people to informally negotiate their own agreements with constituencies lying beyond the SML border.

An open society

From line to social field

Anthropologists have often tended to assume that 'societies' are made up of bounded, static groups. We have known, ever since John Barnes's pathbreaking article on 'African models in the New Guinea Highlands' (Barnes 1962) that such an assumption does not square with the facts of life in Papua New Guinea. Even in those PNG societies which have patrilineal or matrilineal 'rules' of descent, actual groups are formed by other criteria and tend to be flexible in their boundaries and composition. Barnes (1967) went on to challenge the application of 'African models' to the Enga, with their supposedly rigid rules of patrilineal descent and group formation. Roy Wagner's equally provocative article of 1974 shockingly asked: 'Are there social groups in the New Guinea Highlands?'

In this context, Ipili society—anomalous yet also brilliant at every turn, and with an unsurpassed fluidity, openness, and ability to respond organisationally to every contingency without loss of integrity—assumes enormous theoretical importance. Worldwide, cognatic descent is a rarity, the Ipili version is conspicuous in both the New Guinea context and the anthropological literature. Recruitment to the line is through female as well as male members, and all line members can be classified as *tene* ('base people') or *wana* ('girls').[2] This contrast does not distinguish the children of a line of male descendants from all the rest, as would happen in a patrilineal regime. Rather, it separates the children of line men from the children of line women. Thus (as I have been told repeatedly by Ipili themselves), the children of male *wana* are *tene*, and the children of female *tene* are *wana*. What is important is the sex of the linking parent, not the sex of a line of descendants. The distinction, in short, is a matter of gender, not of descent.

Since the children of both men and women are line members, any one person is affiliated with multiple lines: with the lines of the mother and with the lines of the father. Porgerans typically list multiple line memberships, some through their mother and some through their father. The model appears to recognise eight line memberships, four matrilines and four patrilines, although actual listings of line affiliations vary in length. Now, if everyone has plural line memberships, the members of any one line are also members of other lines, and lines intersect or overlap in their memberships.

Consequently, and in stark contrast to unilineal systems, there are no discrete, mutually exclusive groups in Ipili society, nor is the line a functional unit in most (if any) social settings. This is where Wagner's shocking question becomes relevant. The groups that form and function precipitate out of a field of actors that cuts across particular line boundaries, and it is upon such fields that analysis must focus.

How, then, do these fields form? The cognatic rule guarantees that all lines will intersect. These points of intersection are thickened through the express preference for concentrating marriages between lines. Typically, A and B lines intermarry not just once but many times, producing members of line A who are also members of line B, and vice versa—in short, a group of people who are As and Bs. If As and Bs intermarry, then many As and Bs will have joint membership in the two lines. Under the circumstances, As and Bs participate in a field of relations in which some As are also Bs (or vice versa), while some As are not also Bs, and some Bs are not also As. Ipili constantly allude to such fields in their own sociological statements. In Ipili idioms: those who are As and Bs are 'in between' (*tombene nga*) A and B; those who are As but not Bs are 'true' As; and those who are Bs but not As are 'true' Bs. A group which precipitates out of such a field would mostly be comprised of A-Bs, with some 'true' As and some 'true' Bs. Ipili action groups have closely related people (A-Bs, for example) at their core, with 'true' members of other lines represented on the margins of the field. Fields such as this function with respect to marriage sponsorship, local group formation, and mobilisation for a variety of collective efforts.

The formation of such fields is the express purpose of marriage. In explaining line exogamy, Ipili state that, if a man from one line marries a woman from another line, then the cognatic rule means that their children will be 'in between' the two groups. The purpose is to extend and consolidate networks, increasing societal cohesion and peace. A person belongs to all of the lines of both his or her parents, and is thus positioned 'in between' parental lines, equally or impartially committed to one and all. Should war break out between any two lines, those who are members of both lines are expected to maintain their neutrality. Smalley (1983:9) pointed out that cognatic descent 'minimises conflict' because '[a] man cannot fight cognates who reside in other lines within the Ipili'. This pacification effect of cognation is also well documented for Ipili speakers living in the Paiela Valley (Biersack 1980, 1990, 1991, 1996).

Lines tend to have more than one line with which they intermarry. Line A would not concentrate its marriages with line B alone, but would 'exchange women' with several lines—with lines C and D, for example. I use the term 'affinal cluster' to designate a line and all the other lines from which it typically draws its spouses—its 'woman suppliers' (*wanda atata pene*) (Biersack 1995b, 1996). The word 'affinal' indicates that it is specifically marriage that is the source of the cluster's cohesion. Line A may have a cluster that includes lines B, C, and D, but line B may have a cluster that includes lines A, D, and E. In this way, affinal clusters interlock. Each line is positioned within an affinal cluster, and these affinal clusters intersect. This network structure is the real integument of Ipili society.

The cluster and the field in which it is embedded are fluid, open, malleable. They can be expanded through the accretion of further woman-supplying lines, and they can be consolidated through a further concentration of marriages between particular lines. The texture and scope of the network depends upon actual marriages. Clusters come into and go out of existence, expand or contract, depending upon specific events and the aggregated decisions that particular actors take in the face of them. Ipili marriage is best understood as an instrument of self-organisation (Biersack 1991) in the face of ecological and political contingencies. Wars, famines, droughts and pestilence have been among those factors that have governed the choice of spouse; and today mining is also important. To understand Ipili society is to understand the suppleness and historicity of its networks, their flexibility and responsiveness to changing circumstances. Marriage is the specific instrument that allows for event-sensitive adaptation without loss of organisational integrity. However people marry, structured fields will form so long as marriages are concentrated to some degree between lines.

Networks, land ownership and travel

Lines own specific blocks of land (*yu*), and these blocks are subdivided among the lines. The members of any one line are 'owners' (*anduane*) of the block of ground belonging to the line, and may exploit the line's estate by gardening and/or residing on it. Any one person, as the member of multiple lines, may garden and/or reside on any and all of the estates belonging to his or her lines. Ideally, a person visits or resides on all of his or her estates, the estates of the father and the estates of the mother, thus activating the various segments of his or her network. Co-residence for longer or shorter periods is required to preserve ties which tend to lapse with any prolonged absence, as do rights in land (Ipara 1994; Pacific Agribusiness 1987:16).[3] Line members who live 'outside', and who do not come to visit and lend their support to line members living 'inside', on the line estate, can become *persona non grata* in the homeland. But access to estates will also depend on contingencies such as the availability of land and whether the local group is recruiting for military purposes, or fattening pigs for a major prestation, and thus wanting to build up its numbers.

Once a person marries, he or she is expected to visit or reside with members of his or her spouse's lines, no less than with members of the lines to which he or she belongs. Spouses should live together, and they should do so on a range of estates, the estates of the wife's lines as well as of the husband's lines. In a pattern that has also been reported for the Huli to the south (Glasse 1968; Allen 1995), Ipili rotate among kinspeople and affines, visiting for longer or shorter periods, or even establishing dual or multiple residences (Biersack 1995b, 1996). This 'coming and going' (*pua ipu pua*) of spouses anticipates the movements of the couple's children once they achieve adulthood. The children will be 'in between' the parents' lines, and owners of all of their parents' estates, and they will be expected to live on these estates, among their matrikin and patrikin. A husband and a wife rotate among each other's estates in order to introduce their children to all their relatives, mapping through their own itineraries the anticipated travels of their own children. Of course, the children will eventually marry and move among their own affines, and not just among their consanguines, widening still further their social and geographical orbit.

Within this general pattern of movement among relatives by birth and marriage, there is some variation by gender. A married woman is expected to live initially among her husband's kin. This does not always happen, nor is it a strict rule. However, the very expectation that a woman would move to her husband's place upon marriage, and not vice versa, makes sons seem more crucial than daughters to residential continuity and gardening succession, at least in the short term. Over the course of the marriage, the couple is expected to live in the wife's as well as the husband's places, and this means that, in the long if not the short run, residential continuity is achieved as much through daughters as through sons. In general, mobility, flexibility, openness, and network breadth are the ideals, and, all other things being equal, daughters and sons-in-law are as crucial to network building and network maintenance as are sons and daughters-in-law. The expectation that a bride will join her husband, and not the other way around, reflects a certain male (rather than agnatic) bias in the culture, which also assures that men and not women are leaders, and that men rather than women dominate the most important arenas of prestige competition (Biersack 1995b). Today, mining is perhaps the most important such arena.

The special status of the spouse

Spouses have a special line status, not as line members but as line affiliates. A member 'takes' the name of the group's ancestor and is reckoned as a descendant or *mandi yene* (literally 'he or she who has been borne') of the ancestor. Since lines are exogamous, the spouses of members are never *mandi yene*. The spouse of an Angalaini line member is 'woman's husband' (*wana akalini*) or 'man's wife' (*akali wetene*) of Angalaini (and all his or her other lines). As such, he or she is considered as an 'owner' of the estate of his or her spouse's line, and is expected to assume certain responsibilities towards his or her affines. Husbands and wives own gardens and pigs together, and they also give and receive pigs as domestic partners. Together they produce wealth, and together they deploy this wealth to support each other's kin.

Together they also reproduce, and it is as parents that their affiliation with each other's lines is ultimately to be explained. By the rule of exogamy, a Porgeran ideally marries a person who belongs to lines other than his or her own lines. And yet, by the cognatic rule, a married person always bears members of his or her spouse's lines. If an A man marries a B woman, his children will belong to lines A and B, the A man becoming the progenitor of members of his wife's B line and the B woman becoming the progenitrix of members of her husband's A line. In recognition of the A man's role in spawning members of B line, he is *wana akalini* of B line and 'owner' of the estate of the particular grouping within the line to which his wife belongs. In recognition of her role as bearer of the next generation of A people, the B woman is *akali wetene* or 'wife of a man' of A line, and 'owner' of the estate of her husband's particular grouping within the line. Smalley, who 'lived and worked' with Porgerans from the early 1960s onward, reported this feature of the Porgera system in his 1983 genealogical study.

It is a fact, that once the full bride price has been paid, a child produced, the incoming member is accepted as having full title and rights to his wife's land and is entitled to compensation. Conversely, a female, who marries in has title to the husband's land and assets through her offspring (Smalley 1983:6).

Hosts and guests (*epo atene*)

The scope for movement is enhanced through the host-guest relationship. In brief, a person can reside and garden anywhere that a 'landowner' grants him or her permission to reside and garden, and regardless of whether that person is a landowner in the area. Landowners—members of the corporate line as well as their spouses—typically grant use privileges to kith and kin. Let us assume, for example, that there are three men: M1, M2, and M3. M1 belongs to lines A and B, is married to a woman who is a member of lines C and D, and lives on the estate of a particular grouping within A line. M2 is a member of line B but not of line A, and he wishes to join M1 on the estate of the grouping within A line. If M1 grants M2 permission to move in, M2 becomes M1's guest or *epo atene*, 'someone who comes to stay'. Now imagine M3. He belongs to line C, or to lines C and D, but not to line A or line B. He, too, wishes to live with M1. If M1 authorises him to do so, M3 will join him on the estate of the grouping within A line to which M1 belongs as M1's affinal guest. Since spouses 'own' the estates the groupings within each other's line, spouses can also serve as hosts. For example, M3 would be as much the guest of M1's wife as of M1; and the same is true of M2, who is the affine of M1's wife.

Epo atene reside where they do at the sufferance of a host, someone who grants them rights of usufruct and sojourn. The hallmark of the class is not, as Banks (1994a:25) suggests, that guests come from outside the Porgera Valley, but that, regardless of where they originate, they are not owners of the estate on which they reside. Morally, a person is bound to host relatives, and this means that a line functions as a magnet, attracting guests from all sectors of the affinal cluster in which the line participates. The rule of exogamy requires that lines draw to themselves spouses ('men's wives' and 'women's husbands') from the outside; and the ability of landowners to extend hospitality to those of their relatives who are not themselves owners of the particular estate, and who are in search of resources and domicile, means that line members host a number of guests—allies, supporters, neighbours, and friends. The mixed composition of any Porgera hamlet—the juxtaposition of line members, their spouses (also 'owners'), and the guests of both of these—is symptomatic of a sort of open-door policy, a policy that rejects line parochialism in favour of inclusivity.

There is one further aspect of hospitality that is important. By definition, a guest does not belong to the descent unit which owns the estate on which he or she resides. Consequently, the guest may marry in, drawing spouses from the landowning line. A guest who marries an 'owner' of the hosting line becomes himself or herself a landowner, and his or her children will be owners as well—hence natives of the land. Line exogamy facilitates the transformation of a guest and non-landowner into a spouse and landowner, and the cognatic rule ensures that the offspring of such unions will be incorporated in perpetuity as members of the corporate and hosting line. Thus are outsiders converted into insiders.

Marriage and regional networks

Marriage, it is said, creates 'roads' or 'bridges' between lines—idioms that reflect the physical movement between the estates of intermarrying lines which are created by marriage. Lines represent districts, and the full inventory of parental and spousal lines maps the geographical reach of a person's network. The scope of a person's network is always established through a marital history: the marriages of his or her great grandparents, grandparents, and parents, as well as his or her own marriage. The 'roads' that such a marital history creates may be quite long, from one end of the Porgera Valley to the other, from the Porgera to the Paiela valleys, and from as far as Lake Kopiago in the west to various groups of Enga speakers in the east. In principle, these networks may extend to Mount Hagen or Port Moresby, or even to Australia and America.

We know, from consultants and researchers writing in the 1980s, that marriage relations were already far-flung. Writing in the early 1980s, Kundapen Talyaga reported that, in a sample of 15 marriages entered into by the future SML landowners, 36 per cent of the spouses were from Porgera, but 25 per cent were from Paiela, 11 per cent were from Wage (an Enga-speaking area), and 6 per cent from Tari (Talyaga 1984:35). In a larger sample of 32 marriages, Talyaga discovered that 28 per cent of the spouses were drawn from Tari and another 33 per cent from Laiagam and Wabag (*ibid*:47). Smalley's sample was much larger. In a survey of nine lines, he noted that there was a heavy concentration of marriages with Engans, but Huli people from the Tari basin were also chosen as spouses (Smalley 1983:2–3). From my own five-week stay in Tipinini, at the eastern edge of the Porgera Valley, in 1993, I came to know the extent of intermarriage between Porgerans living there and the Enga and Huli people to the east, northeast, south and southwest. Similarly, members of the Kewai line living just north of the Kaiya River are said to have 'links with groups to the east (Enga), south (Huli) and the west (Paiela)' (Banks 1994b:8).[4]

While Smalley's and Talyaga's statistics stem from the 1980s, intermarriage with neighbouring ethnic groups was commonplace in earlier periods. An earlier patrol report (Laiagam PR No. 1 of 1960–61) mentions intermarriage with Enga, Huli, and Duna (see also Biersack 1995a:11–12), and even a cursory reading of the Tiyini (a.k.a. Tieni) line genealogy drafted by Father Phil Gibbs in 1981 (and reflecting previous as well as contemporaneous marriages) reveals the extent of intermarriage between Porgera and the southern end of the Paiela Valley. Of the 708 marriages which he recorded, 284 (or about 40 per cent) of the spouses come from the Paiela Valley, whose heartland, as well as its southern end, are well represented in the sample. In addition, a smattering of spouses came from Tari, Lake Kopiago, and the Hewa country, from Tumbiam, Laiagam, Wabag, and Wage (all Enga-speaking areas), and even from Mount Hagen, the Simbu area, and Australia.

Given the plurality of line memberships and affiliations, and the geographical scope of a person's network, the task of distinguishing Porgerans from non-Porgerans becomes difficult, if not specious. If 40 per cent of the spouses of Tiyini line members are Paielans, then a significant number of the landowners of the Tiyini estate are Paielans, and the children of these will be both east and west Ipili—'in between'. During my two-month stay at Porgera Station in 1995–96, I rarely came across anyone who, though residing in the Porgera Valley, did not have at least one, and often many more line affiliations outside it. These cross-cutting ties enlarge the spatial scale of any one person's activities; they render travel across districts, valleys, and regions safer than it would otherwise be; and they are proactively cultivated for these very reasons. By the same token, they render the Porgera Valley utterly porous.

Marriage and the circulation of wealth

Income is ideally shared among all blood kin. Thus, if a person who is a member of lines A, B, and C receives wealth, then he or she should distribute this wealth to the members of all three lines, not just to the members of one or two of them, even if the wealth has been received through his or her membership of only one of them. In other words, to the extent that cognatic descent positions actors interstitially, it institutionalises a circulation of wealth across line boundaries.

Part and parcel of the diplomatic function of marriage is the flow of wealth which it inaugurates between the bride's and the groom's sides along the 'road' which marriage opens up. Married couples co-own gardens and pigs because they are expected to produce the wealth which funds the prestations of their relatives by birth and marriage. Bridewealth instigates a flow of wealth between the two sides, and this is perpetuated in the next generation through the couple's children and their distributions. The express purpose of the union is to produce 'in between' children—children who, by virtue of their network position, will share their wealth with the father's and the mother's side alike, thus uniting them.

Ipili mores endorse sharing among kith and kin. A major award should never be pocketed; it should be distributed. Individuals have multiple line affiliations, some by birth and some by marriage, and it is the full range of affiliations that is honoured in any distribution. Consequently, wealth flows within affinal clusters and across line boundaries; it does not, and should not, stay within line boundaries. To the extent that marriages are geographically far-flung, wealth circulates at the regional and not just the local level, across valley ridges and ethnic divisions. This aspect of Porgeran society—its tendency to set wealth in motion within a wide network of kith and kin—is fundamental to understanding its traditional dynamics, and it is the key to fathoming the tensions and expectations engendered by today's gold mining era. In brief, any situation which privileges some lines over others, and even Porgerans over non-Porgerans, will create valley-wide and regional conflict.

Porgera today: an open-and-shut case

Porgera social organisation creates tremendous flexibility. A person has many options. He or she may live on the estate of a matriline or a patriline, on the estate of a spouse, or as a guest on the land of a foreign line, provided that some relative who is a landowner extends residential privileges. If a conflict develops among neighbours, it is always possible to find a safe haven elsewhere, among other kith and kin. There are many potential hosts to accommodate altered circumstances. During a war, a person can recruit allies or flee from enemies; during famine, more fertile ground can be sought; if an aid post or school has opened up, a person can move nearby it to make use of it. Marriage itself is a tool for adapting to changing circumstances. Through marriage, new 'roads' can be opened up, new niches exploited, and existing networks strategically expanded. In short, Ipili speakers deploy their system as a contingency-sensitive resource. How, then, have Porgerans and others used it in an era of large-scale mining? Is it equally useful to everyone, or is it problematic for some? Reading between the lines of the other chapters in this volume, one can glimpse a pair of conflicting tendencies: towards a continuing openness, through marriage and hospitality, but also towards the imposition of restrictions and exclusions.

The host-guest relationship today: preliminary observations

Today, Porgerans themselves appear to be shifting closer to the mine (Banks 1993:19), and immigrants flood the area. Fritz Robinson, a former PJV community affairs officer, has estimated that about 3,000 outsiders arrived in Porgera between 1989 and 1994 (Robinson 1994b); and Banks has more recently estimated that *epo atene* comprise 'up to 40 per cent of the population of the [Porgera] valley' (Banks 1996:233). Robinson (1994b) fears that this high level of immigration will place Porgera at risk: newcomers are interested in immediate rewards, rather than in the 'gradual growth of the local economy', and if the trend continues, he predicts that there will be a 'gradual demise of the Eastern Ipili as a discrete group'. Bonnell, too, has warned against the potential for 'chain migration', which 'could cause the Ipili culture to be extinguished through marriage' (1994:65).

Robinson's doomsday prediction reflects the kind of negativity towards the newcomers which Porgerans themselves, overwhelmed by the onslaught of immigrants, sometimes express. Nevertheless, Porgerans appear to be complicit in this immigration. As Banks observes, far from passively suffering the incursions of outsiders

> individual Porgerans must to a large degree accept responsibility for the influx of migrants within the valley…Not only have individuals allowed *epo atene* to reside in their areas, but many must have actively recruited people to the SML (1994a:28).

Bonnell also implies that an understanding of the newcomers as 'squatters' is problematic, because the newcomers live in Porgera at the behest of their Porgeran hosts.

A squatter is a person who settles on land without authorisation. As most non-Porgerans residing in Porgera have landowner permission to reside, it is more accurate to say Porgera has an outsider [rather than a squatter] problem (Bonnell 1994:83).

For all the disadvantages of a heavy influx, Porgerans stand to gain much by tolerating rather than stemming the flow of immigrants. Among the newcomers, Engans are the most heavily represented: 34 per cent are from Mulitaka and Laiagam, 33 per cent from elsewhere in Enga Province, and 28 per cent from the Southern Highlands Province (Banks 1994a:27). The same is true of shorter-term 'visitors': 20 per cent are from Mulitaka and Laiagam, 33 per cent are from other parts of Enga, and 40 per cent are from Tari (*ibid.*). Engans are the ethnic majority in Enga Province, and before the expansion of gold mining operations in Porgera in the 1980s, their political and cultural dominance in the province was unchallenged. Yet today, as Bonnell notes, '[m]any angry Engan people complain they have received no benefits from the PJV' (1994:91), and she alludes to the blackmail to which some Engans have resorted in their quest for a piece of the Porgera pie, as when making the road from Mount Hagen to Porgera impassable, especially for PJV vehicles. 'In order for the PJV to secure road access through Enga province, Engans needed to perceive that they were receiving benefits from the PJV' (*ibid.*). Banks himself links the immigration problem to Engan highway blackmail, reporting that '[t]he most frequently raised response to why they can't get rid of the *epo atene* is the fear of security problems further down the Enga Highway if they did eject people' (1994a:28). As any Engan is quick to point out, especially today, when Ipili gold attracts all the attention, Enga Province belongs to Engans, not to Ipili. Allowing, even encouraging, Engans to live in Porgera might placate a group which substantially outnumbers Ipili speakers and is politically dominant.

Immigration also appears to accord the western Ipili (or Paielans) some access to mining-generated revenues. My own guess is that Paielans account for a significant number of the immigrants whom he labels as coming from 'other parts of Enga'. In his report on the Kewai line living just north of the Kaiya River, for example, Banks notes that 'it was evident that a relatively large number of Paielan-born people had moved into the area in the last 5 years' (Banks 1994b:8; see also Bonnell 1994:83). My own observations the Porgera Valley have certainly left me with the impression that there has been a significant influx of Paielans.

Migration gives people greater access to the benefits of mining. For this reason, Porgerans themselves are moving around, relocating closer to the mine. Banks remarks of the Kewai line members that 'individuals and family groups have utilised their links with Tuanda, Tieni and other [SML] lines to gain better access to the material benefits of the mine development' (1994b:10–11). By shifting their place of residence, people who would otherwise be sidelined have greater proximity to the action and access to the benefits of mining. The Kewai line is not an SML line, while SML line members living in the Paiela Valley—indeed, all people living in the Paiela Valley—are not eligible to receive royalties or compensation. However, as a guest living in Porgera, a Paielan or an Engan has a greater chance of being employed by or through the mine, partaking in the distribution of royalties, living in a relocation house, tapping into mining-generated wealth through entrepreneurial activities, and enjoying the infrastructural, educational, and other improvements which are among the spinoff benefits of mining (see Enga Provincial Government 1989) than they would have if they had stayed at home. Hosts cannot easily say no, and it is good diplomacy to say yes, because a guest is a friend and an ally, not an enemy.

Interethnic marriage

Without a doubt, Bonnell's most interesting finding is that, despite decades of missionisation and exposure to a monogamous European culture, and despite extensive monetisation, polygyny is presently on the rise (see Table 4.9). In families which the PJV has relocated, monogamous men had greatly outnumbered polygynous men before the relocation occurred, but after the relocation, polygynous husbands marginally outnumbered monogamous husbands (see Table 4.8). Males converted compensation money into new wives (Bonnell 1994:70).

Interethnic marriage did not begin with gold mining, as suggested by Smalley (1983:2–3), but it has certainly been intensified with mining (Table 4.9). According to Bonnell (1994:7), '64.5% of the wives acquired after relocation (that is after receiving large compensation payments) were non-Porgerans'. By intensifying marriage with their neighbours, Porgerans arguably deploy a traditional device for creating and sustaining amicable relationships between potentially hostile groups. Marriage inaugurates a flow of wealth between the bride's and the groom's side, initially through the bridewealth which the groom pays to the bride's side, and subsequently through the presentations and sharing that characterise affinal relationships. Despite the fact that the royalties from mining belong to the members of SML lines, and despite all the efforts to favour Porgerans over other groups, interethnic marriage allows the dispersion of mining-generated revenues beyond the boundaries of the SML lines, even beyond the Porgera Valley, along the 'roads' which marriage opens up at the regional level. Also, since a person is considered an 'owner' of spousal estates on the grounds that he or she will bear future line members, marriage effectively widens the group of landowners in the gold-mining context. Like immigration, interethnic marriage creates goodwill and 'security' in an environment that would be destabilised if any group or groups had a monopoly of mining proceeds.

There is an obvious connection between immigration and interethnic marriage. All landowners, including spouses, can host guests. Intermarriage facilitates chain migration, as Bonnell notes. The relationship between marriage and immigration can also work in reverse, with immigration facilitating marriage instead of the other way around. Traditionally, as I have already pointed out, guests sometimes married into the host group, becoming 'women's husbands' or 'men's wives', and thus line affiliates, 'owners' of the line estate, and parents of line members. While the previous chapters do not establish this point too clearly, Bonnell does show that the Engans and Southern Highlanders who are heavily represented amongst the immigrants are also heavily represented amongst the new wives of relocated men. Whereas, before relocation, 10.4 per cent of wives were from Laiagam and 5.9 per cent of wives were from Tari, after relocation, the percentage of Laiagam wives jumped to 17.3 per cent and the percentage of Tari wives increased to 29.4 per cent (Table 4.9; see also Smalley 1983:2–4). After relocation, there were also more than four times as many wives from Kandep as before relocation, although the overall percentage was still under 10 per cent (Table 4.9).

The host-guest relationship and marriage have always had strategic uses. In the past, guests facilitated interline marriage, warfare, and production for exchange. Today, it could be argued, the host-guest relationship and interethnic marriage are key devices for positioning Porgera within a developing regional politics which places pressure on Porgerans, and specifically on members of SML lines, to share their mining-based income with those groups located outside the SML area, even among non-Porgerans (see Jorgensen 1997b).

Rule of custom, rule of law

While it is easy to make the case that the porosity of units has been preserved in the mining context—through the use of marriage and hospitality to incorporate outsiders, for example—it is also true that the various codifications of mining have had restrictive effects, and that there is considerable ambivalence among SML landowners about allowing outsiders to access resources.

Consider, for example, the criteria for determining eligibility for a relocation house. To qualify for a relocation house, a guest living in the SML area had to have lived there for at least ten years, and a member of one of the SML lines had to have lived there for more than three (originally five) years (Bonnell 1994:14–15; Robinson 1991).[5] In the case of both the SML and the Kaiya River LMP just north of it, absentee members of landowning lines were passed over entirely. It was entirely predictable that those who were eliminated from consideration—short-term guests and SML line members who did not meet the residency requirements—would challenge these guidelines.

> These apparently simple criteria were not simple in practice. There were a number of different perception [sic] operating. Someone who had been living with relatives in Paiela or Tari, but who had visited the SML (and perhaps stayed a month or two) considered themselves [sic] fully eligible (Robinson 1991).

Contributing to the level of disputation in the Porgera Valley is the fact that codifications as such, because they narrowly specify criteria and are rigid and insensitive to circumstances and mitigating factors, will always be problematic. Operating principles tended traditionally to be plural, ambiguous, conflicting (cf. Ernst in press; Jorgensen 1997a). There were no principles that could not on principle be challenged; and resolutions and settlements were necessarily negotiated through adversarial processes—hence the Ipili penchant for muscle-flexing and disputation. Any effort to codify, particularly for the purpose of exclusion, necessarily founders on that fact: codification as such will always be contested. Hence, the agreements associated with the two relocation programs could only be hammered out over a protracted period, and the conditions for awarding a relocation house were relaxed again and again. The fact that the number of relocation houses has swelled over the years suggests that narrow codifications and interpretations have been challenged by groups who, although disenfranchised by emerging regulations, have successfully pressured both the PJV and the SML landowners to bend the rules in the name of other values and principles (see Bonnell 1994; Robinson 1991).

Codifications have sometimes subtly reinterpreted received categories in ways which have undermined the openness of the system. Among the Ipili, there is parity between *tene* and *wana*, the children of male line members and the children of female line members. Together with the rule of line exogamy, the parity of *tene* and *wana* guarantees the openness of each particular line, for together they mean that every marriage of every member of a line results in the incorporation of people who are also members of other lines. Yet the procedures of the mining era subtly undermine this parity. Those named as 'agents' to distribute royalties are mostly *tene*, rather than *wana*.

> In accordance with custom, some...Wana landowners and persons with affiliated land rights have also been appointed as Agents to participate in the distribution of compensation payments. This is normally done to ensure that the decisions to distribute compensation in relation to who receives compensation and how much, are made collectively. In the event of a disagreement amongst the distribution committee, a decision of the Yuu tenes will usually prevail (Ipara 1994:14–15).

Typically, then, compensation would flow from the PJV to *tene* and thence to *wana*. In 1995, the Department of Mining and Petroleum's Acting Liaison Officer in Porgera, Morep Tero, assured me that, whereas the 'agents' tended to be *tene*, the *wana* and *tene* received equal shares. However, one son of a Tiyini (a.k.a. Tieni) woman complained to me that he was receiving a smaller share of royalties than were the *tene* of his line. He even suggested that the *tene* had removed the names of *wana* from the lists.

There is also a marked ambivalence towards guests among SML residents, for, however diplomatically useful it is to extend hospitality, guests are competitors for resources and allocations. Robinson (1994b) recounts that landowners have expressed a preference for either keeping the mining-related jobs for themselves or else reserving them for Porgerans rather than for outsiders. Also, some Porgeran landowners appear to regret having to share with mere sojourners the compensation paid for houses, gardens and trees which have been destroyed in the course of mining.

> Compensation is for the damage to improvements...which are owned by the occupier, not for the land itself...but the landowners often argue that they are entitled to a share of whatever is given to their guests (Banks 1996:231).

Although some Porgerans may feel that they cannot live without the 'squatters' and immigrants, others may well feel that they cannot live with them.

For its part, the PJV may place subtle pressure on landowners to restrict the number of people who realise mining benefits, on the theory that its own interests are better served by narrowing the circle of beneficiaries. It is obvious from the evidence presented by Banks (Chapter 5), and also from my own conversations with PJV personnel, that some Porgerans have looked to the PJV for support in curbing the encroachments of outsiders. The PJV has shied away from playing an open and official role in monitoring immigration into the valley, but 'indirectly, PJV has offered to provide advice on procedure to landowners who want to evict unwanted *epo atene*' (Banks 1994a:28). In effect, SML landowners and the PJV are thus colluding in their eagerness to place a limit on the distribution of endowments (see Jorgensen 1997b).

Conclusions

The present mining situation creates vast differences in income between SML-landowning lines and other lines, between places within and without the SML, and even among the SML lines. Compare, for example, the income of Apalaka, which lies within the SML, with the income of Mungalep, Anawe and Kewai, all of which lie just beyond the SML, and again with the income of Tipinini at the eastern perimeter of the Porgera Valley (Table 6.1). Compare also the landholdings of Tiyini (a.k.a. Tieni) line with those of Angalaini, Mamai, Waiwa, or Anga (Table 5.4) for an indication of the range of mining-related income among the SML lines themselves. Likewise, the various groupings within these SML lines have differential landholdings, with a corresponding differentiation in their mining-related incomes. But is conflict best understood in terms of class formation and class antagonism pure and simple, as an antagonism between the haves and the have-nots, or is the source of friction more complicated?

The SML is an artefact of multinational investment and national legislation and, as such, represents the exogenous forces of global capitalism and the nation-state. Yet it has been superimposed upon anterior grids, upon the networks of kith and kin which marriage has generated, and these grids also have causal force. The differences in mining-related wealth and income frequently arise among people who are related by blood and marriage, and among whom sharing is mandated by traditional morality (see Filer 1990). In these cases, economic disparities distinguish rich from poor relatives, people who have and who should therefore give from people who do not have and who should therefore receive. The outcome, at least for the many people living in the Porgera Valley and the wider region who are related to SML residents, would be something closer to 'tribal' war than to class war. This 'tribal' war is provoked in an altered context (Gewertz and Errington 1991), the context of mining and state-legislated jurisdictions and rights, and must be attributed to a conjuncture of the local and the national or global.

One could productively ask why the law and order problem is not worse, why the situation is not more explosive than it is. Today, as before, marriage and hospitality are used to build and exercise networks, but the effort is specifically to undercut any polarisation of rich and poor which mining might create. The point is again the same: this peace, like the war it undercuts or forestalls, is explicable in terms of the duality of forces in play; for the peace, like the war, is made among relatives.

In actual fact, the principal beneficiaries of mining evince conflicting responses to the economic opportunities and social and political challenges which mining creates. On the one hand, the porosity which all boundaries traditionally possessed, given certain mechanisms for inclusion, continues because of the strategic deployment of these same mechanisms. On the other hand, there is a novel tendency towards boundary maintenance and exclusion, and a new and insidious parochialism. The previous chapters portray Porgeran society as poised amid competing precedents, temptations and strategies. There is a mixture of orders of determination which are now in play—a matter of culture and political economy, of contradictory principles, codifications and impulses. This conjuncture is unique, volatile, possibly unstable. Consequently, there is no trajectory, no teleology, no master narrative that can orient us adequately in the process, no development theory that might offer guidelines to the various 'stages' of Porgera's unfolding history. What is needed instead is an ethnography of change which captures the disparate discourses, ideologies, and values in play in an ambivalent and uncertain time.

Notes

1   Fieldwork in the Porgera Valley was conducted initially under an award from the Wenner-Gren Foundation for Anthropological Research in 1993, and subsequently, from December 1995 to February 1996, under a Fulbright Research Fellowship. I have also conducted archival research on Porgera in the National Archives of Papua New Guinea; the PNG National Research Institute, and the Department of Political and Social Change in the Research School of Pacific and Asian Studies, Australian National University. My research among the western Ipili of the Paiela Valley was undertaken initially from 1974 to 1978, and was funded by a National Science Foundation Dissertation Grant and the Rackham School of Graduate Studies, University of Michigan, with write-up support from the Wenner-Gren Foundation and the Center for the Continuing Education of Women at the University of Michigan. Further research in the Paiela Valley was conducted in 1993 and 1995, with Wenner-Gren and Fulbright funding.

2   The term *wanaini* (literally 'girl's son') can be used of the sons of female members.

3   See Allen (1995) and Glasse (1968) for Huli parallels.

4   All page references are to the original consultancy reports, rather than the edited versions included as chapters of the present volume, because the wording of some quotations has changed during the editorial process (Ed.).

5   According to Banks (1996:229), the settlement for housing to those who were relocated was as follows. The landowners received a relocation house, built at a site of their own choosing, K1,000 for the inconvenience of relocating, a K1,400 allowance for the making of new gardens, and the covering of subsistence needs for up to nine months while the new gardens matured. Those *epo atene* who did not merit a relocation house were compensated for their loss of gardens, trees, etc., given K500 for the inconvenience, and shipped back home (see also Chapter 4, this volume).

9

Evidence of the 'new competencies'?

John Burton

In this chapter, I review the knowledge of Porgera history and society that mine management has sought to acquire, since proving the prospect in the 1980s, for use in its dealings with the mine area community. In a more general context, the kinds of skills and knowledge required to do this professionally have been advocated as the 'new competencies' of mining (Davis 1995). Conversely, attention to these matters in the industry is acknowledged to have been patchy over the years, and shortcomings have been blamed for the onset of lesser or greater crises, such as those which have occurred at Ok Tedi, Panguna, and other places. Senior industry figures make a direct link between performance in the 'new competencies' and the exposure of their investors' capital to financial risk, and this is certainly the public face of the mining and petroleum industries in Papua New Guinea.

At Porgera, the resources attached to dealings with the mine area community have not been negligible: over 500 families had been relocated and provided with new houses by 1995, about K60 million worth of business contracts had been let to Porgerans, about K30 million had been paid out in compensation for clearance of bush, crops and houses on land required for mining, and sundry lesser benefits had flowed to the community (Banks 1997). At the same time, more staff were deployed by the Porgera Joint Venture (PJV) in

Community Relations and Lands functions, notably with the realisation that law and order problems on the Enga highway would not be dealt with by state agencies, to the point where about 85 people were thus employed across the province—a far greater number than ever used at any other mining or petroleum project in Papua New Guinea (Bonnell 1994:112).

Nonetheless, the scale of the benefits has only a partial connection with the 'new competencies'. Of the 85 staff positions, only a handful were managerial, and perhaps only two or three incumbents held tertiary qualifications, none at higher than degree or diploma level.[1] Much has been made of the hiring, at all sites, of ex-members of the Australian administration—notably those with long field experience— and it is certainly true that, with the demise of the field services since Independence, more recently trained field officers simply are not available to carry out the practical tasks of day-to-day community dealings. But excellence 'in the bush' at the edges of an organisation is not the same thing as the entrenchment of bush intelligence at its heart.

I must acknowledge the limitations of method that face the reviewer of 'new competencies' in the mining industry. For example, should the scope be limited to mine management, or extended to include the collectivity of junior staff, middle managers, consultants, journalists, church representatives, public relations officers, government staff and others who make up most of the knowable interface between the mining operation and the community? Also, as most managements conduct their business behind closed doors—or, more precisely, publicly document only a few of the myriad decisions that are taken each day—what allowable steps of inference can bridge the gaps that will necessarily be left between public pronouncements and private deliberations? I suggest that the best way to overcome this problem is to focus on the outwardly assessable capabilities and actions of the collectivity of people mentioned above. It would be ideal to have a great deal more inside knowledge, but this should not be a handicap in examining evidence of an organisation's outward actions (Table 9.1).

This exercise can have an orthodox 'research and development' model as its point of departure, in which case the logical direction of argument will be vertically down the table. But one might also adopt company self-interest and protection against mine closure—a well-defined, but minimal performance criterion—as the point of

Table 9.1   Assessable capabilities in relation to social issues at PNG mining operations

Capability	Externally assessable actions
Observation and research of social issues	Demonstrated capacity to collect appropriate knowledge
Analysis and reporting	Demonstrated capacity to conduct analysis of social issues, to interpret correctly and highlight points of relevance, and to present these to others through reporting.
Representation to decision makers	Demonstrated capacity to channel information on social issues to decision-making points within the organisation.
Management emphasis	Uptake of this information in the development of clearly articulated management strategies and policies.
Implementation and follow-up	Demonstrated capacity to make use of information on social issues to in an explicit way to defend the project against unnecessary risk.

departure, in which case the argument may proceed in the opposite direction: 'We need information to defend the shareholder's investment against risk: so what kind of information do we need?' My own view, and that of many mining company executives, would be that the minimalism of this second line of argument means sailing too close to the wind; it is simply reckless.

Unfortunately, agreement at the level of corporate rhetoric ('our programs are second to none') is a far cry from actually meeting objectively sound performance standards. What I want to demonstrate in this chapter is that what managements say that they aspire to, and even believe that they achieve, is different from what they are actually able to achieve. I shall call this difference a 'performance evaluation gap'. Several such gaps are possible, and they have knowable and predictable causes. I should add that the purpose of this exercise is not purely academic; gaps of this nature, if they exist in any area of management, expose business enterprises to risk.

Baseline research during the period of exploration

Prior to the development of the mine, the only ethnographic accounts of the Porgera area which were based on anything more than a short visit to the area (for example, Meggitt 1957) were those written by Father Philip Gibbs (1975, 1977), the Catholic priest at Mungalep mission. On the other hand, very detailed ethnographic work had been done in some adjacent areas of the highlands (see Feil 1987; Ballard 1995).

At all recent mining projects in Papua New Guinea, the Social and Economic Impact Study (SEIS) has formed the basis of the company's dealings with the mine area community. In the Porgera case, it is surprising that the SEIS consultancy team did not include an anthropologist (Pacific Agribusiness 1987). For their discussion of the social environment, the authors evidently made some limited inquiries of their own, but also gave a lengthy summary of relevant information from Biersack's (1980) doctoral thesis on the nearby Paiela people, alternatively referred to as the 'west' or 'western' Ipili in the literature (see Biersack 1995a). One member of the SEIS team later noted the availability of other studies of neighbouring peoples, such as Goldman's work on the Huli, but said that 'Biersack had written the only specifically Ipili work that I could find' (Robinson 1991:1). He added that he was unable to understand it, though he encouraged ethnographers to continue their work: 'If the studies are made and the writing is accessible then the studies will be widely used and have an important and beneficial effect on the people' (*ibid*:7).

This is a clear declaration in favour of applied anthropology, and an example of the 'agreement in principle' with the need to make as much use of available sources as possible. In which case, one wonders why the SEIS team did not consult Wohlt's (1978) doctoral thesis, based on his work at Yumbisa village in Kandep District, which is as close to the southeastern part of Porgera as Paiela is to its northwestern part (see Biersack 1995a: Map 2). Wohlt dealt at length with the dispersal, across the western Engan region, of the branches of a genealogical group known as Molopai, and the rights and obligations of individuals at the various places where members of this group had settled. The same highly flexible social structure is found in Yumbisa as in Porgera, and much the same vocabulary is used for its component parts.[2] Wohlt's genealogies show that the Bipe people of

Kairik (Burton 1991:25–6) are Molopai people, while others are found in Tari, Paiela, Kandep and Laiagam. His analysis throws into question whether the Ipili people even 'exist' in the same way as, say, Motuans or Hageners do—as 'tribal' groups subsuming locally bounded subgroups, whether these be territorial clans or the dispersed cognatic structures found in Porgera. They begin to look far more like the local representatives of regionally dispersed 'genealogical groups', lumped together under one name only because they live in one place as neighbours (see also Wohlt 1995).

The ethnographer's first reflex on discovering such regional links must be to uncover as many as possible and map them out. There are frequent references in the SEIS to the land rights which Porgerans hold in various parts of the valley, by pursuing cognatic links of kinship, and to the flexible manner of reckoning relatedness to other people. The authors were correctly concerned with the 'severe vulnerability' of the system once gold production started (Pacific Agribusiness 1987 Appendix B:6), but do not seem to have grasped the regional breadth or generational depth of genealogical reckoning,[3] and could only make limited suggestions as to how to plan for the impact which this might have. Wohlt's work could have helped them in this respect. In the event, the restriction of access to land within the valley has shown itself to be a minor nuisance compared with the problems caused by the mass immigration of genealogically connected people from Laiagam, Kandep and Tari. This was to become the most serious socioeconomic impact on Porgera within a very short span of time, and was to preoccupy Fritz Robinson in his subsequent work on relocation for the PJV (see Robinson 1991:3–4, 1994b).

Why did the SEIS authors not consider Wohlt's work? Does this count as a 'failure', and was their understanding of Ipili society compromised as a result? What lessons can be drawn for the management of social impact at all mining projects?

First, the quotation above suggests that, if anthropologists only write well, then the results will be 'widely used' by the mining company. Obviously this is not true; Wohlt writes luminously well, but his work was not used.[4] I suggest that the reason only partly lies with the mix of specialisations among the members of the SEIS team and their lack of immersion in highlands ethnography. Their greatest enemy was shortage of time.[5] A single field period of six weeks in April–May 1987, which included the certain distraction of frequent meetings with company and government officials, seems to have been all that was available to the main study team. It is vanishingly unlikely that serious analytical knowledge of the social system could have been obtained under these conditions.

Second, I believe that their neglect of Wohlt's work did count as a failure, and the portrayal of Ipili society did fall short of providing useful insights into Porgeran society. I will not dwell on which detail is correct and which is incorrect, but rather refer to the nature of ethnographic understanding itself. Anthropologists make frequent references to entering the field with an over-simplistic or inappropriate knowledge of the people they are going to study. This leads to periods of intense but unstructured data collection, at which point confusion reigns, the society appears chaotic and patternless, and its members inconsistent and even illogical. Kenneth Read (1965:32), already an experienced field ethnographer, wrote of post-war Goroka that 'for weeks after my arrival I knew the valley only as a visitor knows a strange city'. Peter Lawrence had the same problem among the Garia of Madang Province: he probably unravelled their cognatic kinship system (which bears close comparison with that of the Ipili) during his doctoral fieldwork in 1949–50, but his full account of it (Lawrence 1967, 1984) was delayed for years because his colleagues were not equipped at that time to make sense of the extreme flexibility of Garia social arrangements. If a person of Lawrence's analytical skills required many subsequent visits to the Garia to 'nail' their social system to the satisfaction of his readership, it is very unlikely that a social impact study team, without an anthropologist, would properly characterise Ipili society in a matter of weeks.

To be frank, the SEIS authors should have owned up to this, but instead presented 'data' of a quality that is embarrassing to mention, such as a land tenure survey based on a questionnaire administered to Grade 6 schoolchildren (Pacific Agribusiness 1987 Appendix B:9). When, in the report's findings, it is claimed that 'Ipili society and land tenure were studied in detail' (Pacific Agribusiness 1987:95), the writer or writers are having us on.

Third, important lessons can be drawn from this. At Lihir, Filer and Jackson (1989:43) mused over the inability of managements to judge the competence of consultancy work, and the 'insight [this] gives into the way that an image of traditional social structure is...established [at] a major mining development'. I can confirm that a particular image of the project area became fixed at a very early stage of exploration at many other mining operations in Papua New Guinea (see Burton 1997). The basis of an early impression is serendipitous. Apart from anything else, contacts between company and community during early exploration are likely to be particularly haphazard and unrepresentative of later, more permanent dealings. But a constant bugbear is the hiring of inexperienced consultants in the early stages of exploration, typically followed by the use of a one-stop-shop general consultancy firm which employs well-qualified specialists who are then enjoined to cover fields other than their own. This is harmless enough if, to take a hypothetical case, all urban geographers may be expected to grasp the key issues in major specialisms of this discipline. But asking a neophyte to stray into the ethnography of a previously unresearched society is a reckless practice. The key issues, the fieldcraft, and the complex nature of relationships with informants— to name but a few things—do not come packaged as off-the-shelf knowledge. Let me demonstrate this point with another Porgera example.

The SEIS was preceded by the collection of genealogies among some Special Mining Lease groups by Father Gibbs (1981, n.d.) and by two former PJV employees, whom I shall call A and B, in 1982 and 1984 respectively. Gibbs had basic training in anthropology (1975), had spent many years at Porgera, and had a relationship of a special nature with his congregation: in other words, he had the prerequisites for proper ethnography which I have just mentioned. Having gone over his genealogies myself, I can vouch for the fact that his work was of excellent quality and was highly reliable. But I also had to dissect the shortcomings of A's and B's genealogies when I began work at Porgera in 1990 (Burton 1991:2–3). It is sufficient to say that A counted so many people twice (without noticing) that he made a probable total of 6,000 people into more than 11,000. B, for his part, knew of Gibbs' work, but said it was unnecessary for him to read it. Even worse, his 'agnatic' bias, originating from a place in Papua New Guinea which is organised quite differently from Porgera, led him to discard genealogical connections through women—a critical error in a society where connections through women are very important indeed.

I mention these points, not to put down A and B, but to draw attention to the poor level of performance evaluation in relation to social studies undertaken by company managements when undertaking mine planning studies. This is far from just being a Porgeran problem. Filer and Jackson's remarks above derive directly from the lack of competence which A demonstrated again at Lihir, where Kennecott were his next employers; they describe at some length (1989:43–50) the difficulties which they experienced in undoing A's confusions at this new site. Coming onto the Lihir scene a little later, I still found it necessary to deal at some length with the failings in management strategies for understanding the local land tenure system (Burton 1994a, 1994b).

Yet another amateur genealogist whom I encountered at Porgera in 1990—let us call him C—had been employed by Conzinc Riotinto Australia at the Hidden Valley prospect in Morobe Province. C's work was even worse than A's, and his material on Hidden Valley contained nothing which I have been able to use in any way during my own subsequent work in that area (Burton 1996).

All of these examples demonstrate a corporate inability to review specialist information, and a contradictory attitude to anthropology. The work cannot be 'welcomed' on the one hand, but lie unused and unreviewed on the other. I suggest that this failing is due to the absence of the know-how needed to turn ethnographic observations into management strategies which can be implemented. Elsewhere, I have written (1996:i) that the sentiment expressed in the search for the 'new competencies' is frequently overwhelmed by an anti-academic feeling which is revealed in a propensity to 'fly by the seat of our pants' after all.

Companies can surely do better than this when the stakes are so high. We can argue that they have not yet hired the Masters of Business Administration with first degrees in this or that social science—a fair criticism—and play this off against an accusation that anthropologists write in an 'inaccessible' way (as Robinson complains), but I prefer to point to lack of continuity between the SEIS approval process, the submission and approval (by the state) of an Environmental Management and Monitoring Programme (EMMP), and the actual implementation of that programme. In the Porgera case, the SEIS 'ended' three years before the first gold was poured, and implementation of the EMMP began a year after this event. Hence a four-year 'performance evaluation gap' which coincided with what Bonnell (1994:12) terms the 'period of maximum social disruption' at a mining project—the construction phase. Needless to say, I can only describe these kinds of gaps as having the potential to inflict grave damage on any project. The Community Relations staff will be working flat out during this phase, and cannot be expected to shoulder the extra workload of ensuring a continuity of research and planning functions.

Reporting and planning in the period of operations

The person who is primarily charged with the job of implementing the SEIS at a mining project is the Community Relations Manager.[6] This person is in a difficult position because he (all have been male to date) must get on with the day-to-day dealings between the project and the community, which are 'operational tasks', as well as being responsible for upgrading the knowledge contained in the SEIS and other baseline studies, and for longer range strategic planning in consultation with corporate-level executives. In practice, these tasks do not go together at all. It has been demonstrated at sites throughout the length and breadth of Papua New Guinea that operational matters expand enormously and overwhelm the capabilities of the Community Relations staff to do anything else. What remains is usually called 'fire fighting' by insiders.

The EMMP

In formal terms, what is expected to happen is that the EMMP will be drawn up by the company to implement the recommendations of the Environmental Plan, which in turn may contain as few as a hundred words on social issues distilled from the SEIS and various baseline studies. The EMMP is a document required under the *Environmental Planning Act 1978,* which regulates those projects which have been developed since it came into force.[7]

At Porgera, the EMMP was drafted in 1990, just before production began, and finalised a year later. The 35-page draft EMMP document contains two paragraphs on management of the social environment (PJV 1990b:8.13). In the framework setting out the 12 components of the 'long-term environmental monitoring' programme, which range from 'generated sediment tonnages' to 'trace metals in human scalp hair', social monitoring is not mentioned at all.

It was into this rather unordered state of affairs that I came to start my own work at Porgera in 1990. Although I was not party to it at the time, one of the two sentences in the draft EMMP referred explicitly to my project—saying that it was about to start. With an environmental scientist (Saem Majnep) present for part of the time, I and two students from the University of Papua New Guinea then did social and human ecological mapping and census work over a period of about six weeks between June and October. This included a full census of Porgera, which was carried out by about 25 Porgeran assistants working in parallel with government enumerators during the 1990 national population census.[8] Our reports were completed by May 1991 (Majnep 1990; Burton 1991). In the next version of the EMMP, the paragraphs referring to long-term monitoring of the social environment were changed to read

> [a] demographic survey was carried out in June 1990 to collect data on human settlement in area around the mine. The results will be used in the assessment of changes in the population that are associated with mine construction. The timing of subsequent surveys will be determined by agreement with the PNG Government and will depend upon the significance of any changes determined from the 1990 data.
>
> A socio-economic liaison committee has been formed comprising representatives from Porgera, Enga Provincial Government and PJV to monitor issues of concern to local people. Although communication channels are well established with the local people by means of the PJV Community Relations Department, the committee will establish a formal link between the PJV, the community and the Government (PJV 1991:8.13).

But such correspondence as I have retained shows that our reports languished for 14 months before proposals for follow-up work brought about a formal response. Then, from mid 1992, contacts between Unisearch and the PJV were renewed, and these led to the commissioning of new work by Glenn Banks and Susanne Bonnell which began in November 1992. Even at this stage, there was still no framework for long-term monitoring.

The inaugural meeting of a Porgera Social Monitoring Steering Committee, chaired by the social planning officer in the Department of Environment and Conservation (DEC), was held in Porgera on 4 March 1993. This represented the 'formal link' to the state regulatory body mentioned in the EMMP. The meeting set my colleagues and I the task of writing a plan for what was termed the 'Porgera Social Monitoring Programme', and we completed this task in June 1993 (Burton and Filer 1993). We recommended two streams of reporting

- Stream A to be carried out by specialists (economic modelling study, social change study, census project continuation, health study, etc.); and
- Stream B to be handled by means of internal company, government and non-government organisation reporting.

From 1993, annual reports were to summarise and combine the outputs from both streams.

Since our document was laboriously assembled after consultation with other parties to the Steering Committee, and built on earlier documents which had dealt with similar issues, it was unlikely to have been technically defective. At least, no other party responded by saying so. But here lies the problem—no other party responded at all! The upshot was that some of Stream A proceeded, but other parts were dropped, the Steering Committee failed to establish its own priorities, and there was no supervision of the programme by the company's Environment Manager, who was the designated point-of-entry for EMMP matters. The coordinating role which ought to have been played by the state regulator (DEC) was downgraded to that of a passive receptor, incapable of effective comment, and perhaps politically compromised by events being played out at other mines (see Bonnell 1994:118).

Comparison with other projects

At the time, I had some difficulty in making sense of these outcomes, because my proposed census project was the first casualty amongst the parts of the monitoring programme which were dropped. However, my subsequent involvement in the design and implementation of social monitoring programs at several other projects has now provided me with a broader perspective on these events.

At Ok Tedi, no monitoring programme was required under the enabling legislation, but the political situation by 1991 had made the neglect of basic research downstream of the mine an increasingly untenable course of action. A Unisearch-based monitoring programme, coordinated by Colin Filer and myself, and involving a team of specialist fieldworkers, produced 12 reports over a four-year period from 1991 to 1995 (see Filer 1991, 1997b; Kirsch 1995; Burton 1997). While this may sound like a successful exercise, it proved to have been commissioned by one section of management as a means of stirring another, then somnolent, section into action (Filer 1996). The achievement of the project's goal was also its weakness, because the target of the ploy was antagonised by it, and field officers were denied access to our findings for five years, including the crucial years of the Ok Tedi litigation.

At Kutubu, I wrote a short 'annual report' for Chevron in 1993 (Burton 1993) summarising the equivalent of 'Stream B' data on the company's behalf for presentation to the DEC—though belatedly catching up with 1990 and 1991 data only. To the best of my knowledge, this elicited no comment from the Department. Although I lost track of this project for a long period thereafter, new information confirms that no similar reports were written in subsequent years. The lack of a formal structure for this work was its obvious weakness: the information presented fell into a bureaucratic void, and no action was taken on recommendations to upgrade Chevron's internal reporting system to the Porgera specifications. I presume that this was due to the absence of any local equivalent of the Porgera Social Monitoring Steering Committee, and to confusion about the point-of-entry for such monitoring work.

At Lihir, as already mentioned, the Environmental Plan contained three paragraphs on the proposed management of the social environment (NSR 1992), and the unresponsiveness of Kennecott management, then based far away in Salt Lake City, meant that no initiative was taken to maintain the process of social impact assessment until the Australian government's Export Finance Investment Corporation obliged the new operator, Rio Tinto Zinc, to do so as a condition of the project's sovereign risk insurance. Yet this also seems to have meant that social monitoring reports are hidden under a dysfunctional blanket of confidentiality (see Filer 1998), while the consultant responsible for this work has been hampered by management directives concerning her avenues of communication with company staff and community members.

In each of these cases, we see performance evaluation gaps of several kinds. Management 'turf wars' are evident at most projects as a factor in disrupting the effective implementation of proposals. A serious difficulty everywhere, including at Porgera, is the lack of a clear point-of-entry to the company for social monitoring feedback and reports.[9] All consultants report confusion: reporting is variously to the Environment Manager, to an Executive Manager, to the General Manager, to a steering committee that does not meet (as at Porgera), or to a financial institution. Worse, the point-of-entry can change between proposal and report, or from one report to the next. One thing is clear: at no project have the reports gone, in the first instance, to the Community Relations Manager!

This is a structural form of disruption, but its effect is similar to the gap in time between the SEIS and development of the EMMP. A period of paralysis occurs as various actors consider what to do next. It is very likely that this will coincide with the most critical phase of the project, when realignment of the local political process occurs, and new, unanticipated forms of impact arise. I have mentioned elsewhere the parallel difficulties being experienced by the Community Relations

Manager in the early stages of a new project. A multiple increase in the operational workload, connected with the rush of compensation and lands work at this time, always coincides with an exhausting struggle by the Community Relations Manager to retain the priorities of his department in the face of an increase in the number of line managers during project construction, and the intervention of 'rogue players' engaged in reorganising the management structure in ways that pitch Community Relations staff into unnecessary competition with other sections or departments for the attention of the Mine Manager. I calculated that it took an average of 5.3 years for the community relations managers at three projects to win an upgrading of their department's activities to recover the ground lost since the days when community liaison staff and exploration geologists were the only people on site (Burton 1995:3; also Bonnell 1994:111).

Internal reporting

In light of these considerations, it is not surprising that I have only mentioned the activities of Community Relations departments in passing. It goes without saying that these departments carry the workload of daily dealings with the community, and simple observation shows that this is an exhausting assignment. What kind of internal reporting are Community Relations staff able to accomplish in the course of a year?

At Porgera, different people could come up with different lists of the most important problems faced by the Community Relations Department since the end of the exploration phase. It is worth making a comparison of one possible list with the permanent record we have of each item (Table 9.2).

All staff complete written monthly reports for the Community Affairs Manager, who summarises this for the quarterly reports given to the Joint Venture Partner meetings (Glenn Banks, pers. comm.). This certainly draws attention to immediate needs, and shows what responses have been made to current problems, but it does not provide the 'big picture' of how effective Community Relations programs really are. Theoretically, there is plenty of scope for those involved with the work to do this, because they do possess the most intimate knowledge of what is going on. But it does not happen because staff are too busy with other matters. Among the reports listed in Table 9.2, only the short papers by Robinson (1994a, 1994b, 1994c) and Hiatt (1995) could be said to exemplify this kind of 'in-house' product.

Table 9.2   Principal community relations tasks since exploration

Task	Risk	Value	Reporting
Daily liaison	Stoppages; riots; mine closure; etc	Nil to capital value of mine	Anecdotal accounts; monthly reports; *Ipili Wai Pii* newspaper; mentions in *PNG Resources Magazine*; etc
Relocation	Build-up of social tensions; . undesirable impacts etc	>K11m (move 500+ families into new housing)	Mention in speeches of executives; study in advance of relocation (Robinson 1988); short conference papers (Robinson 1994a/b/c); sections of Bonnell (1994)
Compensation	Disgruntlement of aggrieved, un-compensated parties; 'landowner strikes'	K25.9m (1987–92 only)	Mention in speeches of executives; economic modelling reports in social monitoring program (Banks 1993; 1994a)
Business development	Stoppages; riots; mine closure; etc	K24.4m to Porgeran contractors to Dec 1993	Mention in speeches of executives; Business Development Plan (PJV 1990a); Porgera Business Study (Banks 1994c)
Lands important in mine rehabilitation plan	Stoppages; riots; mine closure etc	See 'Compensation'	No review of tenurial problems to date; for garden surveys. See Banks (1994a), and sections of Bonnell (1994)
Welfare and social development	Longer-term risk, esp. in relation to youth	See 'Daily liaison'	Bonnell (1994)
Enga highway issues	Road blockages, thefts, lost time	K?m	Media reports. Paper to Chamber of Mining and Petroleum by Hiatt (1995)
Hides power line	Potential delay in opening Stage 2; destruction of pylons (~5 to date)	~K1m/day when power unavailable; replacement pylons K?m	No known socioeconomic evaluation to date; subsistence improvement work in some places by John Vail.
Infrastructure Tax Credit Scheme projects	Disgruntlement of areas away from the mine; road blockages etc	K9.8m for period from 1993–Oct. 1996	No known socioeconomic evaluation to date (implementation reports for Tax Office exist); publicity through media coverage
Downstream river impacts	Writ from Porgera River Alluvial Miners Ass'n (1995); ongoing threat of writ from Strickland Kulini Landowners Ass'n	cf. July 1996 Ok Tedi settlement + legal bills	Early technical review by Sullivan et al. (1992); major environmental review by CSIRO (1996)

Two cases are instructive in this respect. Susanne Bonnell was hired to work as a welfare officer in the PJV Community Relations section, and especially to implement the recommendations contained in Robinson's earlier relocation study (Robinson 1988:7; Bonnell 1994:18). When I liaised with her at the time of my census project in 1990, it was obvious that she had no time to set about writing anything, let alone to evaluate her own work. After resigning from this job, and spending some time away from the project, she was re-hired as a consultant to do this type of evaluation without having the burden of operational work.

Another person was one of two experienced former patrol officers on staff in 1990, who was given the job of negotiating land usage agreements along the route of the 80km-long transmission line from the Hides gas project to the Porgera mine. The work was carried out under enormous pressure from landowners and a tight deadline set by the mine development plan. No sooner was the work finished than he was laid off, notwithstanding the fact that most of the agreements had been rushed, and a strong element of 'subjectivity' remained in the land investigations (Robinson 1991:6). My own observations confirmed that there was no time, given the deadline imposed by the engineers, to make the more thorough inquiries that this vital pieces of infrastructure really merited. Close to the anniversary of the relevant agreements, the same officer was taken on as a consultant to handle the annual lease payments, but he was soon idle again, and spent the next two years seeking work before taking up a position in the Community Relations department of another mining company.

Both cases illustrate the inability of staff in salaried positions, who know that they are rushing important tasks, to either slow down and devote more time to them or to achieve anything resembling an adequate level of documentation of what they have done. In the first case, the staff member was permitted the breathing space to do this, and has written a report (Bonnell 1994 and this volume) which should actually have been part of the internal documentation of the operational work of her section. In the second case, the staff member was left high and dry. No evaluation of the power line work was done, and the predicted demolition of power pylons[10] took place a couple of years later. The cost of repairs and downtime for the mine easily outweighed the miniscule savings achieved by laying off the investigating officer before his work was properly documented.

Conclusions

The point of my discussion is not to prove the truth of the old proverb that 'a stitch in time saves nine'—even if the incidence and cost of well-known breakdowns in company-community relations suggest that a stitch in time can actually save the entire suit of clothes. Everyone concerned with social issues in the mining industry already knows this. The problem is that the industry fails to entrench the high priority, continuity of effort, and level of resources which is needed for the management of social issues. Common sense says that this should happen automatically, but in most situations the pace of mining construction far outruns the concurrent capabilities of those who handle these social issues to make credible and appropriate responses as a project evolves.

Explanations

A partial explanation comes from the indeterminate nature of social impact crises, when compared to the more definable parameters of engineering or the physical environment. Bridge designers, for example, face calculable fears about what their creations must withstand, so that their specifications for construction are credible and usually uncontroversial. By contrast, the worries of social planners in relation to mining impacts are frequently as convincing as a vague fear of the dark to the engineers and geologists who form the bulwark of mine management.

A universal problem is that agreements made at a political or legislative level are used by company executives as a guide to internal policy for far too long after they have ceased to reflect current political realities—if they ever did. This was clearly the case at Panguna and Ok Tedi, where the projects were regulated under their own acts of parliament. To overcome this particular shortcoming, a more flexible format was adopted in the guideline agreements for the Porgera project. Following a 'forum process' designed for local stakeholders to sort out their own positions, the agreements comprised a formal contract between the government and the mining company, and a separate set of Memoranda of Agreement (MOAs) between the national government, the Enga Provincial Government, and the local landowners (West 1992). A similarly localised form of bargaining took place over the Lihir project, resulting in an Integrated Benefits Package which the Construction Manager described as the local 'bible'.

But these innovations have done almost nothing to address the problem of making adequate resources available for the urgent tasks of community relations. This department is repeatedly sent into the battle for mine construction without sufficient staff, buildings, vehicles, computers, radios, and other basic facilities (see Bonnell 1994:112; Burton 1995). The ink was hardly dry on the Porgera MOAs when it became obvious that neither the national government nor the provincial government was going to uphold its responsibilities in respect of local development issues. Internal correspondence shows that, in early 1990, the company's senior Community Affairs staff were 'sceptical about the capability of the E.P.G. [Enga Provincial Government] to monitor and address socio-economic problems', and requested an expanded role for their department. They also warned that they personally had no time to spare, given their existing workloads, to pursue this expansion or even to oversee it. It appears that one major distraction at this juncture was a debate with senior executives over the company's localisation plan[11]

> The justification for...long term expatriate incumbents is the Bougainville experience. The BCL Department of Community Affairs had been reduced to a few national officers who were reluctant to convey the approaching storm of malcontent to Management (Hiatt 1990:3).

The Community Affairs Manager won a partial victory, and the expansion required to cope with operational work was achieved—by about 1993. But office facilities had yet to be improved, and Bonnell was still echoing the above comments in 1994.

> Future concerns also include the sensitive issue of localisation...If Community Affairs is totally localised there is a danger of senior mine management becoming isolated from the needs, concerns and attitudes in the community. This would have an adverse impact on both the community and mining operations—which appears to have been the case in Bougainville (Bonnell 1994:112).

In fact, raising the spectre of Bougainville and questions about localisation should have been long dead methods of argument. The principle of 'best practice' applies when any in-country issue— inappropriate legislation, failing administration, and cultural or 'conflict of interest' problems—makes any activity come up short of what can be judged to be the best (and safest) attainable standard. Yet the PJV has been able to mount only intermittent efforts to bridge the research and planning deficit, given that it has proved too difficult to push the national and provincial governments into fulfilling their capacity-building commitments[12] and their obligations to 'develop and monitor the social and economic strategy of the Porgera project' (Hiatt 1990:2). By 1997, action had been taken on only some of the issues identified in 1990, and few of the specific monitoring recommendations made by Banks and Bonnell in 1994 had been implemented.[13]

Comparison with responses to environmental fears

In this context, it worth briefly examining the company response to fears of environmental damage in the Lower Porgera/Lagaip/ Strickland river system. In August 1995, the company contracted a CSIRO consultancy team to undertake a comprehensive review of the mine's impact on the river system; the team reported in December 1996 (CSIRO 1996). I have a particular interest in the issues at stake, having written several reports myself on downstream communities in the Ok Tedi-Fly river system, including the Middle Fly flood plain area (for example, Burton 1994c). As my own knowledge of Ok Tedi Mining Limited's environmental programs would have led me to expect, the CSIRO report called for a significant expansion of the PJV's environmental research and monitoring capabilities, notably an upgrading from 'narrow focused' compliance monitoring (the 'minimalism' I discussed in the introduction to this chapter) to 'monitoring for impact' (CSIRO 1996, Recommendation ES5).

By and large, I have no specialist criticisms to make of the content of this report.[14] It was an appropriate response to the realisation that environmental fears might jeopardise company operations, and the threat of lawsuits from aggrieved landowners (see Table 9.2). But we may also note that the team recruited to undertake this study included no less than four professors and another four Ph.D. holders, and we may wonder why such a battery of 'big guns' was never wheeled out to deal with the social monitoring programme. I appreciate that operational community relations matters are now much better resourced than they were previously, and I hasten to add that the quality of the work undertaken by Banks and Bonnell is not in question.[15] Neither of these things are at issue. The imbalance is between the degree of seriousness with which the two sectors have been taken in the overall process of planning, monitoring and evaluation of company operations.

Various reasons can be put forward to explain this disparity. There is every likelihood that physical environmental data and recommendations fall into a scientific 'comfort zone' for executives with traditional mining industry backgrounds, whereas the same people find it harder to accept the discursive nature of social science as having a comparable validity. At the same time, the socially-generated risks to mining projects, especially in Papua New Guinea, often come to the surface in a political form, thus bringing social research and the formulation of social policies into collision with the prerogative of senior executives to handle the company's external political affairs. This may be termed a problem of managerial demarcation.[16] The result is a reduction of capacity to deal with social issues, both within the company and among government agencies and other organisations involved with the Porgera project. A much greater share of the agenda handled by executives acting intuitively, or using 'common sense', at a level of political relations is really amenable to the more formal treatment we see given to environmental issues. Better performance can be achieved through better information about the social environment, better analysis of it, the development of proactive management strategies, and a more rigorous follow-up (see Table 9.3).

For this to happen, there needs to be a more critical level of oversight by managers, and review processes need to be more systematic than any yet seen at a major mining project. Company staff need still more engagement with what Davis (1995:2) calls the 'soft skills that are, in fact, hard skills', so that they have the expertise to be able to recognise and lose their fear of this engagement. It is regrettable that this can only be achieved, under present circumst-ances, by pulling apart the record of what has (or has not) happened, rather than by offering a forward-looking prescription for how to go about evaluating company performance in social areas. But this will be possible in due course, and I hope to have given a hint here (albeit by pointing to gaps in the record) that the most basics steps are not speculative and are capable of measurement. Indeed, they fall squarely into the realm of management structures, good planning, meaningful consultation, and above all, the precautionary principle and the avoidance of risk. The desired outcomes, if this has not been spelled out already, are a swifter and more sure-footed responsiveness to crisis, more agile organisations able to anticipate and steer away from risks of socio-political origin, and an enhancement of the capacity to bring benefits to both investors and landowner communities on a long-term basis.

Table 9.3   Demonstrated capabilities in relation to social issues at Porgera

Item	Demonstrated at Porgera
Observation and research	Observation: a good capacity to see what happens daily. Research: negligible capacity due to workload; weak interest in matching environmental research capabilities in area of social issues.
Analysis and reporting	In the organisation: poor capacity (other than internal memos, monthly reports). Use of external consultants: at a low level and discontinuously; hampered by shifting points-of-entry and problem of demarcation. Use of external planning team: no interest shown.
Representation to decision makers	A much improved capacity since the start of operations.
Management emphasis	In the organisation: slow visible responses betray inability to escape short-term exigencies. In the industry: declarations not matched by guidelines or definition of standards (e.g. absence of Codes of Practice).
Implementation and and follow-up	Extremely slow. Self-handicapped in aim to be pro-active.

Notes

1   Outside Porgera, in particular, the numbers are generally made up of assistants with a Grade 6–10 education.
2   Yumbisa has the terms *yami* and *tata,* while Porgera has *yame* and *tata,* for 'family' and 'genealogical branch' respectively.
3   A figure of three generations before the present is mentioned, but I did not take long (in 1990) to find a genealogy spanning 14 generations. In point of fact, in Papua New Guinea, the Ipili stand out, along with the Huli, as having notably deep and well-organised genealogical knowledge. Another howler is the statement that 'the Ipili have lost much of their oral tradition in recent decades' (Pacific Agribusiness 1987:5). No serious ethnographer could possibly characterise the Ipili as having 'lost their culture' (in which oral tradition is an integral part).

4   It is not conceivable that his doctoral dissertation was too recent to be noticed. Wohlt was employed by the Enga Provincial Government in the implementation phase of the *Enga Yaasa Lakemana* development programme. Both the baseline study for this programme (Carrad *et al*. 1982) and Wohlt's own technical papers on subsistence farming were mentioned in the SEIS.

5   An acknowledgment of this point appears on the first page of Appendix B, 'Factors shaping Ipili society' (Pacific Agribusiness 1987).

6   'Community relations' and 'section' or 'department' are used generically in this chapter. In fact, the Division of Community Affairs at Porgera comprised three sections: Community Relations, Lands, and Business Development (see Bonnell 1994). Note also that the phrase 'Community Relations Department' is used in the Porgera EMMP (PJV 1991:8:13).

7   Of currently operational mining projects, only Ok Tedi is regulated under its own act, which dates back to 1976.

8   Provincial elections coincided with the national census week in July, and Porgera's census was put off at short notice. My work was a consultancy for the PJV, while operational costs for the assistants were borne by the Porgera Development Authority. Training of the assistants and field coordination were handled in my absence by Susanne Bonnell, and the census was carried out during the week of 1–5 October 1990.

9   I am grateful to Glenn Banks for discussion of this particular point.

10 This was predicted in the course of normal conversation in 1990, because the Bougainville crisis had begun with the demolition of pylons in 1988.

11 I do not possess an archive of PJV's internal memoranda. I happen to have this one because the next two paragraphs requested a census be done and suggested that I undertake it.

12 Notable among failed national government commitments in the area of social and economic development were the non-existent 'long term economic development plan' and the 'Porgera District Hospital'—a joint national-provincial government commitment which was due to be honoured by 1992, but which had not opened five years later.

13 The census of Porgera which I had hoped to complete was a 'vital project' in 1990 (Hiatt 1990:3), was proposed and supported in mid 1991, was accepted in our early 1993 proposals, then dropped again in July 1993. Several company employees did genealogies and censuses in the 1993–94 period, but a 'comprehensive census of the whole of Porgera District' was still being recommended in Bonnell's report (1994:120).

14 Actually, I have a major criticism. The hydrological discussion in Chapter 4, concerning the reversal of flow in the Herbert River between Lake Murray and the Strickland (CSIRO 1996:5–4), fails to

mention the dominant role of El Niño events in the human and natural ecology of the lagoonal systems of the Fly River flood plain (Burton 1994c:9–10, Appendix C). An innocent mistake? I can only hope that the omission has been rectified in the proposed 'program of integrative investigations in the flood plain and the Lake Murray region' (CSIRO 1996, Recommendation ES8).

15 At the time, Glenn Banks was a doctoral student at the Australian National University. He has since completed a dissertation on the socioeconomic impact of the Porgera project (Banks 1997).

16 In my view, the demarcation lines are usually drawn in the wrong place, because the industry is rarely able to distinguish the turmoil *within* a society, which finds outward expression in political form, from the political process of a society's *external* affairs. But there is no space here to examine the incidence and consequences of this failure.

References

AGA (Applied Geology Associates Pty Ltd), 1989. *Environmental, Socio-Economic and Public Health Review of Bougainville Copper Mine, Panguna*, Applied Geology Associates Pty Ltd for Department of Minerals and Energy, Wellington.

Ahai, N., Pilyo, P., Areke, M., Kongoni, M., Sand, L., Yopo, M. and Weeks, S., 1991. *Enga Six Year Education Plan 1992–1997*, National Research Institute (for Department of Enga Province), Boroko.

Allen, B.J., 1982. 'Subsistence agriculture: three case studies', in B. Carrad, D.A.M. Lea and K. Talyaga (eds), *Enga: foundations for development*, University of New England for National Planning Office and Enga Provincial Government, Armidale:93–127.

——, 1995. 'At your own peril: studying Huli residence', in A. Biersack (ed.), *Papuan Borderlands: Huli, Duna, and Ipili perspectives on the Papua New Guinea Highlands*, University of Michigan Press, Ann Arbor:141–71.

——,Hide, R.L., Bourke, R.M., Ballard, C., Fritsch, D., Grau, R., Hobsbawm, P., Humphreys G.S. and Kandasan, D., 1995. *Agricultural Systems of Papua New Guinea—Working Paper 9: Enga Province*, Department of Human Geography, The Australian National University, Canberra.

Atkinson, J., 1998. Porgera Environmental Advisory Komiti—why does WWF-Australia belong?, paper presented to the Mining and the Community conference in Madang.

Ballard, C., 1994. 'The centre cannot hold: trade networks and sacred geography in the Papua New Guinea Highlands', *Archaeology in Oceania*, 29:130–48.

——, 1995. 'Bibliography of materials on the Huli, Duna, and Ipili peoples', in A. Biersack (ed.), *Papuan Borderlands: Huli, Duna, and Ipili perspectives on the Papua New Guinea Highlands*, University of Michigan Press, Ann Arbor:401–17.

Banks, G., 1993. *Porgera Social Monitoring Programme: economic modelling project—first report*, Unisearch PNG Pty Ltd for Porgera Joint Venture, Port Moresby.

——, 1994a. *Porgera Economic Modelling Project—Second Report: gardens and wantoks*, Porgera Social Monitoring Programme

Report 3, Unisearch PNG Pty Ltd for Porgera Joint Venture Port Moresby.

——, 1994b. *Kaiya River LMP Socio-Economic Baseline Study*, Porgera Social Monitoring Programme Report 4, Unisearch PNG Pty Ltd for Porgera Joint Venture, Port Moresby.

——, 1994c. *Porgera Social Monitoring Programme: Porgera business study*, Porgera Social Monitoring Programme Report 5, Unisearch PNG Pty Ltd for Porgera Joint Venture, Port Moresby.

——, 1996. 'Compensation for mining: benefit or time-bomb? The Porgera gold mine', in R. Howitt, J. Connell and P. Hirsch (eds), *Resources, Nations and Indigenous Peoples: case studies from Australasia, Melanesia and Southeast Asia*, Oxford University Press, Melbourne:223–35.

——, 1997. Mountain of desire: mining company and indigenous community at the Porgera Gold Mine, Papua New Guinea, PhD thesis, The Australian National University, Canberra.

——, and Ballard, C. (eds), 1997. *The Ok Tedi Settlement: issues, outcomes and implications*, Pacific Policy Paper No. 27, National Centre for Development Studies, The Australian National University, Canberra.

Banks, G. and Bonnell, S., 1997a. Porgera Social Monitoring Programme: Annual Report 1996, report for Porgera Joint Venture, unpublished, May.

——, 1997b. Porgera Social Monitoring Programme: Draft Action Plan 1997, report for Porgera Joint Venture, unpublished, May.

——, 1997c. Porgera Social Monitoring Programme: Action Plan 1997, report for Porgera Joint Venture, unpublished, September.

Barnes, J.A., 1962. 'African models in the New Guinea Highlands', *Man* (n.s.), 62:5–9.

——, 1967. 'Agnation among the Enga: a review article', *Oceania*, 38:33–43.

Biersack, A., 1980. The hidden God: communication, cosmology, and cybernetics among a Melanesian people, PhD thesis, University of Michigan, Ann Arbor.

——, 1982. 'Ginger gardens for the ginger woman: rites and passages in a Melanesian society', *Man* (n.s.), 17:239–58.

——, 1987. 'Moonlight: negative images of transcendence in Paiela pollution', *Oceania*, 57:178–94.

——, 1990. 'Histories in the making: Paiela and historical anthropology', *History and Anthropology*, 5:63–85.

——, 1991. 'Prisoners of time: millenarian praxis in a Melanesian valley', in A. Biersack (ed.), *Clio in Oceania: toward a historial anthropology*, Smithsonian Institution Press, Washington, D.C:231–96.

——, 1995a. 'Huli, Duna, and Ipili peoples yesterday and today', in A. Biersack (ed.), *Papuan Borderlands: Huli, Duna, and Ipili perspectives on the Papua New Guinea Highlands*, University of Michigan Press, Ann Arbor:1–54.

——, 1995b. 'Heterosexual meanings: society, economy, and gender among Ipilis', in A. Biersack (ed.), *Papuan Borderlands: Huli, Duna, and Ipili perspectives on the Papua New Guinea Highlands*, University of Michigan Press, Ann Arbor:231–64.

——, 1996. '"Making kinship": warfare, migration, and marriage...', in H. Levine and A. Ploeg (eds), *Works in Progress: essays in New Guinea Highlands ethnography in honour of Paula Brown Glick*, Peter Lang, Frankfurt am Main:19–42.

—— (ed.), 1995. *Papuan Borderlands: Huli, Duna, and Ipili perspectives on the Papua New Guinea Highlands*, University of Michigan Press, Ann Arbor.

Bonnell, S., 1994. *Dilemmas of Development: social change in Porgera, 1989–1993*, Porgera Social Monitoring Programme Report 2, Subada Consulting Pty Ltd for Porgera Joint Venture, Thornlands (Qld).

Bourke, R.M. and Lea, D.A.M., 1982. 'Subsistence horticulture', B. Carrad, D.A.M. Lea and K. Talyaga (eds), *Enga: foundations for development*, University of New England for National Planning Office and Enga Provincial Government, Armidale:198–216.

Burton, J.E., 1991. *Porgera Census Project: report for 1990*, Unisearch PNG Pty Ltd for Porgera Joint Venture, Port Moresby.

——, 1993. *Kutubu Petroleum Project, Social Monitoring Programme: analysis of data for the years 1990 and 1991*, Unisearch PNG Pty Ltd for Chevron Niugini Pty Ltd, Port Moresby.

——, 1994a. *The Lihir VPS Database: a tool for human resources planning, social development planning and social monitoring*, Unisearch PNG Pty Ltd and Pacific Social Mapping for Lihir Management Company and PNG Department of Mining and Petroleum, Port Moresby and Canberra.

——, 1994b. *The Lands Trust Concept: a preliminary discussion of ideas for landowners and developers*, Pacific Social Mapping, Canberra.

——, 1994c. *Middle Fly and North Morehead Area Study*, Ok-Fly Social Monitoring Project Report 10, Unisearch PNG Pty Ltd and Pacific Social Mapping for Ok Tedi Mining Ltd, Port Moresby and Canberra.

——, 1995. 'What is best practice?: social issues and the culture of the corporation in Papua New Guinea', in D. Denoon, C. Ballard, G. Banks and P. Hancock (eds), *Mining and Mineral Resource Policy Issues in Asia-Pacific: prospects for the 21st century*, Division of Pacific and Asian History, Research School of Pacific and Asian Studies, The Australian National University, Canberra:129–34.

——, 1996. *Social Mapping at Hidden Valley, Morobe Province, Papua New Guinea: work undertaken in 1995–96*, Pacific Social Mapping for CRA Minerals (PNG) Ltd, Canberra.

——, 1997. 'Terra nugax and the discovery paradigm: how Ok Tedi was shaped by the way it was found and how the rise of political process in the North Fly took the company by surprise', in G. Banks and C. Ballard (eds), *The Ok Tedi Settlement: issues, outcomes and implications*, Pacific Policy Paper No. 27, National Centre for Development Studies, The Australian National University, Canberra:27–55.

—— and Filer, C. with Banks, G. and Bonnell, S., 1993. *Porgera Social Monitoring Programme: plan and objectives*, Unisearch PNG Pty Ltd for Porgera Joint Venture, Port Moresby.

Callick, R., 1993. 'IMF warns PNG against more mining investment', *Australian Financial Review*, April 14.

Carrad, B., Lea, D.A.M. and Talyaga, K. (eds), 1982. *Enga: foundations for development*, University of New England for National Planning Office and Enga Provincial Government, Armidale.

Clark, J., 1993. 'Gold, sex and pollution: male illness and myth at Mt Kare, Papua New Guinea', *American Ethnologist*, 20:742–57.

Clifford, W., Morauta, L. and Stuart, B., 1984. *Law and Order in Papua New Guinea*, (2 volumes), Institute of National Affairs, Port Moresby.

CSIRO (Commonwealth Scientific and Industrial Research Organization), 1996. *Porgera Joint Venture: review of riverine impacts*, CSIRO Environmental Projects Office for Porgera Joint Venture, Dickson (ACT).

Davis, L.A., 1995. New competencies in mining, Paper presented to the Australian Institute of Directors, Melbourne.

Davis Film & Video, 1990. *Sitting on a Gold Mine*, video produced for Porgera Joint Venture.

DLPP (Department of Lands and Physical Planning), 1993. *Prices of Economic Trees/Plantings on Customary Land*, PNG Department of Lands and Physical Planning, Office of the Valuer-General (File RSH/V-78), Port Moresby.

Egan, M., 1994. Business entities at mining and petroleum sites, Paper presented to PNG Chamber of Mines and Petroleum conference on Business Development and Community Relations, Port Moresby.

EPG (Enga Provincial Government), 1989. *The Porgera Agreements (Annotated)*, H. Derkley (ed.), Legal Services Unit, Department of Enga, Wabag.

Ernst, T.M., in press. 'Land, stories, and resources: discourse and entification in Onabasulu modernity', in A. Biersack (ed.), *Ecologies for Tomorrow: reading Rappaport today*, special issue of *American Anthropologist*.

Feil, D.K., 1987. *The Evolution of Highland Papua New Guinea Societies*, Cambridge University Press, Cambridge.

Filer, C., 1990. 'The Bougainville rebellion, the mining industry and the process of social disintegration in Papua New Guinea', in R.J. May and M. Spriggs (eds), *The Bougainville Crisis*, Crawford House Press, Bathurst:73–112.

——, 1991. 'Ok-Fly social monitoring project baseline documentation', *Research in Melanesia*, 15(2):121–87.

——, 1992. Lihir project social impact mitigation: issues and approaches, unpublished report to the PNG Department of Environment and Conservation.

——, 1996. 'The policy and methodology of social impact mitigation in the mining industry', in D. Gladman, D. Mowbray and J. Duguman (eds), *From Rio to Rai: environment and development in Papua New Guinea up to 2000 and Beyond—Volume 4: warning bells*, University of Papua New Guinea Press, Port Moresby:59–80.

——, 1997a. 'The Melanesian way of menacing the mining industry', in B. Burt and C. Clerk (eds), *Environment and Development in the Pacific Islands*, Pacific Policy Paper 25, National Centre for Development Studies, The Australian National University, Canberra:91–122.

——, 1997b. 'West side story: the state's and other stakes in the Ok Tedi mine', in G. Banks and C. Ballard (eds), *The Ok Tedi Settlement: issues, outcomes and implications*, Pacific Policy Paper No. 27, National Centre for Development Studies, The Australian National University, Canberra:65–102.

——, 1998. Social monitoring programs and the management of social risk in Papua New Guinea, Paper presented to the Mining and the Community conference, Madang.

—— and Jackson, R.T., 1989. *The Social and Economic Impact of a Gold Mine on Lihir: revised and expanded*, (2 volumes) Lihir Liaison Committee, Port Moresby.

Finney, B.R., 1987. *Business Development in the Highlands of Papua New Guinea*, Research Report 6, Pacific Islands Development Program, East–West Center, Honolulu.

Gewertz, D. and Errington, F., 1991. *Twisted Histories, Altered Contexts: representing the Chambri in a world system*, Cambridge University Press, Cambridge.

Gibbs, P.J., 1975. Ipili religion past and present, diploma thesis, Department of Anthropology, University of Sydney, Sydney.

——, 1977. 'The cult from Lyeimi and the Ipili', *Oceania*, 48:1–25.

——, 1981. Tieni genealogical statement, unpublished report to Placer (PNG) Pty Ltd.

——, n.d. Tuanda and Waiwa genealogies, unpublished report to Placer (PNG) Pty Ltd.

Glasse, R.M., 1968. *Huli of Papua: a cognatic descent system*, Mouton and Co., Paris.

——, 1992. 'Encounters with the Huli: fieldwork at Tari in the 1950's', in T.E. Hays (ed.), *Ethnographic Presents: pioneering anthropologists in the Papua New Guinea Highlands*, University of California Press, Berkeley:232–49.

Goldsmith, R.C.M, 1993. Kaiya River project: report on the status of Kaiya River relocation investigations, unpublished report to Porgera Joint Venture.Gregory, C.A., 1980. 'Gifts to men and gifts to God: gift exchange and capital accumulation in contemporary Papua', *Man* (n.s.), 15:626–52.

——, and Mules, G.J., 1990. Geotechnical input to the Porgera Gold Project, Enga Province, Papua New Guinea, Paper presented to the Australasian Institute of Mining and Metallurgy 'Pacific Rim 90' conference, Parkville (Victoria).

Handley, G., 1993. 'Early Porgera', *Prospect*, 1(5):2–5.

—— and D. Henry, 1990. 'Porgera gold deposit', in F.E. Hughes (ed.), *Geology of the Mineral Deposits of Australia and Papua New Guinea*, Australasian Institute of Mining and Metallurgy, Melbourne:1717–24.

Hiatt, R., 1990. Memorandum to A. Paton and V. Botts, 5 February 1990.

——, 1995. Problems with the Highlands Highway, Paper presented to PNG Chamber of Mines and Petroleum conference on 'Business Development, Community Relations and Law and Order', Port Moresby.

Hughes, P. and Sullivan, M., 1988. 'Land use study', in Natural Systems Resources, *Porgera Gold Project Environmental Plan*, NSR

Environmental Consultants Ltd for Porgera Joint Venture, Hawthorn (VA): Appendix 7.

Ipara, K., 1993. Kewai genealogies, unpublished report to Department of Enga and Porgera Joint Venture.

——, 1994. Lower Porgera land investigation report, unpublished report to Porgera Joint Venture.

Jackson, R.T., 1986. *Residential Options and Relocation Issues at Porgera*, Department of Geography, James Cook University for Placer Pacific Pty Ltd, Townsville.

——, 1987. *Social Survey: Porgera*, Department of Geography, James Cook University for Placer Pacific Pty Ltd, Townsville.

——, 1993. *Cracked Pot or Copper Bottomed Investment?: the development of the Ok Tedi project 1982–1991, a personal view*, Melanesian Studies Centre, James Cook University, Townsville.

Jorgensen, D., 1996. 'Regional history and ethnic identity in the hub of New Guinea: the emergence of the Min', in J. Barker and D. Jorgensen (eds), *Regional Histories in the Western Pacific*, special issue of *Oceania*, 66:189–210

——, 1997a. 'Who and what is a landowner?: mythology and marking the ground in a Papua New Guinea mining project', *Anthropological Forum*, 7:599–628.

——, 1997b. 'Review of "Mountains of Gold: The People of Porgera" (1993)', *Pacific Studies*, 20:167–70.

Kiri Consultants, 1993. Effects of the continuation of Porgera Mine's fly-in, fly-out policy on the business community of Porgera, unpublished report to the Porgera Landowners Association.

Kirsch, S., 1995. 'Social impact of the Ok Tedi Mine on the Yonggom villages of the North Fly, 1992', *Research in Melanesia*, 19:23–102.

Kyakas, A. and Wiessner, P., 1992. *From Inside the Women's House: Enga women's lives and traditions*, Robert Brown and Associates, Buranda.

Lawrence, P., 1967 (1955). 'Land tenure among the Garia', in H.I. Hogbin and P. Lawrence, *Studies in New Guinea Land Tenure*, Sydney University Press, Sydney.

——, 1984. *The Garia: the ethnography of a traditional cosmological system in Papua New Guinea*, Melbourne University Press, Melbourne.

Majnep, I.S., 1990. *On Vegetation Zones in Porgera*, Unisearch PNG Pty Ltd for Porgera Joint Venture, Port Moresby.

Meggitt, M., 1957. 'The Ipili of the Porgera Valley, Western Highlands District, Territory of New Guinea', *Oceania*, 28:31–55.

Mules, G., 1993. Waste dump options stage 4B, unpublished report to Porgera Joint Venture.

NSR (Natural Systems Resources), 1988. *Porgera Gold Project Environmental Plan*, NSR Environmental Consultants Ltd for Porgera Joint Venture, Hawthorn (VA).

——, 1992. *Lihir Project Environmental Plan: main report*, NSR Environmental Consultants Ltd for Kennecott Niugini Mining Joint Venture, Hawthorn (VA).

O'Faircheallaigh, C., 1985. 'Financial failures in mining: implications for LDC mineral policies', *Resources Policy*, (12):235–44.

Overfield, D., 1993. *Coffee and Smallholder Households in Benabena District, Eastern Highlands Province: economic issues and interim results*, Discussion Paper 10, Industry Affairs Division, Coffee Industry Corporation, Goroka.

Pacific Agribusiness, 1987. *Social and Economic Impact Study: Porgera Gold Mine*, (2 volumes), Pacific Agribusiness, South Melbourne.

Pain, C., Smith J. and Lea, D., 1982. 'Physical environment', in B. Carrad, D.A.M. Lea and K. Talyaga (eds), *Enga: foundations for development*, University of New England for National Planning Office and Enga Provincial Government, Armidale:23–40.

Parker, G., 1992. Study of sediment transport resulting from disposal of black sediments and soft waste in a dynamic dump at Anjolek, unpublished report to Porgera Joint Venture.

Peri, B., 1994. Landownership study: Mt Kare, unpublished report to KarePuga Development Corporation Pty Ltd.

PJV (Porgera Joint Venture), 1990a. Porgera Joint Venture Business Development Plan, unpublished report to PNG Department of Trade and Industry Goods and Services Committee.

——, 1990b. Environmental Management and Monitoring Programme for Porgera Gold Mine: draft, unpublished report to PNG Department of Environment and Conservation.

——, 1991. Environmental Management and Monitoring Programme for Porgera Gold Mine, unpublished report to PNG Department of Environment and Conservation.

——, 1993. Environmental monitoring: January–December 1991, unpublished report to PNG Department of Environment and Conservation.

——, 1994. Quarterly review, July to September 1993, unpublished report to PNG Department of Trade and Industry Goods and Services Committee.

——, 1997. Porgera Joint Venture: project information.

Pomponio, A., 1992. *Seagulls Don't Fly Into the Bush: cultural identity and development in Melanesia*, Wadsworth, Belmont (CA).

Read, K.H., 1965. *The High Valley*, Columbia University Press, New York.

Robinson, F., 1988. Porgera relocation study, (2 volumes), unpublished report for Porgera Joint Venture.

——, 1991. Anthropology and the Porgera Gold Mine, Paper presented to conference on 'New Perspectives on the Papua New Guinea Highlands', The Australian National University, Canberra.

——, 1993. Relocation Study: Kaiya LMP, Internal report for Porgera Joint Venture.

——, 1994a. Selling community affairs to management, Paper presented to PNG Chamber of Mines and Petroleum conference on 'Business Development and Community Relations', Port Moresby.

——, 1994b. Squatters and outsiders, Paper presented to PNG Chamber of Mines and Petroleum conference on 'Business Development and Community Relations', Port Moresby.

——, 1994c. Policy directions, Paper presented to PNG Chamber of Mines and Petroleum conference on 'Business Development and Community Relations', Port Moresby.

Rose, C.J., 1982. 'Preliminary observations on the pandanus nut (*Pandanus julianettii martelli*)', in R.M. Bourke and V. Kesavan (eds), *Proceedings of the Second Papua New Guinea Food Crops Conference*, PNG Department of Primary Industry, Port Moresby.

Runawery, C. and Weeks, S.G., 1980. *Towards an Engan Education Strategy: Education and Rural Development in Enga*, Working Paper 3, University of Papua New Guinea, Education Research Unit, Port Moresby.

Sagir, B.F., 1997. The politics of oil extraction in Kutubu, Paper presented to the conference 'From Myth to Minerals', The Australian National University Canberra.

Scott, G. and Pain, C., 1982. 'Land potential', in B. Carrad, D.A.M. Lea and K. Talyaga (eds), *Enga: foundations for development*, University of New England for National Planning Office and Enga Provincial Government, Armidale:128–45.

Shearman, P., 1995. The environmental and social impact of the Porgera Gold Mine on the Strickland River system, B.Sc. Honours thesis, Department of Geography and Environmental Studies, University of Tasmania, Hobart.

Smalley, I.F., 1983. Porgera genealogical survey and case study of the Ipili people, unpublished report to Placer (PNG) Pty Ltd.

Sullivan, M.E., Galowa, K., Iddings S. and Kimbu, R., 1992. Porgera environmental impacts and compensation, unpublished report to Porgera Joint Venture.

Talyaga, K.K., 1984. Porgera Gold Mine: socio-economic impact study, (2 volumes). unpublished report to PNG National Planning Office.

Taylor, J.L., 1971 (1938). 'Hagen-Sepik Patrol 1938–1939: interim report', *New Guinea and Australia, the Pacific and South-East Asia*, September/October:24–5.

Toft, S. and Bonnell, S., 1985. *Marriage and Domestic Violence in Rural Papua New Guinea*, Occasional Paper 18, Law Reform Commission, Boroko.

Vail, J., 1995. 'All that glitters: the Mt. Kare gold rush and its aftermath', in A. Biersack (ed.), *Papuan Borderlands: Huli, Duna, and Ipili perspectives on the Papua New Guinea Highlands*, University of Michigan Press, Ann Arbor:343–74.

Van den Brand, E. and Parkop, P., 1998. Presentation and discussion of Porgera Gold Mine, Enga Province, Papua New Guinea, Paper presented to the 'Mining and the Community' conference in Madang.

Waddell, E., 1972. *The Mound Builders: agricultural practices, environment, and society in the Central Highlands of New Guinea*, University of Washington Press, Seattle.

Wagner, R.A., 1974. 'Are there social groups in the New Guinea Highlands?', in M. Leaf (ed.), *Frontiers of Anthropology*, Van Nostrand, New York:95–122.

West, R., 1992. *Development Forum and Benefit Package: a Papua New Guinea initiative*, Working Paper 16, Institute of National Affairs, Port Moresby.

Wohlt, P.B., 1978. Ecology, agriculture and social organization: the dynamics of group composition in the Highlands of Papua New Guinea, PhD thesis, University of Minnesota, Minneapolis.

——, 1986. *Subsistence Systems of Enga Province*, Technical Bulletin 3, Department of Enga Province, Division of Primary Industry, Wabag.

——, 1995. 'System integrity and fringe adaptations', in A. Biersack (ed.), *Papuan Borderlands: Huli, Duna, and Ipili perspectives on the*

Papua New Guinea Highlands, University of Michigan Press, Ann Arbor:199–228.

Wohlt, P., Allen, B., Goie A. and Harvey, P., 1981. An investigation of food shortages in Papua New Guinea, unpublished report to the Director, PNG National Emergency Services and Civil Defence.

Index

International Monetary Fund
(IMF) 226
Ipara 193, 197, 265, 276
Ipili 9, 10, 20, 22–6, 27, 44, 49, 53,
57, 63, 93, 94, 98, 99, 107,
121, 129, 131, 143, 145, 151,
155, 156, 162, 196, 211, 230,
231, 233, 234, 235, 244, 246,
253, 259, 260, 261, 262, 263,
264, 265, 269, 270, 271, 272,
275, 276, 279, 283, 284, 285,
299, 300
Ipili Porgera Investments 99,
121, 233, 244

J

Jackson 20, 93, 96, 97, 98, 99, 115,
125, 126, 129, 144, 149
Jorgensen 261, 274, 275, 277

K

Kaiya 191–222, 224, 242
kinship and descent 10, 23, 129,
171, 196, 223, 225, 230, 231,
232, 235, 239, 243, 245, 247,
251, 255, 256, 257, 259, 260,
261, 262, 263, 265, 266, 267,
268, 269, 270, 271, 272, 273,
277, 279, 280, 282, 284, 285,
286, 287, 288, 290, 291, 292,
294, 296, 298
Kirsch 290
Kyakas and Wiessner 56, 57, 152,
153

L

Lae 35, 84, 123, 247, 256, 257
landowners 5, 6, 7, 16, 20, 25, 26,
30, 31, 32, 54, 59, 60, 61, 74,
95, 100, 103, 105, 107, 110,
121, 126, 128, 130, 134, 135,
136, 138, 142, 145, 146, 149,
151, 211, 212, 214, 216, 218,
219, 225, 226, 234, 244, 247,
254, 260, 267, 268, 269, 274,
275, 276, 277, 279
Landowners' Negotiating
Committee (LNC) 78, 130,
132, 157
law and order 6, 16, 21, 48, 50,
53, 60–72, 77, 84, 182, 261,
278, 281
justice system, 60–3
tribal fighting, 60, 61, 63–7
Law Reform Commission, 56
Lawrence 285
Lease for Mining Purposes
(LMP) 128, 146, 191, 192,
193, 196, 209, 214, 216, 218,
219, 221
Lihir 285, 286, 287, 291, 295
lines 260, 262–4, 265, 266, 267,
268, 269, 270, 271, 273, 274,
275, 276, 277

M

Madang 285
Majnep 288, 289
marriage 6, 52–60, 131, 140,
152, 153, 154, 155, 156,
157, 159, 196, 260, 261,
263, 264, 265, 268–9, 269–
70, 271, 273–4, 275, 276,
277, 278
Meggitt 22, 24, 92, 93, 94, 162,
164, 166, 167, 189
mine waste 180
Mining Development Contract
1, 31, 108, 225, 248, 251
Misima 13, 129, 230

W

Y

www.ingramcontent.com/pod-product-compliance
Lightning Source LLC
Chambersburg PA
CBHW040152270326
41928CB00040B/3293